Duke Monographs in
Medieval and Renaissance Studies 12
Editorial Committee
Arthur B. Ferguson, Edward P. Mahoney, Chairman
Lee W. Patterson, David C. Steinmetz,
Bruce W. Wardropper, Ronald G. Witt,
Caroline Bruzelius, Joan M. Ferrante
Published in association with the
Institut für Europäische Geschichte, Mainz:
Veröffentlichungen des Instituts für Europäische Geschichte,
Abteilung Religionsgeschichte, Band 147

DUKE UNIVERSITY PRESS · DURHAM
1992

PILGRAM MARPECK
HIS LIFE AND SOCIAL THEOLOGY

BY

STEPHEN B. BOYD

The Frank S. and Elizabeth D. Brewer Prize Essay of the American Society
of Church History

DUKE UNIVERSITY PRESS · DURHAM
1992

Die Deutsche Bibliothek - CIP-Einheitsaufnahme

Boyd, Stephen B.:
Pilgram Marpeck : His Life and social Theology / von Stephen B. Boyd. –
Mainz : von Zabern, 1992
(Veröffentlichungen des Instituts für Europäische Geschichte Mainz ;
Bd. 147 : Abteilung Religionsgeschichte)
ISBN 3-8053-1159-1
NE: Institut für Europäische Geschichte 〈Mainz〉: Veröffentlichungen
des Instituts . . .

Library of Congress Cataloging-in-Publication Data

Boyd, Stephen Blake.
Pilgram Marpeck: his life and social theology / by Stephen B. Boyd.
Includes bibliographical references and index.
ISBN 0-8223-1100-3
1. Marbeck, Pilgram, ca. 1495–1556. 2. Anabaptists – Biography.
3. Anabaptists – Doctrines – History – 16th century.
4. Sociology, Christian – History – 16th century. I. Title.
BX4946.M3B69 1992
284'.3 – dc20   (B) 90-44076 CIP

To the memory of those mentioned in these pages
and those connected to them who have borne witness to the
»mystery of the cross of Christ.«

CONTENTS

Acknowledgments   IX
Abbreviations   XI

Introduction   1

Chapter 1   Rattenberg: Crisis of Loyalty   5

Chapter 2   The »Mystery of the Cross«: Theologies of Suffering   25

Chapter 3   Strassburg: Social and Religious Radicalism   43

Chapter 4   Marpeck's Theology of the Cross
            and the Christian Community   69

Chapter 5   Interim Years: Struggle for Unity and Institutional Identity   97

Chapter 6   Augsburg: Confessional Pluralism and Political Conflict   127

Chapter 7   *Gerechtigkeit* and Marpeck's Social Theology   147

Conclusion   169

Bibliography   173
Index   193

ACKNOWLEDGMENTS

This book is a revision of a dissertation submitted to the Committee on Advanced Degrees of Harvard Divinity School for the Th.D. degree. I am pleased to express my gratitude to the following persons and institutions which have not only made this study possible, but also enriched it immeasurably.

In writing the original manuscript, I received assistance and am grateful to the following professors: Arthur McGill for the influence his mode of thought has had on my approach to this material; Steven Ozment for suggesting a biographical treatment of Marpeck; Margaret Miles for her inspiration and insightful comments; Clarissa Atkinson for her constant encouragement, critical observations, and attempts to bring style and clarity to my prose; and George H. Williams, under whose watchful eye and probing questions the topic germinated and grew, and for his personal and professional counsel.

Harvard Divinity School and Harvard University provided scholarship aid and a stimulating environment which shaped many of the concerns and methods I brought to this work. I am particularly grateful for a research fellowship (1982-83) from the Institut für Europäische Geschichte in Mainz, under the direction of Professor Peter Manns; to his assistants, Rolf Decot and Rainer Vinke, for their aid in many scholarly and practical matters; and to my fellow Stipendiaten in the Religionsabteilung, who helped me with modern and Frühneuhochdeutsch, as well as paleography and archival research.

I received many courtesies and much assistance in various archives and libraries: Regensburg Stadtarchiv, Augsburg Stadtarchiv (especially Professor Claus Peter Clasen) and Stadtbibliothek, Bayerische Staatsbibliothek, Neuburg Staatsarchiv, Württembergische Landesbibliothek, Ulm Stadtarchiv, Fürstliches Waldburgisches Archiv Zeil, Landesregierungsarchiv für Tirol (especially Mr. Perktold and Mr. Rupert), Konsistorial Archiv Salzburg, Zentralbibliothek Zurich, Appenzell Stadtarchiv, Strasbourg Archives de Ville, the library of the Institut für Europäische Geschichte (especially Paul Hupka, Frau Resch and Frau Ries), the Andover–Harvard Theological Library, the Z. Smith Reynolds Library of Wake Forest University (especially Mr. Paul Ach), and the Wake Forest University School of Law (especially Rachel Hilbun for her technical assistance).

I wish also to thank Michael Birkel, Miriam Chrisman, Joyce Irwin, André Séguenny, and James Stayer for reading parts or all of the manuscript at various stages and for their suggestions; Galen Johnson for helping with the index; Neal

Blough for making his dissertation available to me and for his critical response to drafts of this work; Heinold Fast for his enthusiastic support of this project and his generosity in sharing with me his critical text of *Das Kunstbuch* along with his transcripts of related archival material; and Russell Sizemore and John Collins for their sustaining friendship.

Funds for additional research were provided by the German Academic Exchange Service (DAAD), the National Endowment for the Humanities (Travel to Collections), and the William C. Archie Fund of Wake Forest University, which also subsidized this publication with a grant from its research and publication fund.

I am grateful also for the generous subvention accompanying the Frank S. and Elizabeth D. Brewer Prize awarded by the American society of Church History, which made copublication possible.

Finally, I am most pleased about the appearance of this book in the series of the Duke University Press and of the Institut für Europäische Geschichte – an expression of the breadth of its ecumenical commitment and vision.

ABBREVIATIONS

ABT	Ottenthal, Emil von, and O. Redlich, *Archiv Berichte aus Tirol*
Antwort	Loserth, Johann, ed., *Pilgram Marbecks Antwort auf Kaspar Schwenckfelds Beurteilung des Buches der Bundesbezeugung von 1542*
ARG	*Archiv für Reformationsgeschichte*
Aufdeckung	Marpeck, *Aufdeckung der Babylonischen hürn...*
Bekenntnis	Marpeck, *Bekenntnis an Jan von Pernstain*
CC	Klassen, William, *Covenant and Community*
CH	*Church History*
CS	*Corpus Schwenckfeldianorum*
CV	Marpeck, *Clare verantwurtung*
Confession	*Confession of Faith*, 1532
E	Bünderlin, *Erklerung durch vergleichung...*
KB	Maler, Jörg, *Das Kunstbuch*
KR, 1	Krebs, Manfred, and Hans Georg Rott, eds., *Elsaß*, part I: *Stadt Strassburg, 1522–1532*
KR, 2	Krebs Manfred, and Hans Georg Rott, eds., *Elsaß*, part II: *Stadt Strassburg, 1533–1535*
KU	Marpeck, *Ain Klarer vast nützlicher unterricht...*
LRAT	Tiroler Landesregierungsarchiv
ME	*Mennonite Encyclopedia*
MGB	*Mennonitische Geschichtsblätter*
MQR	*Mennonite Quarterly Review*
MZ	Entfelder, *Von den manigfaltigen im glauben zerspaltungen...*
RPA	Rattenberg Pfarrarchiv
SAR	Rattenberg Stadtarchiv
R.St-A	Regensburg Stadtarchiv
St-A.A	Stadtarchiv Augsburg
S.St-A	Strasbourg Stadtarchiv
TD	*Theologia Deutsch*, ed. Hermann Mandel
TE	Marpeck, *Testamenterleütterung*
WA	Weimar Ausgabe
WPM	Klassen, William, and Walter Klaassen, *Writings of Pilgram Marpeck*

INTRODUCTION

As history, biography has certain limitations and values. Among the limitations is the difficulty, owing to the dearth of sources concerning their inner thoughts, of probing the psychological motivations of most sixteenth–century figures. In addition, biography is often an elitist enterprise, focusing on persons of privilege who could afford the education, leisure, and modes of the production of literary monuments, or who obtained sufficient influence so as to be the subjects of extensive public records. Further, biographical treatments usually ignore the larger social, economic, and political structures which shape the thoughts, decisions, and behaviors of individuals.[1] However, there are contributions biography can make to historical understanding, because history is about not only enduring structures and ideas, but also human acts which are the »causes and consequences of structures and ideas.«[2]

This study focuses on the activity of one sixteenth century layman, Pilgram Marpeck (c. 1495-1556), as that activity relates to the structures and ideas of his time. It attempts to address the limitations of the genre by offering assessments of the causes and consequences of Marpeck's activity, while restraining unwarranted speculation about his psychological motivation. In addition to viewing Marpeck in the contexts of the social and political establishments and some of the learned theological debates of his day, there will be an attempt to relate his activity to the popular movements of religious and social radicalism.

Marpeck's life constitutes an historically interesting focus for several reasons. Whereas many leaders of radical religious groups in the sixteenth century were clerics, educators, or artisans, Marpeck came to this role as a former civil magistrate. From 1522 to 1528 he served his hometown, Rattenberg on the Inn, as councilman, Bürgermeister, and mining magistrate. Throughout the rest of his life he was employed by city governments in public works projects. Consequently, a study of his career reveals the perceptions of the theology and practice of the Old Church and of various reform movements from the perspective of an interested, intelligent, lay German burgher, who was well acquainted with the social, economic, and political interests of his fellow burghers, the nobility, and the commoners.

Further, while most of his writings were effectively lost until their rediscovery and publication in this century, Marpeck influenced the developing Mennonite

---

1 R. Emmett McLaughlin, *Caspar Schwenckfeld: Reluctant Radical*, vii-viii.

2 James Stayer, *Theses on the Resistance Movement of the German Commoners in 1525*, develops an idea originated by Hans–Jürgen Goertz.

tradition by his irenic overtures which led to the Strassburg conferences of the 1550s and 1560s between the High and Low German Anabaptists. Since his rediscovery, that same tradition has embraced him as a central representative of an Anabaptist theology.[3] Part of that interest in him is due to his continued professional activity and his sensitivity to social justice issues, which serves as an alternative to some of the extreme, sectarian impulses of the Swiss tradition.[4] In addition, several central themes of his theological position – the humanity of Christ, the necessary, mediatory role of externals, the sacramental character of the gathered community, and the affirmation of certain of the Christian's civil responsibilities – offer possibilities for ecumenical discussions.

Finally, a biography of Marpeck is useful at this time, because twenty–three works have been added to his corpus of writings since the last comprehensive biographical treatment by J. C. Wenger, published in 1938.[5] The 1955 discovery, by Heinold Fast and Gerhard Goeters, of *Das Kunstbuch*, sheds considerable light on the last two periods of Marpeck's career and contains nineteen of his letters.[6] In preparation of his critical edition, Fast has also collected material related to *Das Kunstbuch* from the Ulm, Augsburg, and various Swiss archives.[7] During his work on Marpeck's hermeneutics, William Klassen located Marpeck's 1531 booklet, *Ain klarer vast nützlicher unterricht...*, and argued for the inclusion of it and the *Clare verantwurtung...* (1531) in the Marpeck corpus.[8] More recently, Walter Klaassen has argued for Marpeck's authorship of the *Aufdeckung der*

[3] Harold Bender, *Pilgram Marpeck, Anabaptist Theologian and Civil Engineer*, 231-65.

[4] For example, see the *Proceedings* of the Marpeck Academy, Washington, D.C., April 18-19, 1980, ed. Paul Peachey and D. Merrill Ewert.

[5] John C. Wenger, *The Life and Work of Pilgram Marpeck*, 137-61. In 1907 Friedrich Roth, *Augsburg Reformationsgeschichte*, 3:248f., 278f., published an informative account of Marpeck's Augsburg stay (1544-56), based on material from the city archive. Some twenty years later, Christian Hege, *Gedenkschrift zum 400-jährigen Jubiläum der Mennoniten oder Taufgesinnten 1525-1925*, 185-281, discovered the *Testamenterleütterung* and edited the *Vermahnung*. The former work dates from the Augsburg period, while the latter comes from 1532-44 (the Interim Years), when Marpeck traveled about in Switzerland and Southern Germany. Johann Loserth, ed., *Pilgram Marbecks Antwort auf Kaspar Schwenckfelds...* (hereinafter listed as *Antwort*), 1-5, 175-76, added new information from the Landesregierungsarchiv in Innsbruck concerning Marpeck's formative years in Rattenberg on the Inn (c. 1495-1528). He also edited and published Marpeck's massive *Verantwurtung*, written during the Interim and Augsburg periods in response to Caspar Schwenckfeld. Wenger meticulously gathered the earlier biographical research, dividing Marpeck's life into the four periods used to organize this study. Most later accounts of Marpeck's life were based on Wenger's work: Jan Kiwiet, *Pilgram Marbeck*, 19-39; William Klassen, *Covenant and Community* (hereinafter listed as *CC*), 23-35; Bender, *Pilgram Marpeck*; and Neal Blough, *Christologie Anabaptiste: Pilgram Marpeck et l'humanité de Christ*.

[6] Heinold Fast, *Pilgram Marbeck und das oberdeutsche Täufertum. Ein neuer Handschriftenfund*, 212-42.

[7] He graciously made available to me a copy of his forthcoming critical text of *Das Kunstbuch*, as well as transcripts of this archival material.

[8] CC, 36-45. Hans Hillerbrand, *An Early Anabaptist Treatise on the Christian and the State*, 29 n. 5, reports his discovery of the *Clare verantwurtung* in the Stuttgart library.

Babylonischen hürn... (c. 1530),[9] and Heinold Fast has suggested that Marpeck wrote the anonymous *Bekenntnis an Jan von Pernstain* (c. 1535-39).[10]

The goals of this study include the following. First, I want to describe Marpeck's transition from mining magistrate to an Anabaptist leader in South Germany, examining both the causes and consequences of his decision to resign his position and forfeit his considerable estate.

Second, I will reconstruct, from his correspondence and archival material, his contacts with and activity among radical groups. Since his career spanned thirty formative years of the development of radical movements in South Germany, his activity sheds light both on the inner structure and life of some of those groups and on the character of the relations among them.

The third goal is to view Marpeck's activity in the context of the ideas and the social and political realities which influenced and were influenced by him. With respect to the intellectual sources of Marpeck's thought, this study will concentrate on the medieval mystical tradition, mediated by the *Theologia Deutsch* and the Anabaptist preachers, Leonhart Schiemer and Hans Schlaffer, as it influenced Marpeck's notion of justice. The influence of other figures and traditions will also be noted. However, religious ideas are not only responses to intellectual antecedents but also answers to questions posed by social problems and are themselves, to a large extent, mediated by a social process.[11] Therefore, attention will be given to the social, economic, and political dynamics of particular settings and the relation of Marpeck's theological positions to the various expressions of religious and social radicalism in those contexts.

Fourthly, one of the results of this study will be the articulation of aspects of Marpeck's social theology – the theological themes, such as ecclesiology, ethics, and political theology, which had a bearing on the social life of those who were in the sphere of his influence.[12]

---

[9] Walter Klaassen, *Eine Untersuchung der Verfasserschaft und des historischen Hintergrundes der Täuferschrift Aufdeckung der Babylonischen Hurn...*, and *Investigation into the Authorship and Historical Background of the Anabaptist Tract Aufdeckung der Babylonischen Hurn*, 251-61.

[10] Regensburg Stadtarchiv, Signatur Eccl. I, 52, 74. Heinold Fast, *Ein Täufer Bekenntnis aus dem 16. Jahrhundert*, 40-50, will publish this with his critical edition of *Das Kunstbuch*.

[11] Klaus Deppermann, *Melchior Hoffman*, 32.

[12] See Thomas Brady, *Social History*, 175.

Chapter 1

RATTENBERG: CRISIS OF LOYALTY

Pilgram Marpeck made a decision to identify with a radical Anabaptist group after a series of volatile events in the religious life of Rattenberg on the Inn – events precipitated, in part, by the conflicting interests of social groups in and around his Tirolean hometown. Because of his civil responsibilities and professional activities, Marpeck was in a position not only to understand those often competing interests, but also to appreciate their effects on the expression of religious ideas within the city. His decision to resign his position as mining magistrate is best understood in this context of social tension and religious upheaval. This chapter focuses on the social, political, and ecclesiastical contexts of that decision, while chapter two explores some of the religious ideas which shaped the decision and his later thought and activity.

SOCIAL BACKGROUND AND PROFESSIONAL ACTIVITY

Marpeck, though not of noble birth, came from a family of some wealth and influence.[1] In 1491, while living in the Bavarian city of Rosenheim, his father, Heinrich,[2] sold Gilig von Münchinau mining and grazing rights to lands around Kitzbühel.[3] Five years later he appears in the sources as city and district magistrate of Rattenberg – a Tirolean mining town on the Inn River, south of

---

[1] Marpeck's family name appears in the records with several spellings: Marichpegkh (1491), Marpeckh (1496), Marchpeck (1506), Marchpegk (1506), Marchpeckh (1509), Marchpegh (1510), Marchpegkh (1514), and Marpeck (1525). Most European scholars write Marbeck. Although Pilgram's own autograph is Marpeckh, I use Marpeck because of its common usage in the English literature.

[2] By surmising that Marpeck's birth date was around 1495, Jan Kiwiet, *Pilgram Marbeck*, 20, speculates that Heinrich Marpeck was his father. The evidence for that identification is conclusive. The Ratsprotokoll (RP) of the Stadtarchiv für Rattenberg (SAR) in the Landesregierungsarchiv für Tirol (LRAT), 167 (2):86^v, records that on March 13, 1514, »Pilgram Marchpekh hat an heut seines vaters aid bestat,« which suggests that Heinrich was Pilgram's father. Further, the seal of Heinrich, found on a Kaufbrief dated April 28, 1511 (LRAT, SAR, Urkunde, no. 167), is the same as Pilgram's seal on the letter he signed upon entering the office of mining magistrate (LRAT, Schatzarchiv, Rattenberg, 1:7344).

[3] Emil von Ottenthal and O. Redlich, *Archiv Berichte aus Tirol*, 4:301 (hereinafter *ABT*). Dated September 18, 1491, the original is in the Schloßarchiv auf Kapsburg.

Rosenheim.[4] After his tenure as magistrate, Heinrich served as a member of the outer and inner councils of the city.[5] In 1509 he and his wife entered the Bergwerkbrüderschaft.[6] He was sent twice to Innsbruck on city business and chosen to represent it in the Landtag.[7] In 1511 he served as Bürgermeister.[8] By 1516 one of the city's five gates was identified in official documents by its proximity to the Marpeck house.[9]

Whether from Heinrich's earlier landholdings or from their stay in Rattenberg, the Marpecks must have accumulated a considerable legacy. On February 1, 1525, Pilgram was one of forty–two men in the city assessed a tax for the princes; he was among seven who paid the most.[10] Further, sometime before April 1, he lent Archduke Ferdinand I the sizable sum of 1,000 Rhenisch guilders, or the equivalent of twenty times the yearly salary of a carpenter.[11] There are also several indications of Marpeck's wealth after he left Rattenberg. A record of the tax for the defense against the Turks lists »Pilgrams beide Häuser.«[12] When Marpeck's confiscated goods were given over to Christoph Philipp von Liechtenstein, they were valued by some at 3,000 guilders.[13]

As for Pilgram's own family, he was married sometime before 1520 and perhaps as early as 1514.[14] His first wife, Sophia Harrer, with whom he had a

---

4 *ABT*, 4:304: June 26, 1496. See also *ABT*, 4:96. Marpeck witnesses the sale of other rights to Gilig von Münchinau, who was then guardian of Rattenberg. It is likely that Marpeck's financial relationship to Gilig is responsible for his move to Rattenberg and appointment, by the duke of Bavaria, to the magistracy. At that time, Rattenberg and Kitzbühel belonged to Bavaria and it is conceivable that when Gilig was transferred, he brought Marpeck with him. Johann Loserth, *Antwort*, 175, based on an interview with Matthäus Mayer, a local historian, says that Heinrich was city and district magistrate from August 10, 1494, until June 18, 1502.

5 LRAT, SAR, RP, 167 (1, 2). He was a member of the outer council in 1506, 1507, 1513, and 1514, and of the inner council in 1508, 1509, 1510, and 1512. Volumes 167(1) and 167(2) contain the only extant minutes from this early period and cover 1506-14. Volume 168 preserves the minutes from 1523-32.

6 Rattenberg Pfarrarchiv (RPA), Urkunde no. 23, 26[v].

7 LRAT, SAR, RP, 167(1):33[r], 108[r]. LRAT, SAR, RP, 167(2):32[v].

8 LRAT, SAR, RP, 167(1):109[r], and SAR, Urkunde no. 168.

9 LRAT, SAR, Schuber 251, Stadtkammer Rechungen (SR), 1516-42, 11[v]: zolhaus und Marchpeckhen turl.

10 LRAT, SAR, RP, 168:73[r].

11 LRAT, Embiet und Bevelch (EuB), 1525, 16[v]-17[r]. See Fridolin Dörrer, *Tiroler und andere Geldsorten* (2. Teil), 19-27. Ferdinand instructs the Rattenberg tax collector to pay Marpeck a yearly interest of 50 guilders on the loan. Another letter from Ferdinand, dated May 17, shows that Marpeck was also to receive 20 guilders per year against the principal. LRAT Schatzarchiv, 1:729. For the value of the guilder, see also Grete Mecenseffy, *Österreich*, part 2, *Quellen zur Geschichte der Täufer*, 50; and M. Schmelzer, *Geschichte der Löhne und Preise in Rattenberg*, dissertation, 402.

12 *Antwort*, 176: also »Pilgrams Tochter 3 fl.« No reference given.

13 Johann Loserth, *Studien zu Pilgram Marbeck*, 139. Without reference.

14 LRAT, RPA, Urkunde no. 23, 31[r]: »Am sontag Invocavit [February 26] anno (15) 20 ist pilgram Marbeck und sein hausfrau zue einen pruder auff genomen.« Since men who became citizens were usually required to be married, it is possible that, when Pilgram confirmed his father's oath in 1514, he was already married. See Konrad Fischnaler, *Aus dem Bürgermiliz– und Schützenwesen in Rattenberg*, 133.

daughter, Margareth, died sometime before 1528.[15] He was remarried by July 1528 – perhaps to the Anna who is mentioned by him in later correspondence.[16] He also adopted three foster children, who may have been orphans of men killed in the mines. After his resignation from office and upon his departure from Rattenberg, Marpeck left most of his money and goods behind and therefore also his children. The orphans were taken by guardians who received money from Marpeck's confiscated estate for their rearing.[17] He requested that his daughter receive the fifty guilders yearly interest from his loan to Ferdinand.[18]

Marpeck's professional life began when he was about eighteen years old. Because of a dearth of badly needed help in the city hospital, the council, in 1513, appointed him to work there for an indefinite period.[19] He must have proved capable, for we next find him active in a similar position with the mining guild. It appears that the Rattenberg *Bergwerkbrüderschaft* was similar to the *Gewerkschaften* of the mines in Central Germany – a relatively small corporation of middle–class investors or older propertied miners.[20] Each mining guild ran a Brüderhaus to care for sick, injured, or retired miners. Every miner contributed one *Kreuzer* per month to a common fund, administered by a house father and two assistants.[21] On October 3, 1520, eight months after Marpeck joined the guild, the Rattenberg city recorder was instructed to procure a receipt from him listing the grain that he had bought and sold for the *Brüderhaus*.[22] It appears, then, that Marpeck served the guild as a secretary or treasurer, responsible for the food supply for its incapacitated members.

15 On January 14, 1528, Sophia's brothers–in–law, Hans Stetner and Lienhart Berndarffer, asked that guardians be appointed to care for Margareth. LRAT, SAR, RP, 168:148ᵛ: »Hans Stetner unnd Lienhart Berndarffer, begerten anstat iren hausffrauen und annder erbin, iren verlassen swägerin und swestern Sophia Harrerin pilgram Marpeckhn hausfraue gewesen, demselben kind Margreth genannt, gerhaben zuverordnen, darauf sind mit zugeben pilgram Marpeckhen zu gerhaben verordnet Hanns Stetner und Erhart guglweit.« She may have been the daughter of Lienhart Harrer, a city councilman 1512-14.

16 Marpeck and a wife are mentioned in a letter, dated July 2, 1528, by Ferdinand. See Jarold Knox Zeman, *The Anabaptists and the Czech Brethren in Moravia, 1526-1628*, 199, 256 n. 57. Anna appears as Marpeck's »matrimonial sister« in letters dating from his Augsburg residence: Jörg Maler, *Das Kuntsbuch* (hereinafter *KB*), no. 13, 240ᵛ; no. 17, 306ʳ; and no. 18, 317ᵛ.

17 LRAT, An den königlichen Majestät (AKM) 1527-29, 479ʳ-479ᵛ,; Von den königlichen Majestät (VKM) 1527-29, 451ᵛ-452ᵛ; and Causa Domini (CD), 2, 1527-29, 504ᵛ-505ʳ. See Mecenseffy, *Österreich*, 2:266, 280.

18 LRAT, Gemein Missiven (GM), 1528, 54ʳ-54ᵛ. See also LRAT, EuB, 1528, 72ʳ, in Mecenseffy, *Österreich*, 2:66. Also see n. 12 where Marpeck's daughter paid the tax against the Turks. See n. 15 for the names of her guardians. Erhart Guglweit was a councilman 1524-28, and Hans Stetner may have been the son of Jorig Stetner, who served the council during the same time.

19 LRAT, SAR, RP, 167(2):57ᵛ.

20 George H. Waring, *The Silver Miners of the Erzgebirge and the Peasant's War of 1525 in the Light of Recent Research*, 231-48.

21 *Schwazer Bergbuch*, in intro. by Ing. H. Winkelmann, ed., *Der Eisenhütte Gewerkschaft* (Westphalia: Bochum, 1956), 153-54.

22 LRAT, SAR, RP, 168, unbound sheet folded twice. These are notes made by Lutzenhofer on his business trip to Schwaz.

Although little is known about his educational background, it must be assumed that it was the best that the area had to offer.[23] In other aspects of professional activity, he was involved in the city's crossbow competition;[24] delivered ore from Schneeberg and Gossensass to Kitzbühel;[25] and accompanied Erasmus Männdl, guardian of Engelsberg, to Hopfgarten in 1521, because of Männdl's claim to wood, coal, and land rights in the area surrounding the market.[26]

CIVIL RESPONSIBILITIES

With a confirmation of his father's oath of citizenship in 1514, Marpeck entered a life in the civil community in which he would serve in both the outer and inner city councils, as Bürgermeister, and as mining magistrate. Marpeck probably became a full citizen of Rattenberg with this oath.[27] It consisted of three provisions. First, among other items dealing with the weekly market, he vowed not to sell weapons or inferior goods; second, he promised not to enter any community storehouse without special permission; and finally, after presenting a letter documenting his birth and estate, he submitted in obedience to the council and the Bürgermeister.[28]

Marpeck attended the city council meetings as early as 1518 and may have been a council member by 1520.[29] He served as Bürgermeister in 1522 and in the inner council in 1524 and 1525.[30] During these years he scarcely missed a meeting and

[23] *Antwort*, 175, quotes Mayer as saying that Rattenberg had a Latin school besides its German one. He concludes from this and other evidence of Latin sentence structure in Marpeck's work that he received a humanistic Latin education. He is followed by Kiwiet, *Pilgram Marbeck*, 20, and Harold Bender, *Pilgram Marpeck*, 232. The current Rattenberg chronicler, Friedrich Stops, disagrees with Mayer. He says that one could only receive Latin instruction during this period in Salzburg or Innsbruck. It is apparent that many Rattenbergers availed themselves of this opportunity because Paracelsus caused a stir when he preferred German to Latin in his lectures during his short stay in Rattenberg. As the son of a prominent citizen, it is possible that Marpeck travelled to Innsbruck for Latin instruction, for his controversy with Schwenckfeld indicates that he had at least a rudimentary knowledge of the language. See *Antwort*, 84.20; 91.36.

[24] LRAT, SAR, Schuber no. 251, SR, 17[v]: November 23, 1515. Marpeck is paid probably for procuring the prize to be given the winner. See Fischnaler, »Schützenwesen,« 151.

[25] *Antwort*, 2. Without source.

[26] *ABT*, 4:192.

[27] See n. 2 for the text. At that time, to become a citizen one was required to pay a fee and swear the Bürgereid. See Friedrich Stops, *Die Chronik der alten Stadt Rattenberg*, 48.

[28] Stops, *Chronik*, 48.

[29] LRAT, SAR, Schuber no. 250, SR, 134[r], and SAR, Schuber no. 279, Brückenamts Rechnungen, 1[r]. Those present at a meeting concerning the distribution of the city's wood included: »Bilgram Marpekh des Rats.«

[30] A Bürgermeister Ambt Tafel, compiled in the eighteenth century and which now hangs in the council chambers of the Rattenberg city hall, lists Marpeck as Bürgermeister in 1522. Since the council minutes for the years 1514-22 are no longer extant, it is difficult to confirm this. However, the other names and dates, which can be verified by extant minutes, are correct. LRAT, SAR, RP, 168:49, 69[r], report the council elections for 1524 and 1525.

took an active role in the affairs of the city. He witnessed the sale of a house in the city, initiated an investigation into the violation of the oath by a Rattenberger, brought charges against a thief, and was authorized to divide and distribute firewood to his fellow Rattenbergers.[31] In late spring and early summer of 1524 he represented Rattenberg at three Landtage called by Ferdinand.[32] As late as November 1527 he sponsored someone for citizenship.[33]

In addition to these activities, Marpeck was involved in the resolution of three protracted disputes having to do with the economic and religious life of Rattenberg. We view here his role in protecting the interests of the city's artisans, while his involvement in the prosecution of the city's two »Lutheran« preachers, Stephan Castenbaur and Wilhelm Kern, is reserved until later.

From 1521 to 1524 Marpeck represented the city council to the Innsbruck administration in a dispute over the rights of artisans to work in the vicinity of Rattenberg. On August 15, 1521, Christoph von Liechtenstein signed an agreement between the Rattenberg council and the »subjects and craftsmen« of the surrounding district of Rattenberg prohibiting them from practicing their trade within a seven–kilometer radius of the city. This measure protected the interests of the city's craftsmen, enabling them to service the needs of not only the city, but also the surrounding villages and mining community.[34]

However, a group of craftsmen from nearby Reith claimed not to have known about the contract and sold their goods within the restricted zone. After failing to persuade von Liechtenstein and the district magistrate to enforce the terms of the contract, the Rattenberg council turned to Ulrich Schmotzer, legal counsel to the Innsbruck administration. In a brief to Ferdinand, dated August 4, 1524, Schmotzer put the council's case before the archduke, requesting that those craftsmen, breaking the terms of the contract, be punished and driven from the area. Ten days later, Ferdinand instructed the Innsbruck administration to authorize his *Vorstmeister*, Albrecht Stamp, to enforce the contract. Between March 1521 and March 1524 Marpeck travelled seven times to Innsbruck to represent Rattenberg's craftsmen.[35]

After serving the mining guild, Marpeck's next professional position – mining magistrate – involved also civil responsibilities. This office was one of the most important and difficult in the mineral–rich Tirol region.

Among what a modern scholar has called »macroeconomic changes in the empire between 1440 and 1510« were an »intensification of long–distance trade« and a »stronger demand for money as an accepted medium of exchange.«[36] The

---

31 *ABT,* 4:97: June 14, 1524. Original in Schloßarchiv zu Lichtenwort; LRAT, SAR, RP, 168:70ᵛ-71ʳ: January 20, 1525; LRAT, SAR, RP, 168:63ᵛ-64ʳ: September 9, 1524; and LRAT, SAR, RP, 168:61ᵛ: August 19, 1525.

32 LRAT, SAR, RP, 168:74ᵛ, 80ᵛ-81ʳ; and LRAT, SAR, Schuber no. 251, SR, 232ᵛ.

33 LRAT, SAR, RP, 168: 139ʳᵛ.

34 LRAT, Hofreg., Reihe A, Abt. XII, pos. 11.

35 LRAT, SAR, Schuber no. 250, SR, 171ʳ, 201ᵛ; LRAT, SAR, Schuber no. 251, 28ʳ, 28ᵛ, 30ᵛ; and LRAT, SAR, RP, 168:28ᵛ, 31ᵛ, 45ᵛ.

36 Jürgen Bücking, *The Peasant War in the Habsburg Lands as a Social Systems Conflict,* 160.

Tirolean silver and copper mines provided most of this currency. One of the empire's chief mints was in Hall.[37] At first, these mines were developed and controlled through private investment involving powerful merchants, nobility, and higher clergy.[38] For example, the Fuggers of Augsburg participated in the Schwaz mines as early as 1448. The Schmelzherren, Hans and Jörg Stöchl, must have done very well as they paid 800,000 guilders in taxes over a period of forty years on their mining profit.[39]

The control of such an important resource by so few, and in many cases foreign, capitalists constituted a problem for Maximilian I and his grandson, Ferdinand.[40] In addition, the princes needed money for an ever increasing territorial bureaucracy.[41] Further, the miners represented to Maximilian an important military asset.[42] It was, therefore, important that their interests be protected against exploitation which might lead to alienation from the prince.

The solution to these several problems was found in the office of the mining magistrate, or *Bergrichter*.[43] The mining laws of the period placed the magistrate in the delicate position of adjudicating the competing interests of the princes, the foreign investors, the local investors of the *Bergwerkbrüderschaft*, the miners, and the nearby cities.[44] The magistrate was appointed by and responsible to the archduke.[45] As the representative of the prince, he could grant exploration and mining rights and mediate all disputes.[46] Further, only he could weigh the ore and thus assure the prince and his administration their *Frohn* and *Wechsel*.[47] After the princes and investors were paid, the smelted ore was divided equally among the miners, regardless of their relative wealth.

Within the mining community, the magistrate had almost complete civil jurisdiction. The miners took an oath that they would not seek justice with any

[37] Ernst Correll, *Anabaptism in the Tyrol*, 50.

[38] Bücking, *Peasant War*, 160-61.

[39] Josef Weingartner, *Aus der alten Schwazer Bergwerkgeschichte*, 161.

[40] Ferdinand became archduke of Austria in 1506 and gained, through his brother Emperor Charles V, the Grafschaft of Tirol in 1521. Officially, he was only Statthalter, or governor of the Tirol, until 1526. See Otto Stolz, *Geschichte des Landes Tirols*, 518.

[41] Bücking, *Peasant War*, 161.

[42] Eberhard Gothein, *Beiträge zur Geschichte des Bergbaues im Schwarzwald*, Zeitschrift für die Geschichte des Oberrheins N. F., 2:436.

[43] Ibid., 438, says that in order to grasp the inner politics and the historical, cultural meaning of the miners one must understand the role of the mining magistrate.

[44] This summary of the mining magistrate's responsibilities is based on the *Bergordnung zu Rattenberg* (1497) (*Bergordnung*, 1497), LRAT, Handschrift no. 663; and the work of Gothein, *Beiträge*, who studied the effects of Maximilian's 1517 reform of the mining laws in the Black Forest, which was based on Tirolean Bergordnungen.

[45] Gothein, *Beiträge*, 437. This relationship was carried out through the Regierung, the assembly of nobles headed by a representative of the archduke, in Innsbruck.

[46] Otto Stolz, *Zur Geschichte des Bergbaues im Elsaß im 15. und 16. Jahrhundert*, 125-26.

[47] *Bergordnung*, 1497, article 59. Articles 46-63 of the Bergordnung are entitled »Von des Perkhrichters Ambt und Hanndlung.« See also Weingartner, *Schwazer Bergwerkgeschichte*, 162. The Frohn was a tenth of the unrefined ore and the Wechsel was a portion of the smelted silver or copper.

but him.[48] The magistrate held court four times a year to hear cases concerning the miners and matters related to the mining community. He was assisted in his judicial responsibility by eleven *Berggerichtsgeschworene.* The *Gerichtsfronbote* carried out the decisions of the court.[49] No group could gather without the magistrate's permission and the magistrate was required to report all disobedience and dissension to the administration.[50] In addition, he was responsible for the care of the widows and orphans as well as the retired miners in the community.[51] Therefore, the magistrate had to be a person of »good understanding and reason, experienced in mining, judicial proceedings and customs.«[52]

It is clear that Maximilian and his successors were the chief beneficiaries of the Bergordnungen. Through the mining magistrate, he took the control of the mines out of the hands of the investors. As for the miner, although he was protected from exploitation by the investor, he had little political leverage.[53] The prince, then, gained money from the *Frohn* and *Wechsel,* faced a reduced threat from the foreign and local investors, and could draw on the mining community as a military resource. However, these advantages rested on the ability of the magistrate to keep the miners both diligent and cooperative.

On April 20, 1525, Pilgram Marpeck was appointed mining magistrate and on June 7 assumed the office from his predecessor, Hans Griessteter.[54] Griessteter retired because of the »frailty of age« but Marpeck must have already assumed some of his responsibilities even before this time.[55] In August 1523 he is called *Perckrichter* in the council minutes and instructed to help present gifts to the administration in Innsbruck as a token of the city's loyalty.[56] During this time, the Fuggers briefly took an active role in the Rattenberg smelting works.[57] Marpeck signed and sealed a letter dated April 21, 1525, in which he confirms his vow to Ferdinand.[58] His responsibilities covered not only Rattenberg but also Kufstein and included the forests, as well as the mining and smelting works. He promised to punish wrongdoers diligently while judging the rich and poor without discrimination. In addition, he pledged to bring the books for yearly inspection or as often as they were required. He would make sure the prince

48 Gothein, *Beiträge,* 438.

49 *Schwazer Bergbuch,* 75-76; and Weingartner, »Schwazer Bergwerkgeschichte,« 163.

50 *Schwazer Bergbuch,* 37; and *Bergordnung,* 1497, article 47.

51 Gothein, *Beiträge,* 439.

52 *Schwazer Bergbuch,* 72.

53 The miners, not being citizens of the cities, did not have representation in the Landtag. This was one of the demands of those who participated in the uprisings during the 1520s.

54 LRAT, EuB, 1525, 68ʳ-68ᵛ, 89ʳ. He was paid 65 marks per year and given 3 marks for the mining magistrate's garb. Two weeks later, Marpeck was replaced on the inner council. LRAT, SAR, RP, 168:86ᵛ.

55 LRAT, Bekennen, 1525, 101ʳ-101ᵛ.

56 LRAT, SAR, RP, 168:35ʳ.

57 According to Max Reichsritter von Wolfftrigel–Wolfskron, *Der Tiroler Erzbergbau von 1301-1665,* 159, Charles V gave over stock in the mines to the Fuggers due to his debt for his election and purchase of Württemberg. He apparently took it back on January 23, 1526.

58 LRAT, Schatzarchiv, 1:7344: »Das ich darauf derselben einer fürstlichen durchlauchtigkait zurgesagt und versprochen hab, thue das auch wesentlich hiemit in crafft ditz briefs.«

received the Frohn and Wechsel and do everything, »a true mining magistrate is bound to do for his lord.«

The records show that he fulfilled these commitments to Ferdinand – at least until late January 1528 when he decided that he would do so no longer. On May 15, 1526, and May 2, 1527, he was called to Innsbruck for the annual review of the books and the mining work in general.[59] Although there are no extant records of the Berggericht, the city council minutes show that his jurisdiction reached even into the city for those connected to the mining community. In May and June 1526 Marpeck was given custody of a smelter and smith, who had been arrested in Rattenberg.[60] The following year an iron worker, who had caused a disturbance outside a city gate, was handed over to him.[61] Marpeck also continued to take part in city affairs. From July to October 1527 he attended the council meeting five times and in November sponsored Matteus Gartner for citizenship. A final entry notes that Marpeck was fined sixteen guilders concerning the Berndarffer case. However, the fine was suspended because of his trip to »Nuremberg and other services he had rendered the city.«[62]

The sources, therefore, profile a man of considerable means, who honored the social responsibilities consequent to his familial, professional, and civil bonds. He defended the rights of his wife's family, spoke for the interests of the artisans, swore and preserved the communal oath, and represented the city in the larger political sphere. In addition to mediating the interests of Rattenberg's citizens on the council, Marpeck accepted a broader responsibility in the mining community. As administrator and judge, he adjudicated the rights and claims of the miners, the investors, and the nobles.

RELIGIOUS FERMENT

After two and one–half years as mining magistrate, Marpeck decided that he could no longer fulfill his oath of loyalty to Ferdinand. The factors affecting his decision included the development of religious movements that spread through the Tirol in the 1520s. These led to several acute crises in Rattenberg in which Marpeck played a significant role. It is important to note that, during this period, the spectrum of opinion within the reform movement was rather broad and the lines delineating specific parties were indistinct. The investigation of this background will be guided, then, by Marpeck's perspective on his own religious and theological development.

---

[59] LRAT, EuB, 1526, 16^r; and EuB, 1527, 6^v.

[60] LRAT, SAR, RP, 168:107^v, 109^v.

[61] Ibid., 168:131^v: July 7, 1527.

[62] Ibid., 168:99^v: January 26, 1526. The nature of Marpeck's involvement in this case is unclear. It seems as though he was held responsible for some of the debts of his brother–in–law, Leonhard Berndarffer, who was forced to leave the city.

On December 9, 1531, a Strassburg clerk made a record of Marpeck's remarks in his first discussion with Martin Bucer before the council:

Afterwards and now, in the whole world, the struggle is only about faith. He was led by his God–fearing parents into the papal church. But he discovered a significant dispute about the Scriptures. Then he experienced a fleshly freedom in the places where the gospel was preached in the Lutheran way. This made him draw back, for he could find no peace in it.... And then he reported that every Christian must yield himself under the bodily word and work of Christ.... Therefore, he stands now and gives the reason for his faith.... And in summary, he received baptism for a testimony of the obedience of faith.[63]

Although initially responsive to the »Lutheran way,« Marpeck indicates that he became disillusioned with the »fleshly freedom« of some of its enthusiasts and was drawn to the baptism of »the obedience of faith« preached by the seemingly more disciplined Anabaptists. Archival material related to the turbulent religious life of Rattenberg during the 1520s, sheds significant light on Marpeck's relation to the various religious movements that touched the city.

ATTRACTION TO AND DISAFFECTION FROM THE »LUTHERAN WAY«

One of the first notices of a reform preacher influenced by Luther in the Tirol is that of Jakob Strauß at Schwaz. Having come from Berchtesgaden in 1521, he preached sermons at open–air services that attracted a large number of miners.[64] From there he moved to Hall where he lectured in Latin on the Gospel of Matthew and then began preaching in the chapel of the women's cloister. His sermons drew so many people from Hall and the surrounding villages that the city pastor, Stefan Seligmann, allowed him to preach in the parish church. On fair days he preached outdoors on the city common which accommodated an even greater number.[65] According to the Hall city chronicler, Strauß had a splendid oratorical style that spellbound the »common man,« but he spoke heated words »against the clerics, such as the bishops, priests, monks and nuns.« Further, he »rejected the sacrament of penance and other ceremonies.«[66]

Strauß was cited several times by the bishop to appear in Brixen. He refused to go and was constantly accompanied by bodyguards for fear of reprisals by Hall clerics. The Bürgermeister and other city officials travelled to Brixen to intercede

---

[63] Manfred Krebs and Hans Georg Rott, eds., Elsaß, part 1: Stadt Strassburg, 1522-1532 (hereinafter listed as KR 1), 352. (Listed hereinafter as KR 2 is Manfred Krebs and Hans Georg Rott, eds., Elsaß, part 2: Stadt Strassburg, 1533-1535.)

[64] Johann Loserth, *Der Anabaptismus in Tirol von seinen Anfängen bis zum Tode Jakob Huters (1526-1536)*, 432. See also Justus Maurer, *Prediger im Bauernkrieg*.

[65] S. Ruf, *Dr. Jakob Strauß und Dr. Urban Regius*, 67-68.

[66] Franz Schweyger, *Franz Schweygers Chronik der Stadt Hall, 1303-1572*, 81.

for him, as did another group before the Innsbruck administration.[67] However, just before Easter in 1522, Innsbruck ordered Strauß to leave Hall. When he announced his departure to those gathered for his last sermon, »most of the people reacted, some with sadness and weeping, others with anger and disgust with the clerics.«[68] The chronicler notes that although Seligmann began preaching again, he had little following among the burghers. Therefore, on September 13 he called Urbanus Rhegius to preach.[69] Rhegius's sermons also led to a confrontation with the bishop and his dismissal in December 1523.

Besides the civil jurisdiction of the church and other ceremonies, Strauß vigorously criticized penance. In his view, its contemporary practice prevented real contrition and, therefore, justification. In a 1522 sermon Strauß calls the »verdamlichen beicht« an impossible human law.[70] By requiring that one perform perfect penance, which Strauß says is impossible, the sophists frighten people and cause them to doubt.[71] The result is that priests rule the believer's »imprisoned conscience«[72] as well as the pocketbook.[73] Then when one has no peace because of imperfect penitence, the priests have another ploy to enslave one – they will instruct the penitent so as to create perfect penitence from the imperfect.[74]

However, Strauß asserts that while perfect penitence is impossible, what is needed is receptivity, not to the work of the priest, but to the word and person of Christ in the sacrament. It is impossible for God to forgive through repentance alone, for »all your doing, and leaving undone, is not only imperfect, but also... sinful and damnable.« Only through the death of God's son, »are you reconciled again to him through his mercy.«[75] Through his body and blood in the sacrament, Christ renews the work of salvation in one and shares the inheritance of the heavenly Father, earned by the outpouring of his blood.[76] Therefore, faith

---

[67] Ruf, *Dr. Jakob Strauß*, 70.

[68] Schweyger, *Chronik*, 82. From Hall, Strauß travelled to Hasslack and then to Wittenberg, where he may have spent the summer as a student. By early 1523 he was pastor in Eisenach, and served until 1525. From there he moved to Nuremberg and Baden–Baden. After 1527 he dropped out of sight. A contemporary, George Witzel, asserted that he reentered the Roman church before his death.

[69] Ruf, *Dr. Jakob Strauß*, 76. Rhegius had served as early as 1520 as cathedral preacher in Augsburg. He was dismissed because of his use of Luther's writings. However, he would return as the leading Reformation figure in that city until his departure in 1527.

[70] F. Waldner, *Dr. Jakob Strauß in Hall und Seine Predigt vom grünen Donnerstag... 17 April, 1522*, 25, 19.

[71] Ibid., 23, and also see 18.

[72] Ibid., 37: »gefangen gewissen«; 24: »Do sitzen dann die andechtigen heyligen vetter, an gottes stadt (wie luzifer) und herschen gewalticklich uber deyn gewissen.«

[73] Ibid., 24.

[74] Ibid., 23.

[75] Ibid., 32: »dann das all deyn thun, unnd lassen, nicht alleyn unvollkumen, aber widder gottes gepott sundlich unnd verdamlich ist... aber alleyn in dem tod seynes suns, wirstu wider mitt yhm durch seyn barmherzickeytt versünet.«

[76] Ibid., 29.

is the confession and belief that Christ died for us and that the sacrament is »our justification [*unsser gerechtickeyt*] and forgiveness of sins.«[77]

Only in this faith »are we justified [gerecht gemacht] and freed from our sins and see that Christ is in us and we are in Christ.«[78] For Strauß justification (*gerechtickeyt*), and being made just (*gerecht gemacht*), are equivalent terms.[79] It is true that Christ, apart from the believer, reconciled humanity to God and earned the Father's inheritance. The acknowledgment of that reality is an important aspect of faith. But this work of Christ's is also renewed in the believer by the reception of Christ and his work in the sacrament. This receptivity is the other aspect of faith. Therefore, Strauß's understanding of faith and justification involves a notion of intimate participation between the believer and Christ. Christ is both *pro nobis* and *in nobis*. True repentance involves, not introspection, which only causes doubt, but looking at the »suffering, wounds, death and outpouring of blood of your Savior and healer our Lord Jesus Christ.«[80] He is a lord who does not remain outside, but who comes in through the sacrament to heal. Strauß called those preachers whose doctrine did not issue forth in good works »pretended evangelists.«[81]

With respect to the sacraments, Strauß focused on the Supper as the bearer of the reality of Christ to the believer. It is little wonder that he later opposed the Zurich formulations so vigorously. In a 1523 tract on baptism, Strauß stressed the importance of inner baptism against what he perceived as an overemphasis on the outer in Luther.[82] He believed infant baptism to be a late development in the church and at times, adult baptism a better solution to the problem of the relation of faith and baptism. However, he advised the continuation of infant baptism on the statement of faith by their parents.[83]

Although Jakob Strauß was never an Anabaptist, he probably appealed to the same people and struck some of the same chords as those täuferische preachers, who also found an enthusiastic hearing among the miners at Schwaz five years later.

During this time, Marpeck became involved in negotiations concerning the imprisonment of an Augustinian prior who was preaching in Rattenberg with as much or more success than Strauß and Rhegius in Schwaz and Hall. Stephan Castenbaur, or Agricola as he was later called, came to Rattenberg in 1520. While there, he performed various functions with the order's houses in Innsbruck, Hall,

---

[77] Ibid., 28, 30.

[78] Ibid., 28.

[79] Ibid., 28: »dann Christus allein ynn glawben rechtfertig macht, wie Paulus sagt, zu den Römern am viertten. Dem der do glewbst ynn den, der gerecht macht, den gottlosen, dem wirtt seyn glawb zu der gerechtigkeytt.«

[80] Ibid., 31.

[81] John Oyer, *The Influence of Jacob Strauss on the Anabaptists*, 67.

[82] »Von dem ynnerlichen unnd ausserlichen Tauff...« (Erfurt, 1523). See Oyer, *Influence*, 69.

[83] Oyer, *Influence*, 69.

Schwaz, and Kufstein.[84] Through these, he doubtless came into contact with Strauß and Rhegius. The first sign of difficulties with the authorities involves objections to two of his public sermons – one on All Soul's Day, November 2, 1521, and the other on Ascension Day, May 29, 1522.[85] In them he is later accused of preaching heresy and rebellion, reading from Luther's *Babylonian Captivity* and *Abolition of the Mass* from the chancel, slandering the Roman See, the bishops, and the clerics, and advocating the violent abolition of all ceremonies.[86] On November 17, 1522, Ferdinand ordered the Bürgermeister and council to imprison the one who preached »Martin Luters lere unnd maynung.«[87] His concern was not just the error in the faith but the »revolt, resentment, and rebelliousness« that accompanies it. There is a report that while under house arrest in the Rathaus, Castenbaur was allowed to preach on November 23. When the miners cried for his release on Saturday, November 29, he jumped from a window to talk to them and broke his leg. They promptly carried him to one of their houses where he convinced them to return him to the custody of the council.[88]

Shortly after Castenbaur's arrest, Marpeck, then Bürgermeister, and two councilmen travelled to Nuremberg to see Ferdinand about the imprisoned preacher. On November 27, carrying orders from Ferdinand, Marpeck conferred with the administrative council of nobles in Innsbruck.[89] A letter of December 4 from Ferdinand to the Innsbruck administration reveals a political struggle between the city and the council of nobles brought to light by the Castenbaur case.[90] He reports that the Rattenberg city officials complained that they had no jurisdiction to hold the prior. The implication is that, because of public pressure, Castenbaur should either be freed or the city council should be given jurisdiction to decide the case. Ferdinand feared that giving them such unprecedented jurisdictional power might lead to insubordination to the council of nobles. Therefore, he concluded that the city should yield to Innsbruck in this and other cases and hold him until further orders.

These orders came from Ferdinand through Innsbruck on December 13. Castenbaur was to be sent to his ordinary in Salzburg.[91] However, it seems that Ferdinand received political pressure from another source, for he tells Innsbruck to postpone the order until further notice.[92] This time the pressure may have come from the Rattenberg miners. On December 22 Ferdinand acknowledged a

---

[84] Josef Schmid, *Des Cardinals und Erzbischofs von Salzburg (1519-1540) Matthäus Lang: Verhalten zur Reformation*, 77. Also LRAT, Inventar des Archives des Klosters Rattenberg, Rep. 446a/III.

[85] Hauthalter, *Cardinal Matthäus Lang und die religiös–soziale Bewegung seiner Zeit*, 323.

[86] Ibid., 325.

[87] LRAT, An und von den fürstlichen Durchlaucht (AVFD), 1521-22, 56.

[88] LRAT, Hofreg., Reihe A, Abt. XII, pos. 1. See Gustav Bossert, *Beiträge zur Geschichte Tirols in der Reformationszeit*, 146-50.

[89] LRAT, SAR, Schuber no. 251; SR, 20^r.

[90] LRAT, AVFD, 1521-22, 338^v-339^r.

[91] Ibid., 74^v.

[92] Ibid., 77^r-77^v.

visit by a delegation from the Rattenberg mining works. The representatives of the miners reported that they had received, from the duke of Bavaria and Emperor Maximilian, certain freedoms to operate the mines. Since the agreement had expired, they had approached Innsbruck about a renewal. When they achieved no success, they turned to Ferdinand. Apparently they persuaded him of the advantages of Maximilian's mining policy and the potential threat of disgruntled miners, for he ordered Innsbruck to renew the agreement citing »a disadvantage or danger to us« if it were not renewed.[93] Considering Castenbaur's popularity among the miners, it is possible that the delegation used its leverage to change Ferdinand's mind about sending him to Salzburg.[94] The day after Christmas, Ferdinand told Innsbruck to have Christoph von Liechtenstein, the guardian of Rattenberg, take custody of Castenbaur until a decision could be made.[95] This decision was not easy. If he sent Castenbaur to Salzburg, he risked the wrath of the miners. But if the monk was released and continued preaching, Ferdinand feared that he would incite rebellion among the burghers as well as the miners.

By late February a decision apparently had not been made, for the Rattenberg council sent two emissaries to Innsbruck, Christoph von Liechtenstein, and the bishop of Salzburg to elicit a solution. On March 1 they reported that, although they had warned that the city was in great danger, neither von Liechtenstein nor the administration had given them an answer.[96] The council then elected Marpeck and Lienhart Vallenperger to take a letter to the archbishop warning him of the threat to the city posed by the miners and requesting Castenbaur's release. After meeting with him in Mühldorf, Marpeck reported that the archbishop refused to comply. When the miners heard of these latest developments, their protests reached such a pitch that the council applied to Innsbruck for armed assistance.[97] This forced Ferdinand's hand, and on March 10 the Bürgermeister and council were called to von Liechtenstein's castle overlooking the city to be informed that Castenbaur was being sent to Salzburg. The next day, when the Bürgermeister broke the news to a gathering of the city, he assured them that the council would send someone to Salzburg to intercede for Castenbaur.[98] At Castenbaur's request, the council sent Marpeck and a townsman to Salzburg on March 21.[99]

Two months later, with Marpeck present, the articles written against Castenbaur and his answers were read before the city council. It was decided to

---

[93] Ibid., 76[v].

[94] Duke George of Saxony faced a similar threat in 1525, when his miners went on strike after the Bergmeister claimed to have no authority to act on their grievances. See Waring, *Silver Miners*, 235.

[95] LRAT, AVFD, 1521-22, 77[v].

[96] LRAT, SAR, RP, 168:4[v], 6[r]-6[v].

[97] Ibid., 168:8[v]-9[r], 9[v].

[98] Ibid., 168:9[v]-10[r].

[99] Ibid., 168:14[v]. Kiwiet, *Pilgram Marbeck*, 21, following Eduard Widmoser, *Das Täufertum im Tiroler Unterland*, dissertation, 43, erroneously dates this trip April 18.

send a representative to confirm Castenbaur's teaching at the hearing.[100] Even after Johann Staupitz, who was then abbot of St. Peter's in Salzburg, wrote an analysis of Castenbaur's answer and several more hearings were held, the case was still undecided by the end of 1523.

At that time, Castenbaur experienced extreme deprivation in an attempt to exact his recantation; it was reported that, when he was starved, tortured, and exposed to cold weather, he daily prayed for God to release him by means of death.[101] Early in 1524 Castenbaur twice renewed his request for help from the Rattenberg council.[102] It appears that in May, partly because of public pressure and partly because of special intercession by Ferdinand's wife,[103] Castenbaur was released.[104]

In response to his accusers, Castenbaur admitted acquaintance with Luther's writings but claimed to have read nothing from the preaching chair except »the Gospel of Matthew and the letters of John, Peter, Paul and James.« When he needed help with a particular passage, he once used Luther, but mostly turned to Augustine, Jerome, or Ambrose. As for the Roman See, he said that he never called it a robber's nest, but only criticized the misuse of the keys. Denying that he incited rebellion, he testified that he always preached unity and peace.[105] Further, he asserted that the pope and emperor had their power from God, if they did not oppose God's will. And, while they could punish disobedience with force, spiritual and civil power should be distinguished from each other.[106]

Castenbaur's removal from the cloister church late in 1522 left a void in the religious life of Rattenberg. During that year the city council began a protracted struggle, lasting until 1527, with the pastor at Reith to secure priests to perform pastoral duties for which the city paid an annual benefice. After several fruitless appeals to Christoph von Liechtenstein, the council complained to the Innsbruck administration that it paid an annual fee of twenty–six guilders to Christoph, the pastor of Reith, for which he was to: 1. appoint a vicar for the city; 2. assure that masses were said twice a week and on high holy days; and 3. send another priest every other Sunday to preach and celebrate.[107]

---

100 LRAT, SAR, RP, 168:23^r-23^v. These articles, published as *Artickel wider den / Doctor Steffan Castenpaur / Eingelegt, auch was / er darauff geann / wort hat, auß / seiner gefen / cknuß, newelich / von im außgangen/ MD XXiii*, are available in the Wolfenbüttel Library.

101 Schmid, *Matthäus Lang*, 83.

102 LRAT, SAR, RP, 168:51^v, 55^r-55^v.

103 This may confirm an earlier biographical tradition, which claimed that Castenbaur was at one time Anna's confessor. See Schmid, *Matthäus Lang*, 86 n. 1.

104 Castenbaur went to Augsburg, took the name Agricola, married, and by 1525 was pastor of St. Anna, alongside Rhegius. He attended the Marburg Colloquy, signed the 15 Articles, and served as preacher to the Reichstag in 1530. In 1531 he became pastor of St. Michael's in Hof and later signed the Schmalkald Articles. He died in 1547 as pastor in Eisleben. See Thomas Kolde, *Stephan Agricola*, 254-55.

105 Hauthalter, *Lang*, 325-27.

106 N. Paulus, *Ein Gutachten von Staupitz aus dem Jahre 1523*, 774-75.

107 LRAT, RPA, Urkunde no. 603.

On March 10, 1523, the council offered Wilhelm Kern twenty – six guilders to serve as a pastor in the city.[108] Marpeck and the Bürgermeister apparently tried to persuade Kern to accept, but he asked for more money and an assurance that the city would support him against the princes when he preached the Word of God.[109] After the council refused his salary demands, the job remained vacant for over a year before Kern filled it in June 1524.[110] By October 18, 1524, Kern was suspected of preaching in a way sympathetic to the evangelical cause and, again, asked the council to shield him from arrest by the Innsbruck administration. Apparently he continued preaching and, perhaps, did so in the chapel of the mining community, for the mining guild took over much of his salary.[111] During this time, there are reports that Kern abolished the mass and that Rattenberg was the scene of violent iconoclasm.[112] In January 1526 he was ordered to appear before the Innsbruck administration to answer questions about his preaching and life – style.[113] Accompanied by Marpeck, then serving as mining magistrate, Kern was interrogated and, because of his marriage, relieved of his office, in spite of warnings of a possibly violent response by the miners.[114]

Throughout this episode, the council continued to pressure Christoph of Reith to provide the pastoral services for which it was paying. Citing a dearth of new priests, Christoph sent an apprentice to serve as vicar in October 1524.[115] Early the next year the young vicar fell ill and the council, receiving a pledge of financial support from Marpeck and others, agreed to supplement his income.[116] In 1525 the council twice complained that Christoph was not providing a priest to celebrate the stipulated masses and threatened to withhold its annual payment.[117] Because of continued difficulty in securing pastoral services in 1526 and 1527, the council turned to Christoph Fuchs von Fuchsberg, the Hauptmann of Kufstein, who negotiated an agreement between the council and the pastor at Reith, which allowed the city to hire its own priest for five years. The pastor at Reith agreed to forfeit his right to payment of the annual benefice.[118]

During these years, Rattenberg experienced violent iconoclasm and the Tirol was the scene of several armed rebellions – both partially justified by some who preached in the Lutheran way.

---

108 LRAT, SAR, RP, 168:11^r-11^v.

109 Ibid., 168:19^r; and LRAT, SAR, Schuber no. 250, SR, 173^r: March 25, 1523.

110 LRAT, SAR, RP, 168:60^r.

111 Ibid., 168:82^v.

112 Bossert, *Beiträge*, 150; Loserth, *Anabaptismus*, 445; and Grete Mecenseffy, *Täufer in Rattenberg*, 198, mention Kern in relation to these reports.

113 LRAT, SAR, RP, 168:99^r: January 24, 1526.

114 Ibid., 168:100^r; and LRAT, SAR, Schuber no. 251, SR, 265: January 24, 1526.

115 LRAT, SAR, RP, 168:66^v.

116 Ibid., 168:73^r.

117 Ibid., 168:82^v: June 14, 168:92^v-93^r: October 16.

118 LRAT, Dekanatarchiv, Reith in Alpbachtal, Urkunde no. 110: November 13, 1527. The contract was extended for another five years on February 14, 1533. LRAT, RPA, Urkunde no. 605.

In the spring of 1525 the miners at Schwaz, among whom Strauß and his followers had found much success, took control of the market by force of arms.[119] Later in May they joined the peasants in a revolt that spread throughout the Tirol.[120] In the south the peasants and burghers controlled Brixen, ousted the bishop, and on May 13 elected Michael Gaismair as their commander. Gaismair, having served as secretary to both Leonhard von Völs, Ferdinand's vice – regent, and Bishop Sebastian Sprentz of Brixen, had access to the highest councils of religious and civil power and, as with Marpeck, experienced disappointment and disillusionment. Maintaining confidence in Ferdinand, he sent ambassadors with the aim of stripping the clergy of all civil power and returning to direct rule by the archduke. This confidence was soon proved to be misplaced. Stalling for time until he could raise money for an army, Ferdinand called a diet to deal with the demands expressed at the unofficial Diet of Meran. In June Gaismair brought an evangelical preacher to Brixen. Although probably from the Zwingli circle, the preacher doubtless represented to Ferdinand the subversive »lutherische weise.« He wrote that these men »preach against God, his saints, and the venerable rites of the church... also against the spiritual and worldly authority... saying impermissible things against our own person, our government and counsellors, through which the common man is provoked to rebellion and disobedience to us, his authority.«[121] By September 7 Ferdinand had borrowed enough to send two thousand mercenaries to bring the uprising to a bloody end. In addition to twenty – eight »knechte« chosen from the city's artisans, Rattenberg contributed sixteen citizens in »guetter Rustung« for »hilff und beistannt wider die aufruerigen.«[122] It is possible that Marpeck's loan earlier in the year helped support the mercenary force.[123]

At this juncture it might be instructive to address the question as to whether Marpeck ever became a Lutheran.[124] In a comment, approximately contempora-

---

[119] Six thousand miners took possession of Schwaz, rejected Ferdinand's ambassador, and set off for Innsbruck to appeal to him directly. He rode to meet them at Hall and they presented him with three major grievances: usury and exploitation by the investors; complaints against and demand for the replacement of the mining magistrate; and desire for an elected, representative body. Ferdinand was forced to agree to act on all three, but asked for patience and obedience from the miners. However, Albert Hollaender, *Ein Bergknappenaufstand zu Schwaz, 1525*, 29-33, observes that »they stood shoulder to shoulder with the peasants to fight for political rights in the Peasant War which broke out a few months later.« See also Schweyger, *Chronik*, 83-87.

[120] The circumstances here must have been somewhat different than in Central Germany where, according to Waring, *Silver Miners*, 239, the competing interests of the miners and peasants kept them, with some exceptions, from forming a solid front.

[121] Walter Klaassen, *Michael Gaismair: Revolutionary and Reformer*, 43.

[122] LRAT, SAR, RP, 168:90^v. See Fischnaler, »Schutzenwesen.«

[123] On July 2 Marpeck received a copy of an order from Ferdinand to the Landrichter instructing him to hire three men to watch for signs of uprisings among the peasants and miners. LRAT, Missiven, 1525, 203^v-204^r.

[124] J. C. Wenger, *Pilgram Marpeck, Tyrolese Engineer and Anabptist Elder*, 25, asserts, »Actually he not only came into contact with it, he actually became a Lutheran.« Kiwiet, *Pilgram Marbeck*, 21, speculates, »Durch Agricola muß Marbeck für die reformatorische Botschaft gewonnen worden sein.«

neous with the 1532 report of the Strassburg scribe, Marpeck says that »the
writings, teaching, and sermons« of the evangelicals released him from the prison
of the papacy's »human laws,« including confession and the many prohibitions
that weighed on his conscience. Further, he reveals that, during this period, he
felt himself to be a »good Christian« and read as much as he could that was
critical of the papacy.[125] It is now clear that Marpeck had ample opportunity, not
only through the pamphlets of Luther and others, but also through the published
and unpublished sermons of Jakob Strauß, Urbanus Rhegius, Stephan
Castenbaur, and Wilhelm Kern, to read and hear criticisms of the church of his
parents, as well as of those civil rulers who supported it with the power of the
sword. He complains, however, that, though he was delivered from the »fleshly
coercion« of the Old Church and its defenders, he was led into »fleshly freedom«
by the evangelical teaching, because it spoke little of »the mystery of the cross of
Christ.« By »fleshly freedom,« he may refer to the violent iconoclasm and armed
rebellion, which were justified by evangelical preaching.[126] By 1527 Marpeck may
have already become disillusioned with the Lutheran way, because its adherents
did not manifest the »obedience of faith« required by those who received the
baptism into the »mystery of the cross of Christ,« preached by the Anabaptist
missionaries, who entered the Tirol as the Rattenberg city council completed the
frustrating negotiations to provide for the pastoral needs of the city's residents.

ATTRACTION TO THE ANABAPTISTS

The earliest sign of Anabaptists in the Inn valley is an account of Hans Hut's
Augsburg hearing in September, 1527. He is reported to have testified that in
May 1526, Caspar Ferber mentioned several brothers in the Inn valley, who had
»let themselves be baptized and were leading a Christian life.«[127] Johann Loserth
cites a March 1527 entry in the Hall council minutes mentioning Anabaptists in
Rattenberg.[128] On April 24, 1527, Ferdinand wrote to the Innsbruck
administration concerning »the strange and annoying sects« in which »a new

125 This testimony comes from the anonymous tract, *Aufdeckung der Babylonischen hürn...*
(hereinafter listed as *Aufdeckung*) (c. 1532), Av^v – Avi^r. Hans Hillerbrand, *An Early Anabaptist
Treatise on the Christian and the State*, 29-47, discovered this tract and recognized its Anabaptist
origins. Walter Klaassen, »Investigation into the Authorship and Historical Background of the
Anabaptist Tract Aufdeckung der Babylonischen Hurn,« 251-61, has argued persuasively for its
inclusion in Marpeck's corpus.

126 Elsewhere in the *Aufdeckung*, Av^v, Aiiii^r, Marpeck accuses the evangelical preachers first
of bidding the common man to take the sword and later of hiding behind the »princes, cities, and
lords.«

127 C. Meyer, *Die Anfänge des Wiedertäufertums in Augsburg*, 224. Heinold Fast, *Pilgram
Marbeck und das oberdeutsche Täufertum. Ein neuer Handschriftenfund*, 220, argues against this
testimony and asserts that Anabaptism arose with the arrival of Leonhart Schiemer and Hans
Schlaffer in November 1527. However, there is evidence from the sources that supports the
supposition of an earlier entrance.

128 Loserth, *Anabaptismus*, 450.

baptism has arisen.«[129] Elsewhere in the Tirol, Innsbruck warned Jakob Trapp, guardian of Glurns and Mals, concerning the movement.[130] These early Anabaptists were probably products of missionary work from the west.[131]

From the east missionaries brought a theology with a different character from that of the Swiss. These were influenced by a practical mysticism mediated through Thomas Müntzer, Hans Denck, and Hans Hut. In November 1527 Leonhart Schiemer entered the Inn valley and encountered a highly charged religious and somewhat confused political situation. He was arrested on November 25 by virtue of Ferdinand's mandate, which had been published only five days before.[132] Recalling the Edict of Worms, the Order of Regensburg (1524), and other strictures against Luther and his followers, it denounced as heretical any deviation from the doctrine and practice of the Roman church. Special attention was given to Anabaptists and those who derided the sacrament. Anyone teaching against the twelve articles of faith and seven sacraments was subject to confiscation, prohibition from making a will, loss of public office, forfeiture of the right to buy and sell, and the right to correspond. Although some offenses, as the derision of Christ and the Supper, were punishable by fire, the mandate was unclear about the precise sentence Anabaptists should receive. In the article dealing with baptism, a use other than that of the Roman church was to be punished with »imprisonment, confiscation and other.« Those who preached against the use of force, particularly against the Turks or other unbelievers, received »imprisonment and other.« The ambiguity of these articles led to much confusion and correspondence between Ferdinand and those who were to enforce the mandate, who were all local and regional officers. As he was the first Anabaptist apprehended, Schiemer and the case against him became a precedent for others in the Tirol.

On November 28 the Innsbruck administration instructed Bartlme Anngst, the Rattenberg city and district magistrate to torture Schiemer to find out who belonged to the sect.[133] Based on his confession, sent to Ferdinand, the duke of Bavaria, and Archbishop Lang, Innsbruck instructed Anngst to call for a trial.[134] In the same letter Marpeck was ordered to be ready at all times for the »apprehension and punishment of the Anabaptists.« The administration, in early January, acknowledged Anngst's letter reporting that Marpeck had asked to be relieved of the responsibility of handing over the Anabaptists, arguing that that was not part of his job. The administration reported that Ferdinand had read the

---

[129] LRAT, Von dem königlichen Majestät (VDKM), 1527-29, 35ᵛ-36ʳ. See Mecenseffy, *Österreich*, 2:3.

[130] LRAT, CD, 1527-29, 27ʳ-27ᵛ. See Mecenseffy, *Österreich*, 2:3.

[131] Georg Blaurock and Felix Manz worked in Chur in May 1525, and later Blaurock appeared in Appenzell and the Grisons in April 1526. See Klaassen, *Michael Gaismair*, 107.

[132] For the text see Mecenseffy, *Österreich*, 1:3-12.

[133] LRAT, CD, 1527-29, 95ᵛ. See Mecenseffy, *Österreich*, 2:28.

[134] LRAT, CD, 1527-29, 100ᵛ-101ʳ: December 14. See Mecenseffy, *Österreich*, 2:32-33.

letter and personally demanded that it order Marpeck to help and report any failure to do so.[135]

During this period of imprisonment in the castle tower, Schiemer wrote seven letters and carried on what must have been, in light of the strength of the Anabaptist congregation after his death, a significant ministry. No doubt his success among the burghers and miners placed Marpeck in a particularly difficult position. Having taken an oath to protect and care for the miners, Marpeck was now asked to hand over to imprisonment and, possibly, death those who responded to a message and discipline with which he was probably sympathetic.[136] After his initial refusal, it appears that he had second thoughts. In a letter dated January 10, the administration, after scolding Anngst for allowing Schiemer to write letters, reported Marpeck's oral agreement to uphold the mandate within the mining community.[137]

On Sunday, January 12, Schiemer was tried before a *Reichstag*, consisting of two representatives from cities in the area. Although no complete roll was taken, Marpeck may have attended. Apparently someone argued that the mandate required only imprisonment and confiscation.[138] However, since Schiemer refused to change his opinion, the court sentenced him to the sword and fire. Two days later he was beheaded in the castle yard and then burned in the embankment behind the tower – two hundred yards from Marpeck's residence.[139] This must have made a deep impression on Marpeck, for he immediately resigned his office as mining magistrate. By Saturday, Innsbruck acknowledged his request to be discharged.[140] It was granted on January 22 and Ferdinand followed it with a personal letter to Marpeck ordering him to turn over the books to Wolfgang Schönman, his successor.[141] By February 8 Hans Schlaffer and Leonhard Frick had suffered a similar fate in Schwaz.[142]

However, this was only the beginning of a phenomenal growth of the movement and the difficulties it caused the authorities. In fact, there was a special appointment made, a Kanzler doctor, Hieronymus von Balding, to deal with issues pertaining to Anabaptists.[143] The administration, Ferdinand, and city officials spent the first four months of 1528 trying to establish a policy for them. It is difficult to determine how strong the movement was in the Inn valley.[144] It

135 LRAT, CD, 1527-29, 116^V-117^r: January 3. See Mecenseffy, *Österreich*, 2:48.

136 One limitation of the mining magistrate's jurisdiction involved capital punishment. For crimes which required that sentence, only the city and district magistrate had jurisdiction.

137 LRAT, CD, 1527-29, 122^V-123^r. See Mecenseffy, *Österreich*, 2:51-52.

138 LRAT, AKM, 1527-29, 151^V-155^V. See Mecenseffy, *Österreich*, 2:70-77.

139 Stops, *Chronik*, 52-53. The castle yard lay on top of a small hill just behind Marpeck's house.

140 LRAT, GM, 1528, 35^V-36^r: January 18.

141 Ibid., 54^r-54^V; and LRAT, EuB, 1528, 342^V: January 28. See Mecenseffy, *Österreich*, 2:66.

142 LRAT, AKM, 1527-29, 151^V-155^V. See Mecenseffy, *Österreich*, 2:73.

143 LRAT, CD, 1527-29, 182^V-183^r. See Mecenseffy, *Österreich*, 2:91, 198.

144 Eduard Widmoser, *Das Tiroler Täufertum*, 1, *Tiroler Heimat* 15:84, estimated that between 1525 and 1627 there were 20,000 in the Tirol associated with the Anabaptists. Taking the 2,064 found in the sources, he multiplied by a factor of six for those who did not appear in the records

is known that there were seventy–one executions in Rattenberg alone.[145] By
June 6 the council minutes report that Rattenberg was being called
»Täufernest.«[146] In Schwaz there is an unconfirmed report that 800 of the 1,200
residents became Anabaptists.[147] Around April, 1528, there was also a group
gathered by a preacher named Paul in the castle of Münchinau near Kitzbühel. Its
owner, Helena von Münchinau, may have been influenced in favor of the
movement by Marpeck, for she later corresponded with him.[148]

Marpeck faced in these days an acute crisis of loyalty. He had taken an oath of
loyalty and obedience to Ferdinand; as a city councilman he had been active in
several attempts to secure pastoral services for his city; as guildsman and mining
magistrate he was bound to protect the interests of his guild and the miners for
whom he was responsible. However, Ferdinand had previously imprisoned two
preachers, Castenbaur and Kern, who, in spite of the neglect of the pastor of
Reith, had met some of the religious needs of the city, and in whose retention
and employment Marpeck had taken an active role. Then the archduke
imprisoned Leonhart Schiemer and required Marpeck's aid in coercing, under
pain of death, the recantation of those miners who responded to the Anabaptist
preacher. Marpeck's refusal and subsequent activity evinced a loyalty to those
Anabaptists who preached and received baptism as a »testimony of the obedience
of faith.«

---

and their dependents. Claus–Peter Clasen, *Anabaptism: A Social History, 1525-1618*, appears to
have used Widmoser's figures from 1525-1618. However, he did not allow for the »invisible«
number and reports the number as 2,012, without explaining the reduction of Widmoser's figure.

[145] Widmoser, *Tiroler Täufertum, Tiroler Heimat* 15:73.

[146] Mecenseffy, *Täufer in Rattenberg*, 205.

[147] LRAT, CD, 1527-29, 422^v-423^r. See Mecenseffy, *Österreich*, 2:249.

[148] Her married name was von Freyberg. Marpeck later sent her a copy of the *Vermahnung*
which she forwarded to Schwenckfeld. See p. 105. It is possible that their acquaintance stems
from his father's relationship to Gilig von Münchinau. See pp. 5-6.

Chapter 2

THE »MYSTERY OF THE CROSS«: THEOLOGIES OF SUFFERING

Marpeck later reported that, during these early years, the Anabaptist preachers won his loyalty because of their »obedience of faith« and their preaching of the »mystery of the cross of Christ.« As we shall see, Marpeck's first theological expressions (the 1531 tracts, the *Confession* of 1532, and the *Aufdeckung*) reflect the mystically influenced theologies of the cross, or suffering, of the *Theologia Deutsch*, Leonhart Schiemer, and Hans Schlaffer.[1] One of the themes that seems to have caught Marpeck's attention in this literature is that of the righteousness, or justice, of Christ which, when incorporated into the life of the believer, leads to a suffering that is believed to have salutary effects for the individual and the community.

The purpose of this chapter is not to trace completely Marpeck's intellectual–historical genealogy, but to examine particular medieval mystical themes in three authors – the anonymous Frankfurter, Leonhart Schiemer, and Hans Schlaffer – who directly influenced Marpeck.[2]

1 *Das Kunstbuch* reveals that the writings of Schiemer, Schlaffer, and probably the *Theologia Deutsch* were among the devotional works circulated by and read in the groups associated with Marpeck. When Jörg Maler collected and edited *Das Kunstbuch* in 1561, he included three writings by Schiemer (*Von der Gnade Gottes* (KB, no. 9), *Über die 12 Artikel und von der wahren Taufe* (KB, no. 10), and *Ein wahrhaftig, kurz Evangelium...* (KB, no. 11); and two by Schlaffer (*Ein einfältig Gebet*, and *Beicht und offenbares Bekenntnis* (KB, no. 12). For bibliographical information on the complete writings of these two, see Stephen Boyd, *Hans Schlaffer*, and *Leonhart Schiemer*. It is possible that Marpeck carried copies of these works with him to Strasbourg and throughout his life and that Maler had access to them in Augsburg. Further, in speaking of Gelassenheit, Leupold Scharnschlager, Marpeck's successor in Strasburg and later collaborator, refers to the ideas of the »teuschen teologi« (KB, no. 32, 257ᵛ). Marpeck cites the *Theologia Deutsch* only in the *Verantwurtung II*, but even his very first works contain ideas and terminology which reflect his debt to the anonymous Frankfurter, the author of the medieval mystical tract. For a brief summary of the attempts to identify the author of the *Theologia Deutsch*, see Bengt Hoffman, *The Theologia Germanica of Martin Luther*, 1-2.

2 Neal Blough, *Christologie Anabaptiste: Pilgram Marpeck et l'humanité de Christ*, has focused on the parallels between the writings of Marpeck and those of Caspar Schwenckfeld and Martin Luther. With respect to the medieval mystical tradition, Werner Packull, *Mysticism and the Early South German–Austrian Anabaptist Movement, 1525-1531*, has convincingly demonstrated the interrelatedness of the thought of Thomas Müntzer, Hans Hut, and Hans Denck, and the dependence of all three on the practical mystical tradition, represented by the *Theologia Deutsch*. A detailed comparative study of the thought of these three, along with that of Schiemer,

Marpeck's appropriation of these ideas in the context of his own concerns will be noted in later chapters.

THE THEOLOGIA DEUTSCH AND THE JUSTICE OF GOD

In chapter thirty‑nine of the *Theologia Deutsch*, the Frankfurter affirms, »If one loves justice, that one wishes to do no injustice.«[3] Although Bengt Hoffman uses righteousness and unrighteousness to translate *Gerechtigkeit* and *Unrecht*, he notes that one might use justice and injustice to express the moral content of the Frankfurter's words, for »the sociomoral component is definitely there.«[4] That component is more obvious in another passage: »The creature should be subjected to God and to all creatures by divine truth and justice.«[5] There is, then, in the divine justice an inner connection between the creature's proper relationship to God and to other creatures. Indeed, the Frankfurter's concept of justice (*Gerechtigkeit*) relates to his notion of order (*Ordnung*) which is grounded in the nature of God.[6]

It is the property of God »to know himself, to love himself and to reveal himself to himself.«[7] Therefore, there is within God a distinction of persons mutually related by the dynamic processes of knowing, loving, and revealing. The Frankfurter calls that dynamic reciprocity the good and says that God »loves himself not as himself but as the good.«[8] Therefore, God loves that reciprocity and desires a further extension of the experience of the good.[9] However, the will, love, justice, and truth is essentially in God, but they cannot become worked or used (that is, become actual) without the creature.[10]

Schlaffer, and Marpeck would shed light on why these figures took a common tradition in revolutionary (Müntzer), quietistic (Denck), apocalyptic (Hut), and critically participating (Schiemer, Schlaffer, and Marpeck) directions. James Stayer, *The Anabaptists*, 145, has called for such a study.

3 *Theologia Deutsch* (hereinafter listed as TD), 39/77.23-24. When quoting the *Theologia Deutsch*, I cite Hermann Mandel's *Theologia Deutsch* (1908) edition of Luther's 1518 text, which was most probably used by Marpeck and his group. The first number in the citation refers to the chapter of *TD*, followed by the page and line number in the Mandel edition.

4 Hoffman, *Theologia Germanica*, 184 n. 177.

5 *TD*, 33/65.9-11. Emphasis added.

6 Ibid., 41/83.16-17: »... so muss alles das da geliebet werden, das guten namen in der warheit hat, als tugent, ordnung, redlicheit, gerechthickeit, warheit und der gleichen.« The Frankfurter here relates virtue, order, rectitude, and justice.

7 Ibid., 30/58.5-7, 9-10.

8 Ibid., 30/61.14-16.

9 Ibid., 35/67.29-30: »Alles, das hie geschriben ist von gottes eigenschafft, die er doch haben wil yn dem menschen, yn dem sie geübt und gewurckt sol werden.«

10 Ibid., 30/60.24-25: »Und ist doch alles ein wesen in got, und es mag deines nymer gewurcket oder geubt werden on creature.«

The purpose of the creation is a wider participation in the good, which characterizes the divine life.[11] But the creature, which has flowed out from God, »is not true being and has no being other than in the perfect.«[12] In fact, »all things are essentially in God and more essentially in God than in themselves.«[13] Therefore, the proper mode of the creature is a participative mode, whereby the creature constantly receives that which is from God. This receptivity and participation characterizes the proper order (*Ordnung*) of creation.[14]

The Frankfurter defines sin as a disruption of this participative order. The creature assumes to the self (*sich an nympt*) »something good, such as being, life or knowledge... as though it belonged to the creature or was the creature.«[15] The creature turns from »the unchangeable good and turns to the changeable.«[16] In this act of self – will or injustice, the mode of the creature changes from one of willing receptivity and mutuality to one of presumptuous grasping – from a dynamic participation to static possessiveness. The result is not only harm to the honor of God, but also to the creature and to the neighbor.[17]

According to the Frankfurter, Christ undid the injustice introduced by Adam and restored human life to order.[18] In his humanity there was no »selbheit,« that is, Christ did not presume to take things into his own possession as though they were his.[19] The Frankfurter describes the new, just mode of Christ with reference to the two eyes of Christ's soul:

the soul of Christ had two eyes, a right eye and a left eye. In the beginning when those were created, it turned its right eye into eternity and into the divine and stayed there immovable in perfect viewing and participation of the being and perfection of God. It remained there unmoved and unhindered by all events... in the outer human. With the left eye, it saw into the creature and there discovered and noted the differences among creatures.... [A]lso the outer human being, or the soul according to the left eye, in its work... was never hindered or weakened by the inwardness. As for them, one does not wait for the other.[20]

It is clear that the eyes of Christ's soul were created and functioned according to their proper nature. Therefore, it was possible for Christ to live in full

---

[11] Ibid., 48/92.20-23: »... und got möchte sich des seinen nydert bekomen und seiner eigenschafft... yn wurcklicher weise, das doch sein sol und gehort zu volkumenheit.«

[12] Ibid., 1/9.18-10.1.

[13] Ibid., 45/89.14-17: »Nu sind alle ding wesenlich in got und wesenlicher dan in ym selber.«

[14] Ibid., 37/69.19-20.

[15] Ibid., 2/10.8-11.

[16] Ibid., 2/10.3-7.

[17] Ibid., 4/12.11-12.

[18] Ibid., 28/56.9-13.

[19] Ibid., 13/32.12-18: »Ja die menscheit Christi was und stund alsso gar an sich selber unnd all, als ye keyn creatur,... und was nit anders, den ein hauss oder eyn wonung gottes. Und alles, das gott tzu gehört und das sie selb menscheit was und lebte und ein wonung was der gotheit, des nam sie sich alles nit an.«

[20] Ibid., 7/16.12-22; 17.13-17.

participation with God, while simultaneously living a full, creaturely existence. One does not preempt or displace the other. They can and must be coordinated or integrated for the life and health of the creature. In the »life of Christ« (*leben Christi*) there is a restoration of order between the creature and God in this particular creature.

When writing of the significance of the life of Christ for other human beings, the Frankfurter mentions two aspects. The first, and most dominant, aspect is an imitatio motif. One must »take that life to oneself« and make it one's own.[21] However, he also alludes to a *pro nobis*, or sacramental aspect of the life of Christ, by which one is enabled, by virtue of what has already been done *for* one, to take that life to oneself.[22] Against the suggestion of the Brethren of the Free Spirit that one can transcend the life and teaching of Christ in the pursuit of virtue, the Frankfurter insists that »virtue, order, and justice« have been done by Christ and are already there.[23] Therefore, these are available to the human being because of what Christ previously accomplished apart from the activity of the human being. As to how that which was accomplished by Christ becomes available to others, the Frankfurter alludes to the solidarity of all creation: »All is one in God and God is one in all.«[24] Because of this solidarity, what was done in Christ affected all of creation and therefore touched all of humanity. The author does not describe precisely how that effect is mediated, but he does insist that the life of Christ continues to be necessary for the human being and is offered in the eucharist.[25]

Since sin happened in the person, that is, from one's own reason and will, the Frankfurter insists that »all the wonders and works and even God himself« will not »make me blessed« if it »happens outside me.« Therefore, God must be »known in me and, by love, had, experienced, and tasted.«[26] However, it is not in God's character to force anyone.[27] Therefore, the will of the human must be changed. This change takes place in a process of purgation, enlightenment, and union.[28]

---

21 Ibid., 54/99.30-100.2.

22 Hoffman, *Theologia Germanica*, 38, notes this *pro nobis* suggestion in *TD*: »The Frankfurter does have an intuition about this part of God's self–disclosure which brings us the 'for you,' the vicarious nature of Christ's suffering.«

23 Ibid., 28/56.9-13: »Sich, alsso was und ist es auch umb all tugent, ordnung und redlicheit und des gleich wan was hiemit zu uberkomen ist und etwas hie mit zu uber komen were, daz ist in Christo alles vor und ist bereit da;...«

24 Ibid., 44/88.2-5.

25 Ibid., 43/87.27-30: »Und wer das enphecht in dem heylgen sacrament, der hat Christum werlich und wol enpfangen, und sso man sein mehr enphecht, sso mer Christus, und sso des mynder, sso mynder Christus.«

26 Ibid., 9/22.3-9.

27 Ibid., 31/63.1-4: »Auch ist gottes eigenschaft, daz er niemant zwingt mit gewalt, zu thun oder zu lassen, sunder er lasst einen yeglichen menschen thun und lassen nach seinem willen es sey gut oder pöss, und wil niemant widersteen.«

28 Ibid., 12/30.6-9.

The human first goes through a period of suffering which is preparatory:

The soul of Christ had to come into hell before it came into heaven. Therefore, the human soul must do the same. But how that happens should be noted. If one knows oneself and looks and finds that one is evil and unworthy of the good and comfort which God or other creatures may give, and indeed finds nothing else there but this, then one is eternally damned and lost and thinks oneself unworthy of even that.[29]

The experience of suffering, or hell, to which the Frankfurter refers, is the confrontation of the human being with that which opposes the self – will and thereby threatens one's sense of self – sufficiency.[30] This pain may lead to the recognition of the futility and presumption of assuming that one is what one is from oneself rather than from the Creator. Therefore, one acknowledges that the good and comfort come from others and that one's own mode is evil. This is true repentance and prepares one for enlightenment.

When one has abandoned one's delusion of self – sufficiency (selbheit), the »unnamed flows into the prepared person« or »God goes in with God's self.«[31] Then, in a brief moment of ecstacy, something of the perfect good is revealed to the soul, »a desire to draw near to the perfect and be one with it is born in the human being.«[32] In the union, or the participation intended by God in creation, the divinized human being (vergottet Mensch) experiences an integration of every aspect of life. The outer aspect is ordered by the inner, so that the outer has no reason or desire but to be only in the eternal will.[33] That is to say, the proper relations of the human being to God and to creation are simultaneously restored; justification and sanctification are conjoined. This reordered human being is the only »true, complete human being« wherein there is »perfect feeling and sensitivity to health and to pain, to love and to suffering, and all that may be felt or experienced.«[34] Therefore, whenever the »divinized human being« sees »injustice [or disorder] in another, he is willing to suffer or do anything to eliminate that injustice to bring the other to justice.«[35]

In 1516 and again in 1518, Luther edited and published the *Theologia Deutsch*, while in the midst of his controversy with Rome concerning the nature and efficacy of the sacrament of penance. He found both the *theologia gloriae* of the scholastics and the penitential forms of the church inadequate. In an article for the Heidelberg Disputation, Luther called those theologians of glory »enemies of the cross of Christ« who »hate the cross and sufferings but who love works and

29 Ibid., 11/25.1-8.
30 Ibid., 22/46.6-8: »Als ein mensch, der nit got ist, befindet und erkennet alles das, das dem menschen wol und wee tut und besunder das yhm wider ist.«
31 Ibid., 53/99.16-17.
32 Ibid., 54/99.19-26.
33 Ibid., 37/71.3-6.
34 Ibid., 22/46.1-3.
35 Ibid., 39/77.24-28.

the glory of works.« Against them, Luther asserted that God »cannot be found except in sufferings and the cross.« Hence Luther, in the Resolutions on the 95 Theses, said that when God »undertakes to justify a man, first he condemns him, just as whom he wants to build up, he destroys, whom he wants to heal, he smites, whom he wants to make alive he kills.«[36] According to Luther, it was precisely this individuating, healing process that was thwarted by the penitential practice of the day. Luther, therefore, sought to restore the personal or individual – the »for me« – aspect of penance. He published the *Theologia Deutsch*, in part, to demonstrate that the Wittenberg theology was not an innovation, but of ancient pedigree. Influenced by his endorsement, many radicals, possibly including Schiemer and Schlaffer, and certainly Marpeck, read the tract with interest, and their theologies of the cross, or suffering, are much better understood with reference to it.

LEONHART SCHIEMER

By his own account, Schiemer was educated in Vienna, though not in a »hoch schuel,« and became a parish priest in Austria.[37] Because he experienced »very little godly teaching and righteous living,« he decided for a better Christian estate by entering a Franciscan monastery. After six years, his disappointment with the »disunity« in the order caused him to leave it and travel to Nuremberg, where he learned the tailor's trade. His search for »godly teaching and righteous living« led him to Nicolsburg. There he must have experienced the dispute between Hubmaier and Hut and was put off by the former.[38] He followed Hut to Vienna although he was suspected by some of being a supporter of Hubmaier. After two days among Hut and his followers, Schiemer reported that he not only heard the Word of God, but that it was manifested in their lives. He soon received baptism from Oswald Glait. From Vienna, Schiemer went to Steyr, where he was called to teach and sent out as a missionary. After work in Austria, Salzburg, and Bavaria, he attended the Augsburg »Martyr's Synod« in August 1527 and then travelled into the Tirol. From his baptism until his imprisonment, Schiemer admitted to having visited twenty – eight cities, in which he baptized over two hundred people.

Schiemer seems to have been something of an independent thinker, who, from the beginning, exhibited a critical distance from Hubmaier and Hut. He was attracted to Hut's teaching and its manifestation in the lives of his followers, but his writings reflect his own appropriation of the medieval *Kreuzestheologie*. His

[36] Martin Luther, *D. Martin Luthers Werke*, Weimar Ausgabe (hereinafter listed as WA), 1:362.25-27, 540.8-10.

[37] Schiemer's affidavit was given before the city council on December 23, 1527. LRAT, SAR, RP, 168:145ʳ-148ʳ. See Mecenseffy, *Österreich*, 2:54-55.

[38] The dispute involved the disagreement of Hut and Hubmaier concerning the time and nature of the final judgment, the divine status of Christ, and the relation of the Christian to civil authority. See Packull, *Mysticism*, 99-106.

analysis of the human condition, Christ's work for and in the human being, the proper nature of human life, and their implications for the sacraments and the exercise of coercive force is perceptibly similar to that of the mystical tradition, represented by the *Theologia Deutsch*.[39]

Sin, for Schiemer, is also a turning from God that treats gifts as possessions, which are disposed of according to one's own will. He writes a polemical interpretation of the Lord's Prayer as experienced by the godless – a creature who in the words of the Frankfurter, »assumes to itself (*sich annemen*) something good... as though... that good belonged to the creature«:

They pray well: give us this day our daily bread. But as soon as God gives it, then it is never ours but mine. And today is not enough for them, but they worry about tomorrow, contrary to God's command.... They worry not only about tomorrow, but also the whole year, and not only the whole year, but about ten, twenty, and thirty. They worry not only about themselves, but also for their children, and not only when they are young but when they get older, that is, who will marry them.[40]

The godless, in a misguided search for security, trust that which cannot carry the weight of ultimate trust – the finite self. An unbeliever thinks: »If I give myself in God, so I am never sure. I must perish. But if I stay in the world, then I am surer and I will not perish so quickly.... God may not nourish me, but... then I will freely nourish myself.«[41] Rather than securing life, these people lose it. Citing Paul, Schiemer asserts that those who seek to control reality and secure themselves are outside God and thus alienated from life.[42]

The key to the human problem is the same as the key to the Scriptures – the cross of Christ.[43] Schiemer calls the work of the cross justice, or *Gerechtigkeit*.[44] Christ's work effectuates a change in the mode of human existence introduced uniquely in the person of Christ. Schiemer says that if this justification happens in us, »it is a great work of God... but it can and may not happen outside Jesus Christ, who is our justness (*Gerechtigkeit*) through his conception, birth, death, and resurrection.«[45] Further, this new mode of existence, made possible by Christ, must be introduced into the life of the believer. The Christian is to share in the justness of God: »Just as water does not quench my thirst if I do not drink it, and bread does not drive away hunger if I do not eat it, so Christ's suffering does not keep me from sinning unless he suffers in me.«[46] In his notion of justice,

---

[39] See W. Wiswedel, *Leonhard Schiemer, der erste Täuferbischof Oberösterreichs*, 184.

[40] Lydia Müller, ed., *Glaubenszeugnisse oberdeutscher Taufgesinnter*, 70.

[41] Ibid., 67.

[42] Ibid., 73-74: »Paulus sagt auch, sie sein entfremdet von dem leben, das aus Gott ist.«

[43] Ibid., 60: »Wer den schlüssl Davidt nit hat, dem ists in ewigkait verschlossen. Das ist das crüetz Christy.«

[44] Ibid., 65: »So hist nun die ander gnad: gerechtikeit. Es ist ein groß werck Gottes.«

[45] Ibid., 65-66.

[46] Ibid., 52.

Schiemer is primarily concerned with the order of human life. The problem is not changing God's attitude toward humanity. That is unnecessary because God's attitude is always the same: »God hates sin but not his creature.«[47] The problem is the disorder or disorientation in the mode of human existence. This does not abrogate the unique *pro nobis* nature of Christ. This new mode was introduced only in the concrete, historical life, suffering, death, and resurrection of Jesus. In fact, the result is a heightened sense of the meaning of the incarnation.

This introduction of Christ's justness into the life of the believer involves the necessity of sharing the suffering of Christ. In a passage that develops his understanding of Hut's »gospel of all creatures,« Schiemer reveals the goal of human life and the necessary process of suffering to that goal:

He (Paul) says further that the gospel I preached to you is preached in all creatures. God created all creatures in five days so that they can be used by the human, who was created on the sixth day. Then the creature has its rest. But the human being was not created to remain a human being on the sixth day, but that he would come to the seventh day, indeed that he become godly, or divinized, and come to God. That is then the appropriate human rest or true day of celebration. And indeed the means by which all creatures come to be useful to the human is suffering. One kills, cuts, and cooks and the creature holds still and suffers for the sake of faith. And just as an animal is not useful to the human for food unless the body dies, so no human becomes blessed, who does not die for Christ's sake.[48]

In his treatise on the three graces, Schiemer identifies the process of suffering, or the cross, as God's second grace and the divinization of the human being as the third grace. The entire process is grace because the Lord »takes us, the creature, sets us naked and bare in the other birth and gives us his spirit and teaches us to know and love him... but such does not happen without pain, suffering, and fear.«[49] Before turning, then, to that goal, the role of suffering in the healing or reordering of the human being deserves closer examination.

Schiemer argues that God neither sends pain nor finds pleasure in it. It is a result of the encounter of the disorder of the human being with the order of creation. He writes: »Not that that [pain, suffering and fear] pleases God, but he allows and endures it for us, as a (doctor endures the stench of a patient), when he heals him, for such suffering and pain comes only from our unbelief.«[50] He compares this pain to that experienced by one who loves an adulteress who leaves him. He is hurt by his inordinate love for her, not because someone punishes him. This is the same for all persons. When one loses, as is inevitable in the

47 Ibid., 46.
48 Ibid., 49.
49 Ibid., 66.
50 Ibid.

created order, »wife, children, father, mother, brother, sister, goods, money, healthy body, or life,« what causes suffering is unbelief, or the inordinate attachment to creatures.[51] This is the pain resulting from treating these as possessions and not as gifts. Schiemer goes on to assert that these disordered relationships cause pain even before they are lost, for example the inappropriate and debilitating anxiety concerning the future mate of one's child. Actually, it is only through the loss of these things »that the human being is purified from the love of all creatures.«[52] Schiemer praises death, or the loss of all things, as the ultimate purification. In it one comes to trust God for one's existence rather than one's own ability to cling to creation. For this process Schiemer employed graphic images from the life of those miners and burghers to whom he preached: »What is needed is a good smelting, a strong refining, a hot rinse, for an uncrucified Christian is like unrefined ore, or a house, for which the trees are not yet trimmed.«[53] And, »The beverage in this bottle is nothing else than a beaten, pulverized, ground, afflicted heart beaten with the mortar of the cross, for the grapes in God's vineyard must all be pressed or smashed under the wine press or feet of affliction. Otherwise no wine is produced.«[54] Through suffering, the old, self–enclosed mode of control and manipulation is broken and one is freed to receive the third grace – the Holy Spirit, who »heals us with the oil of inexpressible joy.«[55] It is the Spirit promised by Jesus, who said that he would »not leave you orphans.« And his Spirit comes into the individual being.

This belief in the reception of the Holy Spirit leads to a major polemic of Schiemer against his understanding of Luther. He argues against Luther's translation of John 1:14, »dz wort ist fleisch worden, und wonet under uns,« saying that every schoolboy knows it should read, »wonet *in* uns, und nit *under* uns.«[56] God does not stay outside, apart from the believer, but comes in. And the believer, no longer alienated from the life of God, does not stay outside of God, but goes into God. Schiemer scoffs that perhaps Luther »hofft *an* Got, und glaubt *an* Christum,« but we »hoffen *in* Got, glauben *in* Christum, haben das wort *in* uns, nit *under* uns.«[57] The goal of the human being is an intimate participation in the life of God. One receives rather than grasps and gives rather than takes. Following Paul, Schiemer says that all his members participate (*sein teilhaftig*) both in Christ's chastisement and in his Spirit.[58] It is this participation in God to which Schiemer refers, when he says one becomes »godly« or »divinized.«[59] In an

51 Ibid.
52 Ibid., 67.
53 Ibid.
54 Ibid., 72.
55 Ibid., 71.
56 Ibid., 61.
57 Ibid.
58 Ibid., 51-52.
59 This relationship should not be seen as a confusion of the human and the divine. or the natural and supernatural as Packull, *Mysticism*, 96-97, claims of Jacob Dachser, an Augsburg Anabaptist influenced by Hut. Schiemer stresses the finitude and, therefore, utter dependence of the human on divine grace. There is always a distinction between the human and the divine.

interesting remark, he says that one should not look only to God's comfort, »but it should and ought to be that a Christian speaks to and comforts another in affliction.«[60]

With his concern for this participation, Schiemer stresses the relational character of faith. For him, faith describes the new mode of receptivity through which the Spirit comes into the believer. Again writing against his understanding of Lutheran theology, he says, »They think that faith is only something that happened in Bethlehem, Nazareth, or Jerusalem... but it does not happen in them.«[61] If that was so, he argues that they could give no account of when or how one comes to faith or what faith is. Faith rather is a new orientation, or change in one's life. It cannot be had with mere words, as though a goldsmith could teach his craft by only talking. It is necessary that one go to the workplace.[62]

Those who say faith comes only from hearing the outer word ignore what the Lord said, »whoever hears it from the Father, and learns, comes to me.«[63] The inner word of the Father in the individual directs one to and confirms the outer work, mediated through the community. There must be a correlation between the outer and inner word.

From Schiemer's perspective, the scribes (that is, the Lutherans), with too much stress on the outer, did not distinguish the inner from the outer word.[64] For that reason, they missed the significance of the entrance of the Spirit and the radical reorientation of one's mode of existence, which must take place. Because Luther »does not want to have anything (Christ, God, faith, or light) in him, but only beside him, under him, at him,«[65] his self-enclosed nature is never changed; the soul remains turned to the flesh.[66] However, »whoever has the true light of the Spirit in him and also hears the word from outside,« that person is easy to teach.[67]

This concern for an inner word and response, present in the *Theologia Deutsch*, led Schiemer to a radical reinterpretation of the theology and practice of baptism. He develops this theology in a tract on the threefold character of baptism. The first aspect is that of obedience. One »pledges himself to be obedient to the

---

With a mystical notion of participation, there is distinction between the divine and human, without separation.

[60] Müller, *Glaubenszeugnisse*, 71: »Jhedoch sollen wir nit allein auf Gottes trost harren, sonder es soll und mag auch ein Christ dem andern in trüebsal zuesprechen un trösten.« Marpeck will develop this concept of Christians as participants in, and concrete, historical conveyers of the work of Christ. See following chapters 5 and 7.

[61] Müller, *Glaubenszeugnisse*, 48.

[62] Ibid., 74.

[63] Ibid., 48.

[64] Ibid., 60.

[65] Ibid., 61: »So wil er ir kains in im haben, sonder nur neben im, under im, an im.« Emphasis added.

[66] Ibid., 63: »Die seel steet in der mitten. Seitemal wir alle sambt, außgenomen Christus, uns haben gewendt zum fleisch mit unser seel, sein wir all gestorben in der seel.«

[67] Ibid., 74.

Father, as also Christ was... unto the death of the cross.«[68] There is, then, an inner call to which one responds with obedience. The second aspect concerns the external act. The baptism of water is a »confirmation of faith and the inward covenant with God.«[69] Therefore, the inner and the outer are correlated in baptism. To baptize an infant who is incapable of a response to the inner word is like sealing an empty letter.[70] Baptism is, for Schiemer, similar to the oath he took upon entering the Franciscan order, as he sought an experience of repentance and change of life. As soon as one commits oneself to this way of Christ and begins to live as a Christian, one encounters the third aspect of baptism – blood.

For those who live in the new mode, »it can, may, and will not go differently than it did with Christ.«[71] Citing Jesus saying that he brought not peace but a sword, Schiemer writes, »the Jews were right when they said that he had caused an uproar from Galilee to Jerusalem.«[72] In like manner, Schiemer, in his affidavit, denies having preached rebellion. He claims to have »taught only the word of God, faith, Christian love, and patience,« which would come to no revolution. However, he was aware that the new mode of existence, as he understood it, would challenge the unjust manipulation and control of others and therefore result in the charge of rebellion as it had with Jesus and Paul.[73] He himself had experienced that conflict and embraced it as a further purification toward a more perfect participation in God.

The combination of Schiemer's reflections on grace and baptism gives a sense of the whole process of salvation. Because of the disorder in one's mode of living, one experiences pain when encountered by the adversities of the created order. This pain jars one to the consciousness of one's own disorder. This is reinforced by the first grace, or light within, which enables one to understand, by comparing one's own plight to that of all creatures, that this process of suffering is necessary. This leads to repentance for one's inappropriate mode of existence and an affirmation of this way of suffering. This is the first baptism, which issues in the public, or outer, baptism of water. The second and third graces alternate in a process of purification – a dissolution of the old mode and the growth of the new. One receives the Spirit and begins to live as a Christian. The result is a different kind of suffering for the sake of Christ, as one begins to live in the mode of Christ. This, in turn, opens one to a greater receptivity to the Spirit.

---

68 Ibid., 77.
69 Ibid., 78.
70 Ibid., 78-79.
71 Ibid., 51.
72 Ibid.

73 Ibid., 51: »Eben dise ursach hett man auch wider Paulum, do die Juden sprachen, wir haben disen man funden schedlich, dan er erregt ufruehr allen Juden auf dem ganzen erdboden und ist ein fürnemer der Natzarener sekten.« Also »geet es auch allen Christen, dan der junger ist nit mer dan der maister.«

As for his eschatological expectations, Schiemer believes that the believer sleeps until the second advent of Christ.[74] Just before the coming of the Son of Man, Christians will experience extreme persecution at the hands of the godless.[75] Then, at the resurrection of the flesh, everyone, living and dead, will be called before the judgment seat of Christ.

HANS SCHLAFFER

In 1511 »im land ob der Enns,« Schlaffer received ordination as a secular priest.[76] He confessed that he had no idea what he preached during that period, for he went sometimes as long as a year without reading so much as a page of the Old or New Testaments.[77] As for the vows of poverty, obedience, and chastity taken before the bishop, Schlaffer reveals that he received forty to fifty guilders per year in addition to board and still wanted more. In addition, he received privileges and freedom from taxes, tolls, and interest. Further, he likened the requirement of celibacy in this context of excess food and drink to someone's putting straw in fire and expecting it not to burn. In spite of this life, he says he thought that he could make himself and others blessed by saying masses and praying.[78] Nevertheless, his conscience often caused him »anxiety and restlessness.« So he thought of becoming a Carthusian and »ran again and again to Roman grace, confession and did things, I know not what.« But, in all this, he could not still his conscience with respect to God.[79] Then, God again opened his eternal word, »through the testimony of the holy Scripture.«

The writings and sermons of Luther and others caused Schlaffer to read »the Bible, the gospels, and the letters of the apostles.« There he discovered that one is not made righteous nor blessed (rechtfertigen noch selig machen) by the work of

---

[74] Ibid., 67.

[75] Ibid., 54-55. Packull, *Mysticism*, 109-13, especially 112, correctly notes that Schiemer's »focus was not on the expected vengeance on the godless,« epitomizing the »transition from a purely internalized cross mysticism to an Anabaptist theology of martyrdom.«

[76] Müller, *Glaubenszeugnisse*, 119.

[77] *Ein einfaltig gebet durch ein qefanngnen armen b(rude)r im herren zu Schwatz gebetet unnd betreubt bis inn denn Tod*, in KB, 117ᵛ-118ʳ: »Wie und was ich aber glernt und gebredigt, o herr, so bekenn ich, das ich inn etlich jaren nit ein blat weder im alten noch neuen testament nach der ordnunng glesenn hab, ja nit wissen kapt, was testament sey.« Having discovered a manuscript of this devotional book of the Marpeck circle, Heinold Fast is preparing a critical edition. All citations from *Das Kunstbuch* are from the notes to this edition, which Fast made available to me.

[78] *KB*, 117ᵛ: »... wolt ich mich nit alein mit meine vermeinten guten werckhen als meslesen und beten (mit fassten ließ ich mir nit wee gschechen) selig machen, sonder ouch andern als ein mitselsorger, darzu hilflich sein.«

[79] Ibid., 118ʳ: »... oft inn angst und unfrid meiner gwissen gstossen... darinnen ich mir zu mermalen furnam, ain kartheiserr zu werden, lief hin und wider inn römischen gnaden, beichtet und thet waiß nit was. Aber inn dem allem konth ich mein gwissen nit zufriden stellen gegen dir, mein ewiger got.«

the law, but alone by »faith in Jesus Christ.«[80] Therefore, he stopped reading the mass and resigned his office. Although, in the beginning, he spoke out against the Anabaptists, he, like Schiemer, was attracted to Hut in Nicolsburg.[81] In the summer of 1527 he made contact with Jacob Wiedemann and Jacob Kautz in Augsburg. In Nuremberg, Ludwig Hätzer and Hans Denck greatly impressed him as »learned and earnest men.« Later, he had contacts with Oswald Glait and Wolfgang Bandhuber zu Linz (Bünderlin) in Regensburg. From there he travelled with Ulrich Moser, an employee of the Fuggers, to the Rattenberg smelting works and stayed with a family friend in nearby Brixlegg.[82] It is not certain how long Schlaffer was in the Rattenberg area, but he undoubtedly made contact with the Anabaptist group there and may even have been responsible for founding the congregation, which received Schiemer so enthusiastically. There is, then, a possibility that Marpeck knew Schlaffer personally. Probably because of Ferdinand's mandate and Schiemer's arrest in late November, Schlaffer decided to go to Hall through Schwaz. There, he was arrested on December 6.[83] During the nearly eight weeks of his imprisonment, Schlaffer wrote all but one of his extant works. The *Ein einfaltig gebet...* was written the night before his execution.

It is possible that Hätzer and Denck introduced Schlaffer to the *Theologia Deutsch* during his stay in Nuremberg, for his writings also reflect its theology of the cross. He sounds, though with different accents, many of the same themes as Schiemer: justice as a reordering of the mode of human existence, the necessity of suffering illustrated by the »gospel of all creatures,« a stress on the inner character of this justness, and baptism as a public repentance.

Christ suffered and died »on account of our sins and rose for our justness« (*Rechtigkait*).[84] There is a twofold work of Christ. Christ's death and blood »achieved an indulgence for your sins... and with respect to the Father... freed and purified your evil conscience.«[85] Further, he arose, »so that one could and should not live in himself, but that Christ might.«[86] Christ's suffering and death purifies the conscience and prepares one to receive the living presence of the resurrected Christ. The problem with the human being is again a living in the self – an isolation from the life of God. Justness is a different mode of living, which ends this isolation by receptivity to Christ.

However, suffering is necessary to change the nature of the human being, turned in upon the self, to one that is receptive or participative. Schlaffer asserts

---

[80] Ibid., 8^r-118^v: »... do befannde ich, das nit die werckh, ja herr, ouch die werckh des gsatz, so du uns durch Mosen geben, ich gschweige von menschen erdachte und gutdunckende werckh nit rechtfertigen noch selig machen mochten, sonnder alein der gloub inn Jesum Christum, deinen einigen sun, o himlischer vater.«

[81] Müller, *Glaubenszeugnisse*, 122-23.

[82] Ibid., 120.

[83] *KB*, 120^v: »... ietz uff Nicloai, do ich alhie zu Schwatz gfanngen.«

[84] Müller, *Glaubenszeugnisse*, 115.

[85] *KB*, 125^v-126^r: »Das ist, wie euch Christus mit seinem tod und plutvergiessen ablaß eurer sunden erlanngt hat und mit dem vaterr, weil ir feind warn, versuent, eure bose gwissen dadurch besprengt und gereinigt.«

[86] Müller, *Glaubenszeugnisse*, 114.

that »whoever does not suffer with him [Christ] will not share the inheritance.«[87] This truth is apparent both in Scripture and nature. Abraham, Isaac, Jacob, and others came to faith only through affliction. Creatures are a living book that teaches the same lesson. For example, »with a hen or fish or other animal, that you want to eat, it is clear that it (according to its own will and pleasure) cannot prepare [rechtfertigen] itself, that is, it may not lay itself out, open itself, clean itself and boil or fry itself. But you must do it according to your will, which it must suffer. You must prepare [rechtfertigen] it according to your will.«[88] The pain routinely experienced by a person as a result of adversity to the will brings the acknowledgment that one is »always turned toward his own desires.«[89] Further, there comes the recognition that one's highest end is not achieved by the exercise of one's own will. The viator sees that »he cannot come farther through himself, for as he knows, a wild tree cannot become better without a gardener.« Rather the human being's highest end involves a participative relationship with something greater than the self – something that cannot be controlled or bent to one's own will. Help must come from outside of the individual. It is God alone »who must make [one] pious, just [gerecht], and virtuous.«[90] Therefore, one »must subject himself to God and suffer his will.« Only through much suffering and affliction does one come »to that for which he was originally created.«[91]

This state originally intended for the human being involves a vital participation, in which one receives from without and goes out of the self into something larger. Schlaffer develops each of these dynamics with his stress on the inward coming of Christ and the outward body of Christ. Like Schiemer, he insists that »the same word became flesh and dwelt in us.«[92] The devil, death, and hell are only overcome »through Christ in us.«[93].

At the same time one is incorporated into a larger body of Christ. According to Schlaffer, through faith, »which is a work and gift of God within us,« one becomes »incorporated, participative, and conformed to the life, suffering, and death of Christ according to the flesh« of the body.[94] Faith seems to refer to the new mode of existence through which participation flows. The body of Christ is »the believing community of Christ,«[95] in which »we are members of his body, of

---

[87] Ibid., 95.

[88] Ibid., 86.

[89] Ibid., 94.

[90] Ibid., 86.

[91] Ibid., 94.

[92] Ibid., 107. Emphasis added.

[93] Ibid., 96. Emphasis added.

[94] *KB*, 124[v]-125[r]: »... essen das fleisch Christi und trinckhen sein plut ist nit anderst dann durch den glouben, der ein werckh und hab gotes ist in uns, Christo seinem leben, leiden und sterben nach dem fleisch eingeleibt, teilhaftig, gleichförmig und ain ding werden... seines reichs ouch teilhaftig werden und erben.«

[95] Müller, *Glaubenszeugnisse*, 109.

his flesh, and of his bones and become two in one flesh.«[96] For Schlaffer, Christ's relationship to the community, not to the bread and the cup, is the »great mystery« of the Christian faith.[97] The community is where the present reality of Christ is experienced – where the new mode of existence of giving and receiving is lived out. The supper is a testimony to one's desire »to have community and be a participant in all things with the body of Christ.« Having received, one is free »to maintain the community, to give for his brother as Christ gave for him.« This participation involves love and suffering, wealth and poverty, honor and humiliation, sorrow and joy, death and life, or »all that has body and life.«[98]

Schlaffer had a concrete, even physical, notion of the sharing of the life of Christ, which issued from his justness. This was the foundation for his rejection of Luther's insistence on the real presence: »They make so many glosses about the word of the Lord in John and want to have the body of Christ or his flesh in the bread and his blood in the cup and say it is not hard or difficult to eat and drink daily. The reason is it creates good and peaceful days and they live in sumptuous eating and drinking... remaining in their fleshly lives.« But, »Christ says, 'Whoever eats my flesh and drinks my blood, remains in me and I in him.'... Here one sees well that the eating and drinking is something new, different from worldly lives.«[99] Again Schlaffer insists that the reality of Christ and his justness is something in which one participates; it reorders the human being's mode of existence. It does not remain outside, embodied in bread and wine; rather it is embodied and mediated by real, flesh and blood people.

Baptism is the means by which one is incorporated into the body.[100] It is the outward public sign of an inner, correct penance.[101] Schlaffer believes that his age was experiencing a renewal of the early church: »Therefore God, in this last dangerous time, through his son, constituted again a public, Christian, holy community. So he also desires that it be made public and before the world through the outer sign of the baptism.«[102] With baptism as the prerequisite for becoming a member of the body, Matthew 28:18-20 seems to have served Schlaffer the same purpose as John 6:48f. served Luther. They can be seen as the

---

[96] *KB*, 122[r]: »Dann wir seyen glider seines leibs von seinem fleisch und von seinem gebein und werden zwey inn einem fleisch sein.«

[97] Ibid., 122[r]: »O, das ist ein grosse geheimnuß inn Christo und seiner gmein. Dieweil nun Christus als das houbt im sterblichen fleisch lept, aber on sundt, must es nur gelitn und getödtet sein. Seyen wir nun seine glider und mitsampt im ein gantzer leib, so muessen jee di glider dem houpt allennthalben nachvolgen, welches aber nit allenthalben mit got, das ist kein glid am leib nit.«

[98] Müller, *Glaubenszeugnisse*, 109.

[99] *KB*, 123[r]-123[v]: »Die machen der glosn sovil uber deß herrn wort im Johanne und wellen den leib Christi oder sein fleisch im brot und sein plut im kelch haben und ist nit hart unnd schwer, teglich zu essen und trinckhen, ursach, es schaffet gut, ruehig tag und leben inn wolessen und trincken, inn allem wollusst und hocher wirdigkeit... doch Christus spricht: Wer mein fleisch isset und mein plut trincket, der pleibt in mir und ich in im.... Hie sicht man wol, das essen und trinckhen ein anders neues, dann wie di welt lebt, ist.«

[100] Müller, *Glaubenszeugnisse*, 117.

[101] Ibid., 122.

[102] Ibid., 93.

words of institution for the only implicit sacrament (though Schlaffer never called it that) he had – the community of baptized believers. For Luther, if one said the words of institution in the presence of believers, Christ promised his presence. So with Schlaffer, if one went, taught all people, and baptized them (that is, those who were taught), then Christ promised his presence in the community.[103] Therefore, for Schlaffer, baptizing infants would be like Luther purposely changing the words of institution, to which Christ had promised his presence.

With regard to the civil order, Schlaffer reveals in a prayer his thoughts concerning the responsibilities which accompany the God–given power. He prays that God will enlighten all princes, authorities, and lords with the divine truth in order that they may use the power to protect the pious, to punish the evil, and not to shed the blood of the innocent.[104] In his testimony to the Innsbruck administration, he affirmed that every true follower of Christ maintains the commands of God, not the least of which is obedience to civil authority. He vowed that neither he, nor anyone associated with him, had ever incited rebellion, but only »laid down the evil old life and in a new life indeed in the holiness and justice of the truth, turned to God.«[105] Though he claimed that it would not lead to armed rebellion, his loyalty to that notion of justice apparently led him to disobey Ferdinand's mandate.

In his extant writings Schlaffer intentionally says little about the eschaton. In fact, he chides those »brothers among us, who have an excessive preoccupation with such questions, particularly in the mysteries of the judgment.«[106] As for the end of the world, the time and day of the Lord's judgment, how and in what form human beings shall be raised, where they shall dwell, and where they are before they come to the judgment, such matters »should be commended only to God in all humility.«[107] Schlaffer probably had in mind certain other Anabaptists, also in the sphere of Hut's influence, who stressed an ultimate apocalyptic vindication of those who endured suffering in the present age.[108]

---

[103] Ibid., 111: »Erstlichen spricht Christus, mir ist geben aller gwalt im himmel und auf erden; darumb geet hin, leeret alle völker und tauft sie (zu versteen, welche ir geleernet habt) im namen des vaters, suns und des heiligen geists und leeret sie halten alles, was ich euch bevolhen hab. Nembt war, ich bin bei euch bis zu ennd der welt usw.«

[104] Ibid., 97.

[105] Ibid., 116.

[106] Ibid., 105.

[107] Ibid., 106.

[108] George H. Williams, *The Radical Reformation*, 226, outlines four distinct types of pacifism in the Radical Reformation: 1, Erasmian prudential pacifism; 2, evangelical pacifism of conventicular separatism (Grebel) based on the Dominical counsels; 3, suffering pacifism which viewed persecution as a confirmation of their elect faith; and 4, provisional, suffering pacifism which stressed the eventual compensation in the bloody eschatological warfare of the saints. Both Schlaffer and Schiemer (nn. 74, 75) represent the third type, in opposition to some of Hut's followers (perhaps Augustine Bader) who embodied the fourth alternative.

MARPECK AND THE »MYSTERY OF THE CROSS OF CHRIST«

In the turbulent years of the 1520s Marpeck was attracted to the notions of justice and the understanding of suffering reflected in the *Theologia Deutsch* and which was preached in and around Rattenberg by the Anabaptists, Leonhard Schiemer and Hans Schlaffer. For them, disorder in the relationship to God necessarily caused disorder in the relationship to the rest of creation and vice versa. The just mode of Christ simultaneously reordered both relationships. According to Schlaffer, Christ's justice does not remain outside, in the bread and wine, but is embodied in the physical lives of men and women. In this view, justice is an intrinsic structure, or ordering, of human life, not an extrinsic judgment about it.[109] This conjoining of justification and sanctification does not reject the *extra nos* character of grace or the historic, *pro nobis* character of Christ's work, but insists that that grace and Christ's justice come *in nos* to reorder the lives of those who receive it. And this internal reordering necessarily manifests itself externally in one's social relationships.

Having been put off by the fleshly freedom of Lutheran believers who had been justified by faith, but whose lives, in his opinion, did not manifest Christ's reordering, Marpeck was drawn to this notion of justice which issued in a change of life, or »the obedience of faith.« When ordered by Ferdinand to aid in the arrest, interrogation, and forced recantation or execution of those in whose lives he perceived the reordering justice of Christ, Marpeck refused to act externally, *coram hominibus*, in such a way as to violate his sense of justice *coram deo*. Further, Schiemer and Schlaffer's theologies of the cross provided a means by which Marpeck could understand their suffering and executions and his own loss of office and property as experienced for the sake of Christ and Christ's justice.

---

[109] Heiko A. Oberman, *The Gospel of Social Unrest: 450 Years after the So-Called 'German Peasants' War' of 1525*, 112, has recognized the medieval mystical tradition as one source of this notion of justice among the radicals, in which there is an inner connection between justice *coram deo* and justice *coram hominibus*.

Chapter 3

STRASSBURG: SOCIAL AND RELIGIOUS RADICALISM

From the introduction of Reformation ideas in 1521 to the establishment of the reformed church by the synods of 1533-35, the imperial city of Strassburg experienced religious, social, and political ferment. Various religious perspectives vied for loyalties formerly held by the Old Church. During the years of Marpeck's stay (1528-31), differing conceptions of the nature of the Christian life, the church, and their relation to the social and political order competed for support and institutional expression.

Marpeck's first theological writings were influenced by and helped shape his activity in the social, political, and religious dynamics of this imperial city. This chapter examines that activity and its contexts, while the next focuses on his theology, articulated in response to opponents on two fronts.

STRASSBURG'S SOCIAL AND POLITICAL STRUCTURE IN THE 1520s

In the bloodless »guild revolution« of 1419, Strassburg's guilds displaced the political domination of the patriciate, or Konstoffler, and became the city's fundamental political units. By limiting the patriciate to one–third of the seats in the Senate and privy councils (13, 15, 21), the 1480 constitution assured the guilds a two–thirds majority.[1] Eligible voters from each of the fifteen guilds elected fifteen Schöffen, who, in turn, selected the members of the Senate. Except for the Council of 15, which named its own, the Senate appointed members of the privy councils, where decisions were made concerning Strassburg's most important business.

By the early sixteenth century a new, guild aristocracy, composed of rentiers and merchants, had emerged as a prominent political group in the city.[2] Because of their financial stability and free time, members of this group held many of the Schöffen positions. In fact, the free election process devolved into cooptation, whereby the Schöffen themselves named their own successors.[3] The guild aristocracy, coupled with the old patriciate, with whom it shared common

---

1 Klaus Deppermann, *Melchior Hoffman*, 141.
2 Thomas A. Brady, *Ruling Class, Regime and Reformation at Strasbourg*, 112-13, 120.
3 Ibid., 166.

economic interests, comprised a powerful ruling regime, dominating the privy councils.

Another group within the guilds exercised some direct political influence but had economic interests different from those of the guild aristocracy. Although in smaller numbers, these working artisans and craftsmen could express their views in the Senate, the privy councils, and the occasional assembly of the three hundred Schöffen.[4] However, they achieved only limited success in their persistent attempts to reduce taxes on goods, such as wine and food; to control usury; and to raise property taxes.[5]

A third group, consisting of journeymen and unskilled laborers, were effectively closed out of the organized political process and faced a difficult economic situation. For example, journeymen had no right to vote, strike, or assemble. The gardeners, the largest but poorest guild, found themselves in an increasingly oppressive economic dependence on the landed patricians and were rarely represented in the privy councils.[6] The Strassburg authorities referred to this third group as the »common man« and were often concerned about its only political recourse – street violence.[7]

In spite of these inner tensions, Strassburg enjoyed a relatively stable social equilibrium due to the wisdom of the *Magistrat* and the city's favorable economic structure.[8] On certain potentially divisive issues, such as the response to the 1525 peasant uprising and the 1529 decision to abolish the Mass, the *Magistrat* called special assemblies of the three hundred Schöffen. It also passed measures to reduce antagonism between groups within the guilds themselves. On behalf of smaller master craftsmen, it discouraged the development of monopolies by larger masters. In 1526, 1529, and 1533 the Senate passed ordinances protecting journeymen and apprentices in the tailoring, weaving, and furrier guilds from attempts by the masters to close them out of a larger profit share and stronger job security.[9] In addition, the city's rich agricultural resources supported a thriving craft industry. Due in part to this stability, Strassburg was able to extend its hospitality to a stream of refugees from religious persecution during the 1520s.

---

4 Ibid., 174-75.

5 Deppermann, *Melchior Hoffman*, 141.

6 Jean Rott, *La Guerre des paysans et la ville de Strasbourg*, 23, says that the gardeners comprised one–sixth to one–fifth of the Strassburg citizens. Depperman, *Melchior Hoffman*, 144, estimates their number at 600 in 1530. Brady, *Ruling Class*, 181, shows that, during the period of his study, the gardeners had no representatives on the Council of 15 and only four on the Councils of 13 and 21. Of these four, three were from the same wealthy family.

7 »Common man« (gemeiner Mann) is a technical term in the Strassburg sources referring to this third, disenfranchised group. For a discussion of the problems involved in a general definition of the common man during this period, see Paul Russell, *Common People and the Future of the Reformation in the Pamphlet Literature of Southwestern Germany to 1525*, 122-24.

8 Miriam Chrisman, *Strasbourg and the Reform*, 23, prefers the use of Magistrat as an inclusive term referring to the political establishment of Strassburg. Although Bürgermeister und 21 is usually used in the sources, Chrisman points out that that formula included other institutions such as the Ammeisters, Stettmeisters, privy councils, and the occasional council of Schöffen.

9 Deppermann, *Melchior Hoffman*, 142.

STRASSBURG'S EARLY REFORM, 1521–25

When Reformation ideas entered Strassburg in 1521, they were developed and promoted by a group of convinced preachers (Zell, Capito, Bucer, and Hedio), members of the small artisans, some intellectuals (Eckhart zum Treübel, Lukas Hackfurt, and Johannes Schwebel of the Latin school), and an enthusiastic »common man.«[10]

In 1521 Mattheus Zell defended Luther from the pulpit of the St. Lawrence Chapel in the cathedral. Because of the canons' support of Zell, the bishop exhorted the council on August 8, 1522, to carry out the punitive measures of the Edict of Worms. Because of increasing popular unrest, the council decided to have its deputies protect Zell.[11] The 1523 tract of the layman, Eckhart zum Treübel, *A Humble Admonition...* , articulated some of the sentiments of a growing anticlericalism in the city and praised the evangelical movement led by Zell. Eckhart asserted that one should have nothing to do with money in the church and criticized the clergy for putting more faith in its assets than in God.[12] In March 1523 the cathedral chapter warned the bishop of a public uproar if Zell was dismissed.[13] The following month Wolfgang Capito, as provost of St. Thomas's the third ranking ecclesiastical official in the city, declared himself for the evangelical movement and bought citizenship.[14]

The tension reached crisis proportions on August 20, when a riot at the Young St. Peter's, one of the parishes with a large concentration of gardeners, caused its canons to flee with their valuables. In September four hundred citizens invaded the Augustinian monastery and brought Conrad Tregor, a pamphleteer among the Old Believers, before the council because of his violation of a mandate prohibiting inflammatory language. Two months later the council sent a delegation to St. Thomas's, attributing the tension to the objection of the »common man« because he was burdened with taxes, from which the clergy was free.[15] In fact, almost every document issued by the council which dealt with the evangelical movement cited the constant threat to the city's peace.

The pressure from below continued in 1524. When the bishop cited six newly married priests to appear before him, they declined, using the threat of a popular revolt as leverage against their ecclesiastical superiors. Because of a bad harvest, the gardeners of St. Aurelian's parish refused to pay the tithe to the canons of St. Thomas.[16] Further, they petitioned the council for the right to call Martin Bucer as their preacher and did so in April, despite the council's objections. The

---

10 Ibid., 149.

11 Chrisman, *Strasbourg and the Reform*, 100-101.

12 William S. Stafford, *Domesticating the Clergy: The Inception of the Reformation in Strasbourg, 1522-1524*, 201.

13 Heinrich Schmidt, *Reichsstädte, Reich und Reformation*, 58.

14 Chrisman, *Strasbourg and the Reform*, 167.

15 Stafford, *Domesticating the Clergy*, 177-78, 133.

16 Ibid., 202.

congregations of Young St. Peter's and St. Stephen's, also with large concentrations of gardeners, quickly followed suit.

By the summer of 1524 a reversal had taken place in the popular mind. Whereas earlier the Old Church had stood for peace and order and accused the evangelists of disruption, now the Old Believers were thrust into the role of disturbing the city's peace and the evangelical preachers, as custodians of the Word or commands of God, were perceived as providing the basis for social unity.[17] A petition to the council in August 1524 manifested this perception asking for the end of old rite services in the churches and the installation of evangelical preachers in every parish. Using a formula of Bucer's the petitioners argued that »without friendship toward God [that is, based only on the Reformer's program], there will never be true friendship among us.«[18]

The evangelical preachers played a key role in shaping the intellectual framework of this popular movement. In his *Christliche Verantwortung* (1523), Zell traced the roots of the irritation between the laity and the clergy to the latter's temporal powers, wealth, and immunity from civil responsibilities. He maintained that the tyranny of the church would subside and social harmony increase if the priests limited their activity to their only legitimate task – preaching the Word of God. Martin Bucer's three booklets of 1524, *Das Ym Selbs*, *Summary seiner Predig*, and the *Verantwortung*, contained his program for reform. In them he asserted that the true gospel was the foundation of social harmony. Faith, grounded on the Word expounded by commissioned spiritual officers, constituted the only source of human »other – directedness,« which is the cement of any society.[19]

On sacramental issues, the Reformers reflected a spiritualistic tendency.[20] Admitting that adult baptism corresponded more closely to the custom of the early church and the Scriptures, they believed that the precise time of baptism was relatively unimportant because »God is not bound to any external thing.«[21] Bucer, in his *Grund unnd Ursach* (1524), acknowledged the argument of those who opposed infant baptism, but enjoined them to avoid destroying the love and unity of the *corpus Christianum*.[22] When Hinne Rode came to Strassburg in the fall of 1524, both Bucer and Capito joined the sacramentarian side of the dispute about the Supper.[23]

The *Magistrat* responded cautiously to these developments and worked out no clear policy for church matters in these early years. This reticence was due not only to the division within the *Magistrat* between an evangelical party (Nikolaus

---

17 Ibid., 210f.

18 Ibid., 218-19.

19 Ibid., 48f., has a description of these works.

20 Deppermann, *Melchior Hoffman*, 152-55, describes these early reflections on sacramental theology.

21 See the 1524 letter to Luther, WA Br. 3, no. 797, 384.97-101; and KR, 1:28.

22 Hans – Werner Müsing, *Karlstadt und die Enstehung der Straßburger Täufergemeinde*, in *The Origins and Characteristics of Anabaptism*, 186.

23 Robert Stupperich, *Strassburgs Stellung zu Beginn des Sakramentsstreites, 1524-1525*, 254f.

Kniebis, Jakob Sturm, Mathis Pfarrer, Martin Herlin, Daniel Mueg, Bernhard Wurmser) and a faction of Old Believers (Martin Betschold, Konrad von Duntzenheim, Wolfgang Böcklin, and Conrad and Friedrich von Gottesheim), but also to the concern for the city's relationship to the emperor, Charles V, the staunch defender of the Old Church. So the council justified its protection of Zell and the married priests by citing the threat posed to the peace of the city by the common man. Of other aspects of the Reform, the *Magistrat* was the grateful beneficiary. The elimination of clerical immunities from the city's taxes, judicial system, and oath of obedience enabled the *Magistrat* to regulate all aspects of secular life. Further, the petition requesting the council to take on the responsibility of the appointment of pastors offered the *Magistrat* significant influence in the spiritual affairs of the city.

THE DEVELOPMENT OF THE RADICAL MOVEMENT PRIOR TO MARPECK'S ARRIVAL, 1524–28

Despite the Reformers' promise of social unity through the preaching of the gospel and, perhaps, encouraged by their spiritualistic tendencies, a radical, lay dissent movement developed in Strassburg from 1524 until the synods of 1533-35.[24] The movement took its inspiration from both native and foreign leaders. Among the various groups and leaders, two major objections to the progress of the city's Reformation emerged. The first manifested a concern for a quicker and more radical amelioration of social and economic injustices embodied in the charge that the preachers' doctrine and practice bore no fruit. The second called for an emphasis on a personal experience of change of heart and a more significant role and sense of participation by the lay person in religious communities. This desire found expression variously as a stress on the subjective aspect of the Supper, the right of any believer to discern and preach the Word of God, an insistence on believer's baptism, or the right of a congregation to select its own pastor.

The activity and writings of the radical gardener, Clement Ziegler, marked the beginning of a split within the evangelical movement. In a 1524 tract Ziegler questioned the baptism of infants for the first time, stressed the priesthood of all believers, and claimed the right to preach because of the direct leading of the Spirit.[25] Living in the southern Krutenau district on lands owned by the convent of St. Nicolaus in Undis, Ziegler denounced the rent and tithe in the outlying

---

24 It should be noted that the evangelical preachers acted, often without success, on behalf of the common man. Hedio (1524) exhorted the city's prelates to suspend voluntarily the tithe, Bucer and Zell attempted to play a mediating role during the peasant uprising (1525), Bucer commissioned a report on usury by Fridolin Meyger (see p. 54), and appealed to the council to reduce the interest rates (1528). See Deppermann, *Melchior Hoffman*, 150-51.

25 »Von der waren nyessung beyd leibs und bluts....« See Müsing, *Karlstadt*, 173. For a general account of the development of the radical movement during this time see George H. Williams, *The Radical Reformation*, 241f.

villages.[26] Although he drew back from the violence of the peasants in 1525, Ziegler sought a more thorough application of the Bible in the social sphere. He remained an important leader among the dissenters and as will be noted, had an ambivalent and, at times, critical opinion of various Anabaptist groups in the city.

It is possible that the brief stay of Andreas Bodenstein von Carlstadt in October 1524 prepared the ground for the later Anabaptist movement in the city. Since 1523 »brother Andreas« had strongly identified with the common man and encouraged lay piety. From the reactions of the preachers Capito and Gerbels, Carlstadt must have raised questions concerning the social dimensions of the gospel, the province of civil power, the nature of the presence of Christ in the Supper, and the efficacy of infant baptism.[27]

By the summer of 1525 there appears to have been a small group of Anabaptists in the city. They were doubtless influenced by Balthasar Hubmaier's tract, *Von dem Christlichen Tauf der glaubigen* (July 1525), and advocacy of a restoration of the economic and social customs of the early church, including the community of goods.[28] Six months later, the small group received impetus from the arrival of several Anabaptists fleeing Waldshut and Zurich. One of these, Wilhelm Reublin, the former priest from Basel who had baptized Hubmaier and led peasant resistance to the tithe in Witikon and Hallau, resided with the tailor Jörg Ziegler.[29] Located on the northern Steinstrasse in Capito's the Young St. Peter's parish, Ziegler's home became one of the centers of Anabaptist activity. Of the discussions between them, Capito reports to Zwingli that Reublin avoided a public debate on baptism, while Reublin claimed that Capito had made many concessions which the preachers feared to make public.[30]

In May 1526 the council interrogated Hans Wolff, a weaver who had arrived the preceding month from Benfeld. Wolff declared that the »doctores, meister und rabbi« lay behind walls wearing good shoes, having enough to eat and seeking only their own advantage; their preaching directed the people only to external things without producing the fruits of the gospel; he denounced the baptism of infants who, according to the Scriptures, were incapable of it; and finally, asserted that no Christian, whether in or out of civil service, should wield the sword. On June 10 he interrupted a sermon in the cathedral, demanding that Zell yield to his own utterance through the Spirit.[31] By July priests baptizing infants were subject to derision in parts of the city. Toward the end of the year,

---

[26] Chrisman, *Strasbourg and the Reform*, 183. See also Franziska Conrad, *Reformation in der Bäuerlichen Gesellschaften*, 125-28.

[27] Müsing, *Karlstadt*, 183, 190.

[28] Chrisman, *Strasbourg and the Reform*, 183. Müsing, *Karlstadt*, 194, argues against Chrisman that Hubmaier himself never came to Strassburg.

[29] See James Stayer, *Die Anfänge des schweizerischen Täufertums im reformierten Kongregationalismus*, 30ff., 42ff.

[30] Hans–Werner Müsing, *The Anabaptist Movement in Strasbourg from Early 1526 to July 1527*, 92.

[31] Ibid., 93-97. See also KR, 1:52-54.

several prominent leaders entered the city and circles began to coalesce around them.

Hans Denck, Ludwig Hätzer and, later, Jakob Kautz influenced several circles, but particularly more highly educated Strassburgers. Denck arrived from Augsburg in November 1526 and gained a considerable following. Four hundred citizens attended his disputation with Bucer and the other preachers in December at the Dominican cloister. According to Bucer, Denck set the inner experienced Word above the literal Scripture and stressed the interpretation by the Spirit in the believer. Further, Denck minimized original sin and stressed the experiential Christ in the Spirit, denigrating as uniquely salvific, the work of Christ on Calvary. During this time, Ludwig Hätzer, a Hebraist from Basel arrived and worked with Cellarius on a translation of the Old Testament. He was disappointed with the Anabaptists and called Sattler a »sly and evil lurker.«[32] Attracted to Denck, he accompanied him to Worms after Denck was expelled from the city in late December. In Worms they won Kautz to their spiritualizing position and collaborated on translations of the prophets, Baruch, and a new edition of the *Theologia Deutsch*.[33]

After their departure, two leaders with connections to the Swiss movement were active in the city. The first, Jakob Gross, a furrier from Waldshut, was arrested with Jörg Ziegler, Jörg Tucher, Wilhelm Ecksel, and Matthis Hiller.[34] Gross had baptized two people in the house of Tucher's father – in – law and one person in Ruprechtsau, where Clement Ziegler then worked. Gross complained that though the preachers had preached their gospel for four years, they had no fruit to show for it. Rather than instructing the sincere believers like themselves, they banned them, put them in the tower, closed them out of the churches, and excluded them from communal life without a hearing. Tucher, a secretary for the police authority, testified that those in the group who had jobs shared freely of what they had. In the meetings someone read the Scriptures and then each spoke, encouraging each to do God's will and love the neighbor. Tucher said that there was a difference of opinion in the group about disobedience to the worldly authorities. Gross appears to have taken a centrist position in these matters. Adducing Jesus's prohibition of oaths in Matthew 5, he refused the civil oath. However, he expressed the willingness to bear arms and keep watch, but refused to kill anyone. Acknowledging that the civil government was given the sword and commanded to punish evil and encourage the good, he stated his intention to obey it insofar as it did not require anything against God (that is, killing another). Tucher, apparently, took the oath. Gross also called baptism a covenant of good conscience, so that children, who cannot die to the flesh, should not receive it.

32 Müsing, *The Anabaptist Movement*, 99-100.
33 J. F. G. Goerters, *Ludwig Hätzer*, 99f.
34 KR, 1:62f.

Michael Sattler, the Anabaptist leader recently expelled from Zurich, probably associated with this group during his brief stay in Strassburg.[35] In a letter to Bucer and Capito on behalf of those still imprisoned, Sattler expressed a position to the left of that of Gross concerning the obedience due civil authority. From an almost dualistic framework contrasting flesh and spirit, earth and heaven, and Belial and Christ, Sattler asserted that »believers are redeemed out of the world, and, therefore, hate the world.« Because their citizenship is in heaven, Christians do not swear civil oaths, carry weapons, or participate in civil government.[36] This position reached full expression in Articles 6 and 7 of Sattler's Schleitheim Confession of February 1527.[37]

In the year preceding Marpeck's arrival, groups met at the two syphilis hospitals in the western part of the city and at the home of Fridolin Meyger. Albrecht Wanner, an Anabaptist expelled from Schlettstatt and Benfeld, testified that Lukas Hackfurt asked him to preach at the small syphilis hospital because »otherwise no one else would go to the poor people as it did not suit their taste.«[38] Among the listeners were Meyger, Hackfurt, and Johannes Schweblin, an associate in Hackfurt's Latin school. Schweblin, like Wanner who lived with him, denounced the civil oath and both were expelled from Strassburg. Later, in a letter to the council from Basel, Schweblin showed a change of heart saying that it was wrong to say that the oath was unchristian.[39] It is possible that Wanner's opinion influenced those who, according to Capito, refused to raise their fingers at the annual renewal of the oath in January 1528. At about the same time the congregation at Ruprechtsau elected Clement Ziegler its pastor and asked the council's confirmation.[40] On April 22 Michel Ecker testified that 250 people, including Hackfurt, gathered each Sunday at Meyger's house. Holding a position similar to that of Gross, Ecker confessed a willingness to obey the authorities but did not wish to kill or take the oath. He admitted to having been baptized on faith and having received visions which he desired to share with the council.[41] In the summer a group of 100-500 Anabaptist refugees entered Strassburg from Augsburg.[42]

The two objections to the reformers' program – the concern for social justice through more fundamental social change and the concern for personal transformation – were embodied in various ways. The radicals and their relative commitments to these concerns are best seen on a spectrum. On one end, there were those – some of the mystically disposed spiritualizers – whose emphasis on

---

35 Sattler was executed together with Matthis Hiller four months later in Rothenburg.

36 KR, 1:68-70.

37 See Williams, *The Radical Reformation*, 185.

38 KR, 1:131-33.

39 Ibid., 178-79.

40 Ibid., 145-46.

41 Ibid., 154-55.

42 The precise number of Augsburg refugees is difficult to determine. Friederich Roth, *Augsburg Reformationsgeschichte*, 1:125f., cites a contemporary witness who said that 500 Brüder emigrated from Augsburg to Strassburg; see KR, 1:181 n. 7.

voluntary, personal transformation led to social quietism. On the other end, there were the peasant resisters whose emphasis on radical and immediate social change led to violently coercive activities. In between lay the vast majority of Strassburg's radicals, among whom there existed differences of opinions as to the relative weight given to each of the concerns, how they might be combined, and what communal forms best fostered their actualization.

Thus, on the eve of Marpeck's entry into Strassburg, the radical movement exhibited an increasing vitality. Although united against the evangelical preachers' reform, the movement was not without inner tensions and disagreements. Clement Ziegler and Eckhart zum Treübel denounced the exclusivity of some of the Anabaptist groups, whose members would not »greet or thank anyone... and live[d] in extreme unfriendliness to other human creatures of God.«[43] As indicated by the testimonies of Tucher and Schweblin, the attitudes of the radicals concerning the oath and civil responsibility varied. To Denck, Hätzer, and Kautz, such questions about external relations were relatively unimportant, while Sattler and Wanner made the refusal of the oath and of participation in the civil community a decisive characteristic of the Christian life.[44] Gross held a moderate position, by which he refused the oath but accepted some of the claims of the civil community outside the conventicle.

Some of the radicals, such as the two Zieglers, Meyger, and Hackfurt, seem to have been willing to countenance those who refused the oath, perhaps as a form of protest against the patricians, rentiers, and merchants who dominated the *Magistrat*, but repudiated that refusal if it involved a demonization and rejection of all civil authority and, thus a renunciation of all civil and social responsibility. Therefore, the position of Gross might have found more sympathy among these radicals than those of Denck or Sattler. As we shall see, Marpeck's position might have had even more appeal.

MARPECK IN STRASSBURG, 1528–32

Professional Activity

Before turning to Marpeck's Strassburg activities, two matters demand attention. The first concerns the whereabouts of Marpeck between his January 1528 resignation from the mining magistrate's office in Rattenberg and the

---

[43] KR, 2:384. See also KR, 1:573, for Ziegler's complaint that the Anabaptists damned anyone outside their particular fellowship.

[44] To the *Magistrat* and others, such a rejection of the oath might well have represented a claim similar to that of clerical immunity, which had previously crippled the city's ability to rule itself and caused so much dissension among its citizens. From this perspective, Anabaptists like Sattler seemed to encourage a radical clericalization, not laicization of religion.

appearance of his name in the Strassburg Bürgerbuch on September 19, 1528. The second involves the time of his submission to adult baptism and therefore his public identification with the Anabaptist movement.

After his resignation, Pilgram and Anna apparently travelled up the Inn and Moldau rivers to Krumau, a Bohemian mining town. On July 2, 1528, Ferdinand I, also king of Bohemia, wrote to officials of that town saying that he had received reports that Marpeck and his wife were there.[45] There seems to have been a significant Anabaptist congregation in Krumau at this time, for eighty to ninety »Brüeder zu Behemischen Kromaw« migrated to Austerlitz in early 1529.[46] Marpeck may have carried a communal order composed by Schiemer for the Rattenberg congregation in 1527.[47]

According to Thomas Adolf, an Anabaptist convert from Speyer, Marpeck's close associate, Leupold Scharnschlager, reported that Marpeck received a commission from the Moravian congregation to go to Strassburg and baptize.[48] It is possible, then, that Marpeck visited Austerlitz before going to Strassburg. Therefore, when he entered Strassburg in the late summer of 1528, Marpeck had already received baptism on faith and came as a commissioned elder.[49]

Citizenship and Guild Participation

On September 19, 1528, Marpeck bought citizenship in Strassburg and swore obedience to the council and city magistrates.[50] Due to widespread persecution of Anabaptists elsewhere in the empire, he was one of an abnormally high number of 260 new citizens that year.[51] For a person not born in Strassburg or married to

[45] Jarold Knox Zeman, *The Anabaptists and the Czech Brethren in Moravia, 1526-1628*, 199, 256 n. 57.

[46] A. J. F. Zieglschmid, ed., *Die Älteste Chronik der Hutterischen Brüder*, 91.

[47] Robert Friedmann, »The Oldest Church Discipline of the Anabaptists,« 162-66, and *Mennonite Encyclopedia* (hereinafter listed as *ME*), 4:252-54, identified this order as the work of Schiemer. Williams, *The Radical Reformation*, 231-32, suggests that it served as a constitution of the proto–Hutterites in Austerlitz. It is possible that the 80-90 brothers, who arrived in Austerlitz just before Hutter returned with his Tirolean refugees, brought this order with them from Krumau.

[48] Manfred Krebs, *Baden und Pfalz*, vol. 4 of *Quellen zur Geschichte der Täufer*, 422.18-30.

[49] Marpeck was most likely baptized in the spring or summer of 1528 in Krumau or Austerlitz. An earlier date, perhaps the fall of 1527, is possible, for his property was confiscated by the city – a measure taken against the Anabaptists in Rattenberg. In 1609 Johannes Walch, reported that Marpeck taught mining techniques in Augsburg and other German cities before coming to Strassburg, KR, 1:186.14-18. However, he probably reversed the order of Marpeck's activities in the respective cities as his description fits closely with Marpeck's work in Augsburg during his later residence there (1544-56).

[50] Strasbourg Stadtarchiv (hereinafter listed as S.St–A), Bürgerbuch 1:635: »Bilgram Marckber von Rotenburg auss dem Inthall hatt das burgrecht kauft unnd dint zun gartnern under wagnern.«

[51] Deppermann, *Melchior Hoffman*, 143, says that the average number of applications per year from 1500-30 fluctuated between 50 and 100. The number jumped to 485 during and after the Peasants' War in 1525, and to 260 in 1528.

a citizen, the law required that one live in the city, be registered with a guild, pay the citizenship tax, and swear an oath of loyalty and obedience to the city, its councils, and its magistrates. The primary responsibilities of the citizen included the payment of city taxes and the military defense of the city. After 1450, when campaigns outside the city became a rarity, the latter duty ordinarily involved participation in the watch on the city walls. In the event of attack, each burgher used his own weapon in the defense led by leaders of the guilds and certain councilmen. Two additional responsibilities involved the aid of a fellow citizen, particularly in the case of fire, and the yearly renewal of the oath to the newly elected council on the cathedral square.[52] This annual oath was not »one institution of city law among others, but the very foundation of the same.«[53] The oath was the center of civil life. With his oath, then, Marpeck vowed to carry out his responsibilities for the good of the civil community.

As required by law, Marpeck also entered one of the city's fifteen guilds, the »gartnern under wagnern,« before becoming a citizen. An initial membership fee and annual dues provided for banquets which concretized the communal life of the guild. Involved mostly in truck farming for the city market, the gardener – wagoners were one of the subdivisions of the large gardener guild. Their guildhall was located in the western part of the city in St. Aurelian's parish, while the other two gardener groups were centered in the northern area of the Steinstraße in the Young St. Peter's parish and in the southeastern Krutenau district near St. Stephen's.[54]

As has been noted, the gardeners found themselves on the margin of Strassburg's economic and political life. They were strapped variously by usurious interests and rents to patrician landowners and tithes to the ecclesiastical establishments, while also dependent on unpredictable weather and harvests. It is not surprising, therefore, that radical social and religious ideas found fertile ground among them. In the early stages of the city's reform they probably participated in, and may have led, the riot in 1523 against the canons of the Young St. Peter's. After a bad harvest the next year, the gardener – wagoners refused the payment of the tithe and called Bucer to be their preacher at St. Aurelian's. Their colleagues at the Young St. Peter's and St. Stephen's did the same.

By the time of Marpeck's arrival in 1528, the predicament of the common man, and the gardeners in particular, had not changed significantly. From the perspective of some, the new gospel had made little progress in establishing justice and social harmony. In a report on usury, commissioned by Bucer, Fridolin Meyger wrote:

52 See François – Josef Fuchs, *Le Droit de Bourgeosie à Strasbourg*, 21-23. A text of the annual oath sworn in 1594 appears in S.St – A, Extract der Stadt Strassburg Bürger – Ordnungen in Das grosse Ratsbuch der Stadt Strassburg, no. 863, f. 66.

53 Otto Brunner, *Souveränitätsproblem und Sozialstruktur in den deutschen Reichsstädten der früheren Neuzeit*, 50:338.

54 Ulrich Crämer, *Die Verfassung und Verwaltung Straßburgs von der Reformationszeit bis zum Fall der Reichsstadt (1521-1681)*, 99.

I am plagued by the devilish curse of usurious loans. Persons, who nevertheless consider themselves good Evangelicals and hear sermons daily, engage in this activity; they want most of all to make a pile of money.... I know very well that this usurious practice is the support, the very lifeblood of the nobles who go about town.... [All] courts and law deal with usury.... Come to the courts if you would see it; see how the courts and law treat widows and orphans – or how they mistreat them – all because of usurious interests, rentes, and tithes.[55]

Therefore, at the *Stammtische* at the gardener–wagoners' *Stube*, Marpeck probably heard long and bitter complaints about the city's evangelical usurers.

Strassburg's Poor Relief and Marpeck's 1528 Arrest

Upon his arrival, Marpeck also associated with a group involved in a communal collection for the care of Strassburg's poor and refugees from religious persecution. On October 22, 1528, he was arrested with the social radical Fridolin Meyger and the Anabaptists, Jakob Kautz and Wilhelm Reublin, because of a gathering of Wiedertäufer which met in his house. During the interrogation, Marpeck stated:

The gathering took place for the simple reason that many foreign people had come and were driven here and were too great a burden for the city's alms collection. Therefore, they collected money among themselves to give to Luxen [Lukas Hackfurt] to distribute or to keep in the chest in order to help these people. This was done publicly and with the knowledge of Bucer and Capito.[56]

In his association with Meyger and Hackfurt, Marpeck had access to an insider's view of the economic and social tensions and divisions within the city.

Coming from the middle level of Strassburg society, both men were dissatisfied with the apparent lack of social conscience in the church reform to this time. In words similar to those Marpeck would use two years later, Meyger testified that he had always had a great zeal for God.[57] Although raised in the *bapstlich* faith of his parents, he discovered many abuses through Luther and Erasmus. However, the movement was soon torn apart and, with it, his conscience. His attraction to the Anabaptists apparently had to do with his disillusionment with the evangelical movement which left the usurious practices of the upper class Strassburgers untouched. As a notary in the episcopal chancery, Meyger's job was to draw up their contracts for rentes and other types of debts. As has been seen, his own participation in these transactions weighed on Meyger's conscience. But, in the Anabaptists he found a middle way between Luther and the papacy.

---

55 KR, 1:222-23. I follow the translation given by Brady, *Ruling Class*, 150-51.
56 KR, 1:185.
57 Ibid.,1:235-36, for Meyger's letter of appeal to the council (March 1529).

Among them, he experienced »a good Christian life... with sincere love of God and neighbor.« They stressed a change in the inner person according to which the outer should be ruled.[58]

Lukas Hackfurt, a former vicar at the Münster cathedral and early enthusiast for the evangelical cause, accepted the appointment in 1523 as the city's *Almosenschaffner*, chief administrator of the welfare office.[59] As noted, he persistently pleaded with the council to give more confiscated church property to the poor, asked wealthy artisans to train unskilled boys, and invited Anabaptists to preach to the poor in the hospitals because the evangelical preachers would not. From his diary it is apparent that Hackfurt analyzed the deeper structural problems which caused deprivation and suffering among the lower class Strassburgers. These problems included: a high inflation rate; pressure and competition from immigration; pressure on the land, driving people to the city; and unemployability among youngsters, whom artisans refused to train.[60]

Between 1525 and 1528 the problem caused by immigration became acute. The 1523 *Almosenordnung* restricted begging to one hundred children and established a community chest to take care of the balance of the city's poor.[61] However, during the peasant uprising of 1525, an estimated three thousand poor people, widows, and orphans poured into Strassburg. In 1527 Hackfurt argued that the city should receive everyone, whether they bought citizenship or not.[62] The next year refugees from religious persecution, including Marpeck and at least one hundred Anabaptists from Augsburg, flooded the city. According to Marpeck's October 1528 statement, the increasing number of foreigners constituted an impossible drain on the already strained community chest.

In addition to the collection, Marpeck's testimony reveals that he and Meyger housed certain of the refugees and attempted to establish a voluntary order for the group. Marpeck may have used Schiemer's 1527 Rattenberg church order as a guide in the collection and organization of the group.[63] Further, Marpeck signed to cover the debt of two immigrants, Christlin and Barbel Herwater of Salzburg, in order that they might receive treatment at the syphilis hospital.[64]

There is no report of the outcome of Marpeck's case, nor of his precise whereabouts in 1529. On October 26 the councilman Hans Sturm ruled that those being held must take an oath, or be banned from the city or be given a hearing.[65] Kautz and Reublin remained imprisoned until their hearing on December 14. Meyger was released on his oath to obey the council and never

---

[58] Ibid., 1:236.18-19.

[59] Warnfrid Werner Grams, *Die Straßburger Almosenordnung von 1523 im Spannungsfeld der Geschichte*, dissertation, 170.

[60] Miriam U. Chrisman, *Urban Poor in the Sixteenth Century: The Case of Strasbourg*, 63-67.

[61] Otto Winckelmann, *Das Fürsorgewesen der Stadt Strasbourg*, 83.

[62] Chrisman, *Urban Poor*, 60, 62.

[63] See chapter 3 n. 47.

[64] S.St–A, Spital–Archiv, 1477, 200ʳ.

[65] KR, 1:188-89.

attend another Anabaptist meeting.[66] Marpeck is never mentioned as having taken an oath or having participated in a hearing. In fact, he later reports that, though Capito visited and talked with him, he refused the oath and encouraged others to do the same. Further, he admitted to having baptized a brother during this period.[67] It seems reasonable to assume, then, that Marpeck was either banned from the city or pardoned.

Activity as Holzmeister

If Marpeck had been expelled from Strassburg in the late fall of 1528, he may have moved to the Kinzig Valley.[68] At any rate, he was in a position, in 1530, to advise the city to buy land there in order to alleviate a chronic wood shortage.

According to Johannes Walch, »This Pilgram was in Strassburg at that time when a lack of wood afflicted the heavily populated city. He offered his advice and help and ordered around 6,000-8,000 trees cut down from the vast mountain pasture in the untouched area of Fürstenberg.«[69] He reports that this lumber was bound together and floated into Strassburg by means of aqueducts and the Kinzig and Rhine rivers. Further, he says that Marpeck was given responsibility not only for the wood cut from the forest, but also »authority over the land and jurisdiction over the silver.«[70] Unfortunately because of the 1871 shelling of the Strassburg city archive during the Franco–Prussian war, there is little direct documentation of Marpeck's work for the city council during these years. However, there are some direct and indirect sources with which to check and expand Walch's account.

Since the thirteenth century, Strassburg had invested in land and canals in the Black Forest for a supply of wood as well as other natural resources.[71] While some necessities came from the Murg Valley to the north, the Kinzig Valley, just across the Rhine, provided Strassburg with the bulk of its raw materials. Because of the narrow roads in this mountainous region, the Kinzig River became the major artery for the transportation of these resources. In 1485 three small cities on the Kinzig – Wolfach, Hausach, and Haslach – developed, with the permission of the Fürstenbergs, a guild constitution regulating the life and

66 Ibid., 1:185-86. He did not keep that oath, for he was arrested again in March 1529. At that time he expressed disagreement with some Anabaptists who stressed the inner person to the point that they destroyed »law and order, under which the outer person should be held.«

67 Ibid., 1:351-52.

68 Count Frederick von Fürstenberg had hired the Tirolean Jakob Täntzl in 1525 to run the thriving mining works centered around Haslach and Hausach in the Kinzig Valley. He brought a large group of miners from Schwaz with him. See Eberhard Gothein, *Wirtschaftsgeschichte des Schwarzwaldes und der angrenzendes Landschaften*, 607-8, 664.

69 *Decas fabularum*, in KR, 1:186.19-29. Walch was a former deacon at Nürtingen who settled in Strassburg and became involved in the Anabaptist group there by 1597. See Gustav Bossert, *Herzogtum Württemberg*, vol. 1 of *Quellen zur Geschichte der Wiedertäufer*, 517, 527, 697, 1109.

70 KR, 1:187.9-11.

71 Gothein, *Wirtschaftsgeschichte des Schwarzwaldes*, 440.

conduct of those involved in the river commerce. By 1500 logging had become a significant local industry and led to a dispute between the counts of Fürstenberg and the duke of Würtemberg.[72] The *Wolfacher Schifferschaft*, drawn up in 1527, settled the dispute and set down more definite laws governing the commercial activity on the river.

It was not unusual that Strassburg would look to the Kinzig Valley for wood. However, it is possible that, with the increasing regulation of the Kinzig River within the Würtemberg and Fürstenberg territories, this wood became increasingly expensive by the time it reached the market at Kehl – the confluence of the Kinzig and Rhine rivers. Apparently Marpeck suggested that Strassburg buy land and transportation rights in the Fürstenberg territory in order to obtain wood more cheaply using the city's own labor force.

On April 2, 1530, Strassburg, through Councilman Bernhard Wurmser, bought woodland »in Einbach by Husun.« Einbach refers to both the mountain stream feeding into the Kinzig at Hausach and the small community on the stream.[73] According to the contract, the Strassburg forest extended north from Einbach bounded on either side by Newenbach and Eichwald. For a period of thirty years the city had the right to cut an unlimited amount of lumber and firewood from this forest and float it down the Kinzig toward Strassburg without paying any tolls. Further, the residents of the valley were forbidden to obstruct the transport, which took place twice a year.[74] Marpeck received principal administrative responsibility for this project and might have been called *Holzmeister*.[75]

The process of cutting and delivering the wood from Einbach to Strassburg was both difficult and dangerous. After the logs were cut, they had to be moved to the Kinzig River. The Einbach is a small mountain stream, neither wide nor deep enough to float lumber. Marpeck supervised the building of a series of dams, which collected the water from the winter snows. Therefore, when the dams were opened, the stream swelled large enough to carry the logs down to the Kinzig.[76] Once at the Kinzig, the logs were bound together to form rafts, which ranged in width from about seven to twenty feet. These rafts were then connected front–to–back in a large flotilla, reaching up to six hundred yards in

---

72 Ludwig Barth, *Die Geschichte der Flößerei im Flußgebiet der oberen Kinzig*, 28, 35f.

73 Husun has been called Hausach since 1622. The Strassburg archive has two slightly different copies of the letter of contract: S.St–A, 3:120/1, and 5:145/16.5.

74 See Barth, *Die Geschichte der Flößerei*, 18-19. A 1439 regulation prohibited lumber rafting from St. Martin's (November 12) to St.Matthew's (February 24).

75 Barth, *Die Geschichte der Flößerei*, 53, based his account on the Fürstenberg archive at Donaueschingen. He asserts that the Holzmeister lived in the Kinzig Valley and that he was released in 1531 because of questionable business practices. He never mentioned Marpeck's name but, based on other evidence, this Holzmeister must have been Marpeck. Apparently Laurenz Klausrath, the Strassburg clerk in 1609, had documentary evidence that the council hired Marpeck for the job in 1530: »meiner herren vorfahren beredt, dass sie den wald im Einbach gekaufft und das holtzflötzen auff der Kintzig hieher in anno 1530 angestellt hat, Pilgram Marbeckh, ein burger alhie, gehiessen.« S.St–A, MS 850, 126r.

76 Georg Sölch, *Die Holzbringung im oberen Kinzigtal*, 158.

length. Raftsmen, standing on these great floats, navigated them with long poles down river to the city lumber yard at Kehl on the Rhine. People in and around Strassburg called these wood rafts *Pilgerholz* or *Pilgranholz* even into the seventeenth century.[77]

At the stockyard at Kehl, by the Rhine bridge leading to Strassburg, the building lumber was divided by a tariff agent and sold, with private burghers receiving priority over carpenters and auctioneers.[78] The firewood was transported by carts into the city wood market on the *Barfüsser Platz*.[79] The city wood commission exercised authority over this process and acted through its agent, the *Holzknecht*. It is likely that some of Marpeck's fellow gardeners worked for him and the commission in the cutting and transportation of this scarce resource.

Although Walch mentions that Marpeck had responsibility for the silver mined in the area, the dearth of documentation prohibits more specific knowledge concerning this aspect of Marpeck's activity. Upon his dismissal in 1532, Marpeck did mention that he still had business to finish with those who worked with him in the »berckwerck.«[80] He later corresponded with fellow Anabaptists in the Kinzig as well as in the Leber valleys.

As *Holzmeister*, Marpeck was required to swear a professional oath upon entrance to his office. Although his contract and oath is no longer extant, there are texts of oaths required of people in similar positions. In 1541 a Holzknecht swore »to God almighty to be true to that which he was ordered to do concerning the wood« and to bring any irregularity to the attention of the Council of 15.[81] As was the custom of the day, Marpeck would have given his right hand upon swearing the oath. In addition, he probably swore lesser oaths in a similar fashion in the daily transactions of business having to do with his responsibility as *Holzmeister*.

Marpeck was directly responsible to the Council of 15. This important privy council dealt with domestic affairs including the regulation of guilds, the control of the city treasury, and the supervision of the public works.[82] It consisted of five patricians and ten guild representatives. However, as has been noted, even those from the guilds tended to be from the merchant – rentier class. Since these council members were replaced by cooptation (that is, it appointed its own members from the lower assemblies), the power of the Council of 15 remained firmly in the hands of the ruling class.

---

[77] See again Klausrath's note from 1609, S.St–A, MS 850, 126[r]: »Pilgranholtz, woher is den namen? Vide under den zollsachen sub rubrica: Zoll uff der Kintzig.« T. W. Röhrich, »Zur Geschichte der strassburgischen Wiedertäufer in den Jahren 1527-1543,« 16, reports the usage of »Pilgerholz.« In the Kinzig Valley these rafts were called Bachflössen or Kinzigflössen.

[78] Crämer, *Die Verfassung und Verwaltung*, 116.

[79] The city passed an ordinance on November 25, 1532, regulating the price of the wood from Einbach and the places where it could be sold. S.St–A, R 3, 215[r]-215[v].

[80] KR, 1:362.27-29.

[81] S.St–A, Stadtordnungen, 4:473.

[82] Chrisman, *Strasbourg and the Reform*, 22.

During his stay in Strassburg, Marpeck moved and worked among the gardeners. Although virtually closed out of the political process, this group, like the mining community in Rattenberg, constituted a powerful political force by virtue of its number and potential for violence. When he entered the employ of the Council of 15, Marpeck assumed a similar role to that of *Bergrichter* in mediating the interests of the council and his fellow gardeners. He must have been well acquainted with the tensions which existed between these two groups. Marpeck's intimate contact with both groups makes intelligible his later objections to Bucer's strategy and the use of coercion by either group in the name of the gospel.

DEFINITION OF DIVERGENCE AMONG THE RADICALS

As early as 1528, a visible distinction appeared among the Anabaptists. In the hearing for Wilhelm Reublin and Jakob Kautz, both agreed that the preachers' teaching produced no fruit and that the evangelical church was not the true church. However, Reublin »showed himself to be not in agreement with every point of Kautz.«[83] With the advent of Hans Bünderlin, Christian Entfelder, and Sebastian Franck between 1529 and 1531, this distinction grew into a cleavage finally completed by Marpeck's two polemical tracts of 1531. These Spiritualists or Spirits (*Geister*), as Marpeck called them, followed the spiritualizing tendencies of Denck, Hätzer, and Kautz and stressed the inner, spiritual reality of the human over the external physical aspect.[84] The arrival of Melchior Hofmann introduced still another grouping.

Hans Bünderlin arrived in Strassburg from Nicolsburg early in 1529. By March he had published two tracts and taken a leading role in convening an Anabaptist group, including Meyger, in the home of Claus Bruchen.[85] These first two works contain the seeds of his rejection of all religious externals. Though an Anabaptist, Bünderlin suddenly raised questions about the ordinance of believers' baptism. He directed his next book, *Explanation through Study of the Biblical Writings, that Water Baptism and All Other External Ceremonies Used in the Apostolic Church Are Currently Being Reintroduced without God's Command or the Testimony of Scripture* (1530), against his former Anabaptist associates.[86]

---

[83] KR, 1:195.28-30.

[84] The term, Geister, becomes a technical term which Marpeck uses in later writings. At this stage he does not refer to any specific names, but evidence from his 1531 tracts indicates that he included Bünderlin, Entfelder and, perhaps, Hofmann under this rubric (chapter 4). He later included Franck and Schwenckfeld (chapter 5).

[85] KR, 1:226-27. The two works were entitled: *Ein gemeyne Berechnung über der Heiligen Schrift Inhalt*, and *Aus was Ursach sich Gott in die nyder gelassen und in Christo vermenschet ist....*

[86] *Erklerung durch vergleichung der Biblischen geschrifft / das des wassertauff sampt andern eusserlichen gebreuchen / in der Apostolischen Kirchen geubet. On Gottes befelch und zeugniss der gschrift...* (1530).

Sometime in 1529 Christian Entfelder came to Strassburg where he may have associated with Bünderlin. He had served as *Vorsteher* 1526-27 in an Anabaptist congregation in the Moravian village Eibenschitz.[87] He published two books in 1530 and a third in 1533. In the first, *On the Many Divisions in the Faith*, Entfelder reacts to the disagreements among the Reformers reflected at Marburg and Augsburg, as well as the many divisions among the Anabaptist groups. His solution was to stress the internal unity of the Spirit in contrast to the external ceremonies and forms, about which so many held various opinions.

Sebastian Franck, the former Lutheran pastor at Ansbach–Bayreuth in 1526, had become increasingly dissatisfied with the *solafideist*, magisterial reform and left the ministry. In 1529 he came to Strassburg »a programmatic Spiritualist.«[88] He identifies, in his earlier *Türkenchronik*, three new splits in the church, the Lutheran, the Zwinglian, the Anabaptist, and a fourth then taking shape, the Spiritualist. He further clarified his position in a letter to John Campanus, in which he highly recommended Bünderlin.[89] Because the antichrist entered the church with Constantine, Franck says that the Roman church and magisterial reformers mix the Old and New Testaments. For example, they justify war and treat heresy with the sword rather than the Word. According to Franck, in the New Testament the Spirit alone teaches and baptizes – the outer or external things have passed. Therefore, following Bünderlin, he opposes those who would reinstitute the ceremonies and customs of the apostolic church. Franck's distinction between the Old and New Testaments, his rejection of the practice of infant baptism (in his *Chronica* of 1531), and his criticism of the exercise of coercive force by Christians since Constantine became valuable elements of Marpeck's position.[90] However, Marpeck opposed Franck's spiritualistic conclusion that all external ceremonies and customs must be abandoned.

Still another important radical leader, Melchior Hofmann, found his way to Strassburg in 1529. Taking up residence with Katherine Seid, Hofmann associated with the Strassburg prophets Lienhard and Ursula Jost, for whose visions he wrote an introduction in 1530. Similar to the prophets and Hans Hut, Hofmann looked forward to an apocalyptic, political, and military victory of the true church. For him, Strassburg was the spiritual Jerusalem, the center of the gathering of the 144,000 faithful (Revelation 14:1f.). The free, imperial city would be the scene for the final, bloody siege and victory of the persecuted church.[91]

---

[87] For a biographical sketch of Entfelder, see André Séguenny *Christian Entfelder*, 37.

[88] Williams, *The Radical Reformation*, 265. For a more recent treatment of Franck, see André Séguenny, *Sebastian Franck et la Philosophie Spirituelle*, 293-313.

[89] KR, 1:301-25. February 4, 1531.

[90] Reflecting Franck's direct influence, Marpeck claimed that Christians during the apostolic age before Constantine did not wield the sword and that the pope had created the antichrist by marrying the church to the beast, or temporal power. See *Aufdeckung*, Bviii^V – C^r (Hans Hillerbrand, *An Early Anabaptist Treatise on the Christian and the State*, 44). Quotations from the *Aufdeckung* are taken from the Stuttgart edition followed by a citation in parentheses referring to the photostatic copy of the Augsburg edition reproduced in Hillerbrand, *An Early Anabaptist Treatise*, 29-47.

[91] Williams, *The Radical Reformation*, 263; and Deppermann, *Melchior Hoffman*, 179-80, 185-86.

Hans Frisch of Horb, who also arrived in Strassburg in 1529, observed that the Anabaptists there were »divided into three groupings, namely those who followed opinions of Hofmann, Kautz, and Reublin, with those of Hofmann and Kautz sometimes confused.«[92] Although this testimony comes from 1534, these distinctions were certainly already present in 1530 and were given further definition by Marpeck in his two tracts of July 1531. Before the examination of Marpeck's position, defined in those works, his status within the Anabaptist groups needs clarification.

Marpeck came to Strassburg a commissioned elder. The record of his hearing of December 18, 1531, named him an Anabaptist *Vorsteher*, a term used in Schiemer's 1527 Rattenberg church order to denote, among other things, an elder chosen to look after the poor.[93] We know that Marpeck baptized several persons during his stay in Strassburg. Among them, we know of a man who was in prison with him in 1528, and of several who were imprisoned in 1533, as well as of Cornelius Schehe from Babenhausen, arrested in 1536.[94]

Clearly by 1531 Marpeck was the leader of an Anabaptist group in Strassburg.[95] Many of those in his group had probably been associated with Reublin before he was expelled in early 1529. In a letter from Reublin, who was then in Moravia, Marpeck is asked to greet five people including Leupold Scharnschlager.[96] Scharnschlager, a Tirolean from Hopfgarten near Kitzbühel, came to Strassburg in 1530 and took responsibility for the group after Marpeck's expulsion in 1532.[97] In addition, Reublin asked that the letter be sent on to brothers near Zurich. Marpeck, therefore, was probably identified more closely with the Swiss Anabaptists than with any other group. However, he did have contacts with the Augsburg refugees in the city. Further, as will be seen later, there existed important differences of opinion among those included under the rubric, »Reublin« group. Other members of the Marpeck circle, who later became Marpeck's correspondents, were Sigmund Bosch, Christman Steiger, and Gilg Brenner. The latter two replaced Marpeck in the lumbering at Einbach.

There is only indirect evidence concerning the internal structure and order of the Marpeck circle. At the time of his first arrest in 1528, the group met in Marpeck's house and developed an order. As has been suggested, the model might have been the order drawn up by Schiemer for the Rattenberg congregation the

---

92 KR, 1:288-89. See also KR, 2:299.

93 KR, 1:359.23, fürstehern. See Article 5 in the translation of Friedmann, »Church Discipline,« 164.

94 See KR, 2:210.19-20, and the forthcoming third volume by Rott, no. 469, June 28, 1536. M. Jean Rott provided this reference. Judging from his later changes to Bernhard Rothmann's *Bekenntnisse* in the *Vermahnung* it is possible that Marpeck baptized by sprinkling.

95 If Marpeck had been expelled in 1528, perhaps he had been allowed to come back into the city when he signed the contract to work for the Council of 15 in 1530.

96 See an English translation of the letter in J. C. Wenger, »A Letter from Wilhelm Reublin to Pilgram Marpeck, 1531,« 67-75.

97 See William Klassen, *Leupold Scharnschlager's Farewell to the Strasbourg Council,* 211-18.

year before.[98] According to that order, everyone »in one another's presence agreed to regulate everything in the best possible way.« The brothers and sisters pledged to meet together four or five times per week and pray for each other. If any led a disorderly life, he or she was admonished and punished by the group. All gifts of God were to be held in common and each contributed to the needs of others. The elders, or *Vorsteher*, administered this collection. In the gatherings, one person spoke at a time and the others listened and judged what was spoken (*Sitzerrecht*, 1 Corinthians 14:23 ff.). The gathered brothers and sisters were understood as »being one body and one bread in the Lord« and therefore kept the Lord's Supper »as a memorial of the Lord's death, whereby each one shall be admonished to become conformed to the Lord in obedience to the Father.«

Although the hearings of Marpeck and his close associates do not reveal much about the group's inner life, it is reasonable to assume that this order, even if used in a modified form, indicates the nature of that communal life.[99] Responsibility for the life, discipline, ministry, and worship of the group lay in the hands of each participant. Marpeck's notion of the body of Christ (chapter four) was the theological foundation for this radical ecclesiology.

In the summer of 1531 Marpeck published two tracts, *A Clear Refutation* and *A Clear and Useful Instruction*, directed specifically against Bünderlin's *Explanation* and Entfelder's *On the Many Divisions in the Faith*, published the preceding year.[100] Motivated by pastoral concerns, Marpeck developed a theology of the cross and suffering with which he criticized these *Geister*. According to Marpeck, they made the kingdom of God »too spiritual« and therefore ignored the physical suffering and social injustices endured by others. Marpeck also objected to those who spoke too loftily of Christ and refused to submit humbly to the human feet of Christ. Besides the *Geister*, Marpeck might have had in mind Hofmann in reference to his monophysite Christology as well as his exclusivistic apocalyptic visions. Further, Marpeck implicitly distinguished his position within the Reublin Anabaptist group as he refused to demonize civil authority and to reject all civil and social claims of those outside his group. As has been seen, Marpeck willingly swore the city oath, as well as those oaths required in daily business and professional transactions. He also served the needs of the larger community through his work as Holzmeister.

Marpeck's tracts, then, had two important effects within Strassburg's radical movement. First, they further defined the growing distinctions among the Spiritualists, the Melchiorite Anabaptists, and the remaining two groupings of Anabaptists. Second, they manifested a theology of the cross, which integrated a desire for a personal experience of a change of life and participation in the

---

[98] For the following discussion I use the translation of Friedmann, »Church Discipline,« 162-66.

[99] People from other closely related groups confirm aspects of this description. For example, see Hans Frisch, KR, 1:289, and KR, 2:299. Fridolin Meyger denied that the group held all things in common, KR, 1:234.21-23.

[100] See *CC*, 36-37, for Klassen's arguments for the attribution of these tracts to Marpeck.

religious community with a concern for social responsibility. Therefore, Marpeck's position integrated some of the religious and social concerns of Strassburg's radicals. Thus, on the eve of his debate with Bucer, it appears that Marpeck had emerged as an intellectual leader among the radicals – one with the potential to unify various segments of the movement.[101]

MARPECK AND THE STRASSBURG REFORM: DEBATE WITH MARTIN BUCER, DECEMBER 9, 1531 – JANUARY 12, 1532

From the beginning of the reform movement in Strassburg, there was disagreement among the evangelical preachers about the role of the civil magistracy in the Reformation. The principal difference existed between the approaches of Bucer and of Wolfgang Capito. In his earliest writings, Bucer expressed the conviction that the work of the magistracy included not only the adjudication of temporal rights, but also the protection of piety to assure the praise of God and the true faith in the city.[102] The church in Bucer's *Das Ym Selbs* was the church of the whole Strassburg community. The clergy, as representatives of Christ, successors of the apostles, and interpreters of God's law, stood at the top of a hierarchy of authority. The civil authorities followed just below the clergy, ruling according to God's law.[103] Bucer's notion of an indivisible Christian community determined his stance on baptism and his method of dealing with the Anabaptists. He saw their insistence on believers' baptism as destructive of the love and unity of the *corpus christianum*.[104] In the interrogation of Jakob Gross, Bucer was concerned not primarily with baptism, but with obedience to civil authority and the willingness to bear the sword and to swear the annual oath. Bucer mobilized the council with these issues and was supported by the preacher, Caspar Hedio.

Capito, however, took a different, more pastoral approach insisting that the power of civil authority was limited to external, temporal matters, while the spiritual unity of the city was secured only by teaching and persuasion.[105] The large number of radicals concentrated in Capito's Young St. Peter's parish has been noted. Here, Capito and his assistant, Wolfgang Schultheiss, received many radicals and gave them a sympathetic ear. Among those invited to Capito's own home for discussions or longer stays were Reublin, Wolff, Denck, Cellarius,

---

101 In the opinion of Deppermann, *Melchior Hoffman*, 237, Marpeck was »der geistig bedeutendste Täuferführer Strassburgs.... Er wäre vermutlich der einzige gewesen, der Hoffmans apokalyptischen Phantasien mit Erfolg hätte entgegentreten können.«

102 See Klaus Deppermann, *Die Strassburger Reformatoren und die Krise des oberdeutschen Täufertums im Jahre 1527. Eine Antwort auf J. H. Yoder, 'Der Kristallisationspunkt des Täufertums,'* 27. See also Henry G. Krahn, *Martin Bucer's Strategy Against Sectarian Dissent*, 176.

103 Chrisman, *Strasbourg and the Reform*, 203.

104 Müsing, *Karlstadt*, 186.

105 Deppermann, *Die Strassburger Reformatoren*, 27. See also James M. Kittelson, *Wolfgang Capito from Humanist to Reformer*, 187f.

Hätzer, Sattler, Kautz, and Schwenckfeld. It seems that Capito was more interested in the theological issues and sought common understanding among those persons related to his parish. After the execution of Michael Sattler in 1527, Capito wrote a letter of reproach to the council at Horb. Praising Sattler's zeal for the honor of God and community of Christ, Capito maintained that the council should not punish a lack of understanding but only things that disturbed the peace of the city, such as stealing or causing a public uproar. He consoled the congregation at Horb, calling them brothers with whom he could live in mutual admonition. Further, he acknowledged that the issues, including their rejection of the oath, on which he disagreed were not critical, so long as they agreed that one should obey the civil authorities.[106] This conviction was reflected also in his insistence, contrary to Bucer, that a distinction should be made between Anabaptists who were misguided, but who could be led back with patience and gentleness, and those who were malicious and denied that the civil authority could be Christian.[107]

In the years immediately preceding his debate with Marpeck, Bucer and the Strassburg reform faced difficulties, which reached crisis proportion by December 1531. The obstacles threatening Bucer's reform included developments both outside and inside the city.

Outside of Strassburg, the evangelical movement suffered several blows to its unity and the strength of its leadership. In January 1530 Bucer wrote of his disappointment with the failure of Luther and Zwingli to reach agreement on the Supper at Marburg. At the Diet of Augsburg, the Strassburg reformers found themselves isolated in a position between that of Luther and Zwingli and formulated the Tetrapolitana. This weakened Strassburg's political alliance with the Swiss and isolated the city from other German cities. Then, in October and November 1531, the Swiss movement lost two of its major exponents, Zwingli and Oecolampadius. A letter dated December 11, 1531, from Bucer to Ambrosius Blaurer reflected his growing anxiety about the success of the movement. He wrote, »If it were not for you and what is left of those in Zurich who knows what might happen?«[108] Apparently his concern for a continued solidarity with Blaurer, in Constance, prompted a series of letters in the second half of 1531 to Blaurer's sister, Margaret. Evidently she had had some contact with Marpeck or his ideas, and expressed her admiration of him to Bucer.[109] Bucer responded with three letters admitting that Marpeck and his wife had a »fine irreproachable manner« but warning that his strictness threatened to divide the church.[110]

Inside the city, Bucer faced further difficulties in the form of Capito's sympathy for the position of certain Anabaptists and in the growing strength of

106 KR, 1:81-91.

107 Ibid., 1:179-80, Capito to Zwingli, and 1:184, Capito to Ambrosius Blaurer.

108 Traugott Schiess, ed., *Briefwechsel der Brüder Ambrosius und Thomas Blaurer, 1506-1548*, 299-300.

109 It is possible that Margaret Blaurer had read one or both of Marpeck's tracts, since they were published a month prior to her exchange with Bucer.

110 KR, 1:338-39, 342, 350.

the movement. We have noted Capito's openness to a critical perspective of civil authority which did not demonize or totally reject such authority. His openness to the critique of infant baptism, expressed most clearly in his *Hosea Commentary* (1528), caused Bucer much discomfort. Capito asserted that faith was grounded on the »inner Word« of God and that Old Believers, Lutherans, and Anabaptists all made the mistake of valuing the external ceremonies too highly. He defined baptism as that act by which one commits oneself before one's brothers to kill the flesh and follow the Spirit. However, he maintained that, because one is predestined to the kingdom of God, rebaptism is unnecessary.[111] On June 24, 1528, Bucer complained to Zwingli that the latter's arguments had not yet convinced Capito unequivocally to acknowledge the validity of infant baptism.[112] In fact, according to Capito, the Anabaptists had had a healthy effect on Strassburg in that they had made the people more careful and the preachers more alert, so that the offices were being better fulfilled.[113] There is also evidence, from Bucer himself, that Capito was attracted to Marpeck's notion of the division of the Testaments, which stressed the descent of the Spirit in the incarnation, and the full remission of sins through the outpouring of the Spirit in Christ's death.[114] The tension between Bucer and Capito surfaced in the spring of 1531, when Capito objected to Bucer's attempt to have the regime suppress the Anabaptists without any distinction among them.[115] By the end of the year, Bucer was so concerned about Capito's intention to marry Sabina Bader, the wife of the executed Anabaptist leader, Augustin, that he wrote several letters encouraging friends to dissuade him.[116]

It is difficult to estimate the precise strength of the various Anabaptist groups at this time. Records from extensive hearings in October 1530 reveal the following centers of activity and estimates of the number of participants: the Barfüsser Platz, the Pflug Tavern on the Steinstrasse, the Butcher's Gate (2,000), the yard beside the convent near the cathedral (20), and the house of Wendeleng von Zabernn (20-30).[117] By 1531 Bucer was alarmed that »very few« came to the sermons so that it became impossible for the preachers to state their case to the common man against the Anabaptists.

Faced with disunity among the evangelical preachers, strong Anabaptist activity and dwindling church attendance, Bucer turned to the council for help. In February the preachers presented to the council a petition calling for a synod

---

111 Deppermann, *Melchior Hoffman*, 171-72.

112 KR, 1:163-64.

113 Ibid., 1:152.

114 See Bucer's letter of February 2, 1532, to Blaurer in Schiess, *Briefwechsel*, 322-23. Here, Bucer encourages Blaurer to refute Marpeck's denial »that the ancients have remission of sins and righteousness through faith,« when Capito visits him. This and other considerations have led me to question the conclusion of Kittelson, *Wolfgang Capito*, 182, that Capito's »comparatively tolerant policy toward the radicals was not founded upon any theological agreement with them.«

115 KR, 1:331-33.

116 Schiess, *Briefwechsel*, 317.

117 KR, 1:268-78.

to work out a confession of faith and a *Magistrat*–supported church order.[118] Complaining that the Anabaptists spread their views freely and that the city mandates were not being carried out, the petition called on the council to see that God's will was done by its subjects. Quoting Romans 12, 1 Corinthians 12:28, and 1 Timothy 2:1, the preachers called on the council to exercise God's gift of governing to God's honor. Among other things, the petition demanded that everyone must attend at least one sermon on Sunday, all young people must be brought to weekly catechetical instruction, and the Anabaptists must be opposed for the sake of unity. A committee of three laymen, or *Kirchenpfleger*, were to oversee the behavior and doctrine of the pastor as well as the discipline of the parish community. According to one observer, Bucer was concerned not so much about general parish discipline as about the oversight and control of the pastors.[119] He intended to unify the pastors, to reform their behavior, and therefore silence the Anabaptist critique and get the council more directly involved.[120]

The council was dubious about the kind of direct involvement demanded by Bucer. It was concerned about the civil implications of the refusal of some Anabaptists to take the oath and the threat to the city's peace resulting from public attacks on the evangelical preachers. Therefore, the council acted to expel each leader with whom there was potential for a mass movement.[121] However, the regime, motivated partially by a minority of Old Believer's fearing religious persecution, was careful to restrict Bucer's sphere of power.

The issue of public debates with the Anabaptists brings to the fore the differing purposes of the preachers and the regime. With respect to the pace and extent of the reformation of religious life in Strassburg, the Protestant councillors were divided into two camps, defined by socioeconomic interests. The »politiques« – composed primarily of the guild aristocracy and old patriciate – because of their connections with territorial nobles and concern for a wider imperial consensus, favored a more deliberate and tolerant approach to reform. The »zealots« – the working artisans and smaller merchants – wanted a faster, more tightly disciplined reform of the church, which would embody their ideal of *corpus christianum*.[122] The preachers, supported by the zealots, were faced with decreasing attendance at sermons and catechetical instruction and sought a means of winning the support of the common man to their position. The politiques wanted to be rid of anyone who might garner enough public support to cause political instability, but not at the expense of too greatly strengthening the hand of the evangelical preachers. A public debate was therefore out of the question.

---

118 Ibid., 1:327-30. See also Krahn, *Martin Bucer's Strategy*, 170f.

119 Chrisman, *Strasbourg and the Reform*, 209, quotes Wendel.

120 Krahn, *Martin Bucer's Strategy*, 172.

121 Denck (1526), Reublin and Kautz (1529), Marpeck (1532), and Hoffman (1533). See Deppermann, *Die Strassburger Reformatoren*, 29-30.

122 R. Emmett McLaughlin, *Caspar Schwenckfeld: Reluctant Radical*, 150-51, summarizes the analysis of Brady, *Ruling Class*, 241-45, of these groups and their relation to the city's reform.

So, when Bucer requested a public hearing with Marpeck in December 1531, the council decided to limit the audience to its own members.

There follows here a brief chronology of the debate; chapter four includes a more extensive analysis of the issues, Marpeck's position, and its relation to Strassburg's social and political dynamics.

On Saturday, December 9, 1531, Marpeck met Bucer for the first discussion behind the closed doors of the council chambers. On the following Wednesday the council heard a second debate between Marpeck, a companion, and four of the evangelical preachers. At its conclusion, the preachers asked the council to publish an opinion for the common man, to maintain better order and to punish the blasphemers and strip them of their citizenship. The clerk noted disagreement among the councilmen about whether such uniformity should be enforced. Three days later the preachers petitioned the council for an open debate. Complaining, again, that few attended the sermons, they argued that a public debate would restore »one teaching and religion« to Strassburg. The council refused the request on Monday, December 18, and adopted Jakob Sturm's recommendation that Marpeck be expelled from the city unless he was willing to retract his assertion that infant baptism was unchristian and to abstain from rebaptizing.[123] Sturm revealed that, in the judgment of the council, Marpeck had not sufficiently grounded in the Scripture his three accusations against the preachers. In a letter dated the same day, the council informed Countess Elizabeth von Fürstenberg that Marpeck had been dismissed and replaced by Christman Steiger and Gilg Brenner.[124]

On December 19 Marpeck informed the council that he, having been »bodily« obedient, respected its decision but could not promise not to return »if he were driven or led here by the Spirit.« He also asked for a postponement of his expulsion until he could sell his household effects and receive payment for his work in Einbach. The council granted him two weeks. In the meantime, Marpeck asked Bucer for a written defense of infant baptism, which he received just after the first of the year. Intending to write a response, Marpeck asked for and received a second two-week grace period. By January 10 he had finished his *Confession* and approached Bucer for a third discussion. In a letter dated about the same time, he asked the council to reconsider his case in light of his and Bucer's written arguments. On January 12, 1532, the council agreed to a third hearing, which took place sometime the following week before a select group and ended with Marpeck's expulsion.[125]

---

123 Sturm was a »leading politique« who persistently sought to limit the power of the clergy. See McLaughlin, *Caspar Schwenckfeld*, 152.

124 For documents related to Marpeck's first and second hearings and subsequent dismissal and expulsion, see KR, 1:351-61.

125 For the period December 19, 1531, to Marpeck's final expusion, see KR, 1:361-63, 529-32. For Marpeck's *Confession*, see KR, 1:416-518 (herinafter cited as *Confession*, followed by the page number).

Chapter 4

MARPECK'S THEOLOGY OF THE CROSS AND THE CHRISTIAN COMMUNITY

Marpeck forged his first publicly expressed theological ideas in Strassburg, where different social theologies competed for loyalty, in relation to, among other intellectual influences, the theologies of the cross of the *Theologia Deutsch*, Leonhart Schiemer, and Hans Schlaffer. His conception of the cross of Christ and its implications for the suffering of the human being will be viewed in the context of his notions of sin, the person and work of Christ, the regeneration of the human being, and the nature of the realm of Christ. There follows an examination of Marpeck's criticism of those in Strassburg who, he believed, made the realm of Christ »too spiritual« (namely, the Spiritualists, or *Geister*) and those who made it »too fleshly« (namely, the evangelical preachers).

SIN

Marpeck's description of the nature of sin parallels, conceptually and linguistically, that of the Frankfurter. He consistently characterizes sin as one's »own invention or presumption [aigen ticht und annemen].«[1] In an important distinction, Marpeck says that »sin, death, and hell and their rule and mastery consist purely of self–enclosed knowledge [aigen wissen] not in unknowing [unwissen].«[2] According to Marpeck, this self–enclosed knowledge was introduced through Adam and Eve, in whom the human became »an enemy to his own life.«[3] All of humanity and all creatures were ruined through disobedience to God and to the Word. Reminiscent of the *Theologia Deutsch*, Marpeck defines that disobedience as the desire »to be one's own lord and god.«[4]

---

1 Pilgram Marpeck, *Ain Klarer vast nützlicher unterricht* (hereinafter listed as *KU*), Aiii^v, D^r. See *TD*, 47/90.23-26, where the Frankfurter describes the »eygener will« and *TD*, 2/10.8-11, for the often employed »sich annemen« (1528). See Klaus Deppermann, *Melchior Hoffman*, 150-51.

2 *Confession*, 428.3-4. Cf. a similar notion (*TD*, 47/90.23-26). The Frankfurter says that hell and the Devil are found only where there is »eygener will.« See chapter 5 for Marpeck's interesting use of the mystical *unwissenheit*.

3 *Confession*, 429.1-3.

4 Ibid., 427.1-7. See chapter 7 where Marpeck explicitly adduces the *Theologia Deutsch* for his notion of sin.

Falling from the mind and will of God in unknowing, the human was snared by the cunning, deceit, and will of the snake. Therefore, the ensuing knowledge of good and evil reflected a selfish reason (*aigen vernunfft*) bent on self–rationalization and control.[5] He claims this self–seeking use of human reason (*aigens ticht* or *menschen ticht*) is at work in the positions of his opponents – the prophets (Spiritualists) and the learned scribes (preachers).[6]

For Marpeck, the problem of sin is not with the unknowing child, but the knowing adult whose reason is dominated by a self–obsessed mode of life: »every human being eats and takes for himself from the forbidden fruit, without the fault of Adam and Eve, in the knowledge of good and evil, otherwise it must follow that Christ did not restore the fall of Adam in us as [he did] in the unknowing children. Although a root of sin is in the unknowing, according to the mode of the flesh, it is not sin itself.«[7] He supposes a point at which the individual willingly participates in the sin and therefore guilt of Adam. In these first reflections on original sin, Marpeck displays a characteristic concern for the importance of individual participation, but does not deny a certain pervasive, inherited root of sin. Since the guilt of sin lies in this conscious complicity (*wissenhait*), the ridding children of that guilt through baptism is unnecessary. Marpeck later develops this notion of the root of sin (chapter five) and a countervailing inherited grace (chapter seven).

The effect of the »Adamic mode and fall« is the imprisonment of the »spirit and inward life under the gloom and darkness of the flesh.«[8] Flesh, in Marpeck's vocabulary, refers, then, to this self–enclosed, self–rationalizing mode of existence in which all of humanity was trapped. The knowledge of good and evil is that by which the human being seeks to justify and secure the self in the world. One seeks a self–sufficient existence, without reference to any reality beyond the self. It is this *aigen wissen* by which sin, death, and hell reign and the prince of this world holds the human being bound according to his own will (*aigen will*).[9] According to Marpeck, this gloom and darkness »may not be opened or released in anyone with any assurance without an external key.«[10] The key which unlocked the self–enclosed existence of humanity is the humanity of Christ.[11]

---

5 *Confession*, 427.8-10.

6 *KU*, Aii^v: »Got geb wie hoch ihr vernunfft unnd aigens ticht die geschrifft maistert / auss welcher vernunfft sye billich maister der geschrifft genannt werden«; Aviii^r: »Aber ihr vernunfft und aigen ticht ist der grundt ihres glaubens.« Cf. *TD*, 18/40.21-26, for a polemic against the »naturlich vornunfft« which ascends in its »eigen leicht und yn yr selber.«

7 *Confession*, 460.6-461.6.

8 *KU*, Avi^v: »Dann ihe die Adamisch art unnd fal den geist unnd innwendigs leben / under die finsternuss und tunchklheyt dess fleysches / Roma. am 7. gefangen hat.«

9 *Confession*, 427.1-10.

10 *KU*, Avi^v: »... das es inn keinem menschen mit kainer sicherhait / on einen ausswendigen schlüssel (der da ist die menscheyt Christi) auff gethan noch erlost mag werden.«

11 Marpeck may have taken this notion from Schiemer who called the cross of Christ the key of David which opened eternity to the human. Cf. chapter 2.

CROSS OF CHRIST

A number of scholars have recognized the pivotal role played by the incarnation in Marpeck's systematic theological reflections.[12] In clarifying his understanding of Christ's cross, it is important to examine Marpeck's conceptions of the person and work of Christ, and its *pro nobis* character.[13]

As with the Frankfurter, the incarnation represents for Marpeck a new reality or mode of existence, in which the created order is restored in the person of Christ. As the key to the human being's self-enclosed prison, the humanity of Christ is »our mediator to his divinity« (Timothy 2).[14] In another place Marpeck says, »the Lord Christ became to the natural human being a natural human being, so that he [the person] might be translated, through the natural, into the supernatural and heavenly being [wesen].«[15] There is, then, a union of the human and the supernatural, or heavenly wesen, in Christ, which the human being comes to share. Before examining that participation by other human beings, we need a closer look at the participation of the human and heavenly in Christ.

Because God deals with creation according to order and fairness, God responded to the disorder introduced by Adam. The human spirit, which was ruined and died in Adam, was made alive in Christ who brought everything to order.[16] In the human Christ, the presumptuous, self-obsessed mode of human activity ceased and the order intended in creation was restored. That order consisted of an integration of, or participation between, the human and the divine, which ceased with the fall or turning of Adam from the divine. Of this order in Christ, Marpeck writes: »the natural realities must precede, even today, the victory and maintenance of the natural human being in the supernatural (which begins here in the restoration of destroyed nature) through the natural obedience brought again in the order initiated by Christ, in which he [the human being], shall be held, so that the natural and the supernatural might exist together.«[17] Marpeck calls this new order the teaching and order of Christ (*ler*

---

[12] Blough, *Christologie Anabaptiste*, 20, cites observations by Hans-Jürgen Goertz, William Klassen, Heinold Fast, and Torsten Bergsten.

[13] Although Marpeck did not use Luther's technical terms such as *pro nobis, extra nos, in nobis,* or even their German equivalents, I employ them where appropriate as interpretive tools.

[14] *KU*, Biii[v]: »(dann eben die menschait Christi ist unser mitler gegen der gottheyt / I Timot. 2. und nit die gotheyt gegen der menschait).«

[15] Ibid., Bvi[v]: »Also ist der herr Christus dem natürlichen menschen ein naturlicher mensch worden / auff das er auch wider durch das natürlich ubersetzt würde auss der zerstörung der natur / in das ubernatürlich und himlisch wesen.« Cf. *TD*, 3/ll.12-19, for a similar affirmation by the Frankfurter, who calls this supernatural state »vergottet.«

[16] *KU*, Av[r]: »dann es Johannes nit / sonder alleyn Christus (dem die krafft und ehr gebürt / alles zu recht bracht hat / Rom. v.«

[17] Ibid., Bvi[v]: »Also müssen noch auff heut / die naturlichen wirckligkaiten zu der gewinnung und erhaltung dess naturlichen menschen vorgeen / ehe er in das ubernaturlich (welches hie in widerbringung verstörter natur anfahet) durch naturliche gehorsam wider in Christi fürgestellte ordenung gebracht / und drin erhalten werd / damit das natürlich und ubernaturlich bei einannder bsteen mog.« Marpeck's use of the word *übernatürlich* is somewhat unusual in Frühneuhochdeutsch. Grimm, *Deutsches Wörterbuch*, 11:2, 435, cites its usage by Luther (WA

und ordnung), the established witness of Christ (*furgestellten Zeugkhnus Crissti*), or the justice in Christ (*gerechtigkait in Chrissto*).[18] The justice of Christ, then, is a state in which the human no longer exists in a self – obsessed, grasping isolation but lives in reciprocal participation and harmony with God and other creatures. Gerechtigkeit is a proper ordering of reality which has reference not only to the disposition or mode of the individual (justness) but also to social relationships (justice). As did Schiemer and Schlaffer, Marpeck insisted that the justice of Christ coordinated these two aspects and that the proper ordering of one was impossible without the other.[19]

Important in his argument against the Geister, Marpeck asserts that the incarnation is not a »contradiction to created nature... but allows that nature to stand undisturbed its real power [*krafft*].«[20] Only the humanity of Christ could take »captivity captive« and establish the justice which restored the human to strength and life. This was accomplished in the »obedience of the untarnished, pure, mortal flesh and blood of Christ.«[21] The problem, then, was not the flesh as created matter, but the disorder in the human will and mode of existence. Following the Frankfurter, Marpeck describes the disorder as disobedience and the new order in Christ as obedience.[22]

We turn now to the work of Christ *pro nobis*, by which the new order or justness in Christ is shared with others. According to Marpeck the Spirit of Christ, which is the true sanctification (*fromachung*), was not poured out before his suffering and death.[23] The apostles did not wish to go the way of Christ's suffering and death because that »Spirit of power [*craft*] and strength [*sterkh*]« had not yet been received. This innovative understanding of the implications of Christ's cross is at the heart of Marpeck's position and requires more detailed examination.

In the incarnation the Spirit is more powerful than in the time of the Old Covenant.[24] Further, Marpeck says that the serpent cannot be trampled and

---

7,19: »syntemal keuscheyt so ein seltzam übernaturlich gottes krafft und gabe ist«), but identifies its origin in the mystical writings of Suso.

[18] *Confession*, 517.12, 447.22-25, 514.14-15, 18-20. Cf. Schiemer in chapter 2, for a similar notion of justice.

[19] Marpeck's notion of order reflects that of the Frankfurter, see chapter 2.

[20] *KU*, Bviʳ: »Er ist nicht ain widersprecher der geschaffen natur / so vom vatter (durch ihn als ainen herren der natur) erschaffen seindt / sonnder lasst die selbig unzerbrochen stehen inn ihrer wircklichen krafft / biss auff die letste zeit da alle natürliche wurckligkait auff hört.«

[21] Ibid., Bʳ: »under die ghorsam dess unvermailigten / rainen / sterblichen fleisch und blüt Christi.« The Frankfurter also stresses the obedience of Christ as the means of establishing the new order, *TD*, 13/32.12-18.

[22] His christological debate with Schwenckfeld forced Marpeck to formulate more clearly his understanding of the participation of the human and divine in the person of Christ. See chapter 5.

[23] *Confession*, 439.15-16.

[24] Pilgram Marpeck, *Clare verantwurtung* (hereinafter listed as *CV*), Ciiʳ. See below, note 119. The title page of the *CV* bears testimony to the centrality of this notion of the qualitatively new availability of the Spirit in the incarnation and cross of Christ. After the ceremonies and

killed without the suffering and death of Christ.[25] Elsewhere he quotes Jesus telling the disciples that the Comforter will not come to lead them into godliness and truth until he dies.[26] Therefore, his willingness to die represents an offer to share or make available that Spirit to others.

Christ submitted and gave himself as prisoner to the inventions and self–enclosed reason (*dichten und aigner vernufft*) of the serpent. Or, as Marpeck writes, Christ, »was trodden under by our sin, carried our weakness, and was raised on the cross.«[27] Rather than oppose with force the self–obsessed mode of existence, ruled by the serpent, Christ chose to subject himself to that mode and its offer to him – death: »while he submitted everything to death, even eternal death, he was, himself, also subjected for the delivery in death.«[28] His death effectuated the delivery of those who waited in their guilt. Apparently, through that death, the Spirit of power and strength was made radically available to humanity.[29] Through that Spirit, the human being gained release from the prison of self–obsessed isolation, received a share in the divine life and thereby a reordering of existence in the world. Out of death comes life; out of darkness, light.[30]

There are several aspects of this cross theology which need attention. First, although Christ conquered sin, death, hell, and the serpent, the nature of this conquest (*uberwindung*) is crucial. According to Marpeck, the Spirit conquers not with force but with patience.[31] This has important implications for Marpeck's distinctions between force (*gewalt*) and strength (*krafft*), the realm of the world and the realm of Christ, as well as his position concerning the use of force by the Christian. Second, the availability and mediation of the Spirit needs further clarification. Although he concedes that elect persons before Christ's birth had this promised Spirit, their share was not as rich as that of persons who came after. Further, even Christ's contemporaries did not have full access to this more powerful Spirit. The Spirit became available to humanity only in the outpouring

commands of Christ, Marpeck says that the tract deals with the »aussgiessung dess heyligen Geystes.«

25 *CV*, C[r]: »Dann eyner schlangen den kopff zertreten / todt mans am beldisten / Darumb ist vom kopff gesagt. Wie wol sie Christum im auff sie tretten / inn die ferssen beisst / das ist / on leiden unnd creutz nit kann zertretten odder todt werden.«

26 *Confession*, 440.2-4.

27 Ibid., 445.26-29.

28 Ibid., 445.29-33. See also *Aufdeckung*, Aiii[v]: »Dann Christus ist under allem gewalt / hat sich kains gewalts nie verwidert.« Citations of the *Aufdeckung* are from the edition held by the Augsburg Stadtbibliothek and are followed by the corresponding page number of Hans Hillerbrand's photostatic copy published in »An Early Anabaptist Treatise on the Christian and the State,« 29-47.

29 Although implicit at this stage, Marpeck states this explicitly in his argument with the Swiss Brethren (chapter 5).

30 *Confession*, 446.23, 17. Marpeck reflects, here and elsewhere, Johannine themes and terminology. Marpeck also says that Christians are married to Christ »through his cross, blood, and tribulation.« *Aufdeckung*, Aii[v]. (Hillerbrand, *An Early Anabaptist Treatise*, 36).

31 *CV*, Ciii[r]. Cf. *TD*, 35/67.4-10.

of the Spirit at Christ's death and most fully with the ascension and at Pentecost.[32]

However, the reception of that Spirit is not a strictly individual experience: »For God, the Father, is in no member of the body of Christ... as in a member for itself... but so they are together put under the head [Christ] in the purification of his Spirit.«[33] Also, »Paul says here, all is given to us with Christ through faith in him, yet according to the gift and measure of the body of Christ.«[34] The Spirit, poured out by Christ's death is mediated by the concrete, living body of Christ; that is, it is borne and made available in the lives of those who have received it. Just as John the Baptist prepared the way to the bodily Christ or humanity of Christ, through his teaching, life, word, ceremonies, and deeds, the bodily Christ prepared the way and was the way itself to the inner Christ – and is still the way through his members.[35] Marpeck conceives of the gathered community and its ceremonies as a prolongation of the incarnation.[36] The Son of Man »moves and acts on earth, according to his bodily nature, through his members.«[37] His intention is to underscore the inclusion of the corporeal and the communal in the restoration wrought by the Spirit.

For Marpeck, Christ's work of atonement is directed toward the human being, not toward God. Because Christ shared the nature of the human being, that nature was opened or received the capacity (*vermugen*) to share in the divine life. Therefore, created reality, including the material, became, in the person of Jesus Christ, the mediator of that capacity and participation. Through Christ's death this capacity became available to other humans whose nature he shared. It appears that Marpeck, following the lead of Schlaffer, developed the

32 Ibid., C^v: »Solchen verhaissen geist (als geist dess glaubens / Galat. iii.) haben alle ausser-welten vor Christi gburt gehebt / Heb.xi. aber nit so reichlich als seither«; *CV*, bviii^r: »Es stet geschrieben Joel.ii. Act.ii. Es soll gschehen in den letsten tagen / spricht Got / Ich will aussgiessen von meinem geist auff alles fleysch. Das ist das new Testament davon Heb.viii. Jerem.xxxi. gesagt wirt. Die letsten tag seines geystes weder vorhin«; *CV*, cii^v: »Es kunnt auch solcher krefftiger geist Christi / als geist der verheissung der letsten tag nit kommen / weil Christus noch personlich auf erden by seinen jungern was / Joh. xii.xvi«; and *CV*, ciii^r: »Diesen geist haben all Apostel gehebt / und derst uberkommen nach der himelfart Christi.«

33 *KU*, Aiiii^v: »Dann Gott der vatter ist inn kainem glid dess leibs Christi (welcher leip biss zur ende der welt raicht) als in eynem gliedt fur es selbs / alles in allem / sonder so sie zusammen gethan werden under dem haupt inn der verainigung seins geists.«

34 Ibid., Aiii^v-Aiiii^r: »dann Paulus sagt ihe / es sei unns alles mitt CHRISTO geschenckt durch den glauben inn ihn / doch nach der gab unnd mass der glieder des leibs Christi.«

35 Ibid., Cvi^r: »Wie Johannes /... ain wegberaitter gwest ist dess leiplichen Christi / das ist / der menschait Christi. Also ist der leiplich Christus oder die menschait Christi den seinigen leiplicher weiss durch sein leiplich / lere / leben / wort / ceremoni und thaten / wie obstet / ain wegberaitter / und der weg selbs / gwest / dess geistlichen innerlichen Christi.«

36 Blough, *Christologie Anabaptiste*, 60: »Cette humanité du Christ est présente dans la vie des être humains, c'est-à-dire dans la vie de ceux qui acceptent de suivre Jesus-Christ.« In pp. 57ff. he has a helpful discussion of ceremonies as a prolongation of the incarnation and the conjecture that Luther's anti-Spiritualist writings may have been a source for this development.

37 *KU*, Bii^v-Biii^r: »O es verdreusst die flaischlich hoch hart / das dess menschen sun nach leib-licher weiss durch seine glieder 1. Cor. 6. als Act. 13. 1. Corinth. 12. Eph. 4. seinen leip / ja / Ephe. 5. sein flaisch und bain / auff erden handeln und wandeln sol.«

Frankfurter's *extra nos* character of the *leben Christi* with reference to the concrete existence of the Christian community.[38] For him the gathered community (*leib Chrissti*), not the supper or baptism, mediated that grace of God in Christ.

Here it is important to note that Marpeck's thought includes both universalistic and particularistic aspects. Before the advent of Christ all of humanity and creation shared the ruination of Adam's fall. And Marpeck argues, »Christ is the reconciliation, not for one part or half of the world, but for the whole world's sin (1 John 2). Also, just as the light enlightens everyone who comes into the world (John 1), through his ordering [*rechtfertigkait*], justification [*rechtfertigung*] has come over all (Romans 5).«[39] That justness or order embodied in Christ and made available in his death, restored the fall of Adam in all of humanity, that is, in all unknowing children. Having not yet personally eaten from the tree of the knowledge of good and evil, they do not share the guilt of Adam and Eve.[40] His notion that the Spirit is given to the community and the affirmation of the physical interdependence of humanity are further aspects of this universal tendency.

However, the community mediating the Spirit is a gathered community. Disagreeing with the *Geister* who claimed that the Spirit was poured out on all in the apostolic age, Marpeck says, »The Spirit of God was not at that time poured out everywhere, but only over the apostles and Christians. The others were unbelievers.«[41] Just as one eats for oneself of the tree of the knowledge of good and evil, so must one receive for oneself the Spirit of power and strength which reorders and heals. In his notions of sin and salvation, Marpeck manifests a persistent concern for individual participation, albeit in the larger social context of which the individual is a part.

---

[38] See chapter 2 for Schlaffer and the Frankfurter. Luther's emphasis on the real presence against Zwingli, Carlstadt, and Schwenckfeld reflects a similar concern to affirm the mediatorial inclusion of material reality.

[39] *CV*, bvi^r: »Wie auch CHRISTUS nit für ein odder halben tail / sunnder für der gantzen welt sünde die versünung ist / I. Johannis 2. auch als das liecht alle mennschen inn diese wellt kommende / erleucht / Johan. 1. unnd durch sein rechtfertigkait die rechtfertigung dess lebens uber sie alle kommen ist / Roma. v.« Marpeck's notion of justification is not far from that stage in the development of Luther's thought, in which he stressed the passive nature of God's justice – that justice by which God makes the human being just.

[40] *Confession*, 461.1-3. George H. Williams, *Popularized German Mysticism as a Factor in the Rise of Anabaptist Communism*, 295f., and »Sectarian Ecumenicity: Reflections on a Little Noticed Aspect of the Radical Reformation,« 154f., discusses this universalistic aspect within the theology of several radicals. He traces possible sources to the thought of Rhegius and Melancthon on the Mass, Zwingli's doctrine of original sin, and the historic and experiential aspects of Christ's work in the *Theologia Deutsch*.

[41] *CV*, bvii^v: »Der geist Gottes ist doch der selben zeit / Ac. 2. / nit uber all / sonder nur uber die Apostel unnd Christen aussgossen / die andern waren unglaubig.«

NEW BIRTH

Marpeck maintains that the »out–pouring of the Spirit of God in another person next to me or in the apostles does not help me.« Therefore, God must »also pour the Spirit into my heart according to the general salvation [that is, through the mediation of the community].«[42] But this reordering of the human and the divine happens not through a »fleshly coercion or a forcing together,« but through Christ's »unconstraining Spirit« (freiwilliger geist).[43]

We turn now to that uncoerced, »free and willing« process by which the *pro nobis* justness of Christ comes *in nos* and *in me*. As with the Frankfurter, Schiemer, and Schlaffer, suffering plays a key role. In his *Clare verantwurtung*, Marpeck maintains that wisdom does not enter an evil mind (gmuet) and that the unwilling, disobedient human receives »so little of the Spirit of God as he participates in the reconciliation [*versunung*] of Christ.« Then, he describes the process of coming to that participation:

That one who gives himself through repentance, i.e. through faith in Jesus Christ in co–suffering under the hand and discipline of God [Job 12:9], will also participate in the suffering and reconciliation of Christ and the Spirit of God will be poured out over him (Proverbs 1) through faith ([Galatians 3:14] John 7 [:39]). That is the rich Spirit of understanding or knowledge of Christ in our hearts.[44]

Suffering, or the process of repentance, prepares one for the inpouring of the Spirit through faith and the true knowledge of Christ.

Like the Frankfurter and Schlaffer, Marpeck stresses the necessity of suffering on the way to justness and participation in the divine life.[45] For him, one must suffer with others and thereby share the suffering of Christ before one is able to receive the gift of the Spirit. In suffering – a discipline of the spirit – »all deficiency and partialness« is revealed and acknowledged so that »one learns for

---

42 Ibid., bviii[r]: »Die aussgiessung Gottes geists in einen andern menschen neben mir / oder inn die Apostelen / nützet mir groben / rohen menschen nit / er werde dann in mein hertz auch also gossen nach gmainem hail zur seligkait.« Emphasis added. For a similar insistence on this personal nature by the Frankfurter, see *TD*; and Schiemer and Schlaffer, chapter 2. George H. Williams, »Sanctification in the Testimony of Several So–Called Schwärmer,« 6, has also documented this *in nobis* concern.

43 *CV*, avii[v]: »Wie auch itz dieser zeit an viel orten geschehen / unnd noch geschiecht zu erweckung und widerholung der rainen ordenung Christi / durch sein freiwilligen geist / nit mit fleischlichen zusamen nötten oder treiben / sunder frei / selbs willig.«

44 Ibid., bviii[v]: »Darumb wirt der unwillig / ungehorsam mensch / gleich so wenig Gottes geist emphehig / als wenig der versönung Christi tailhafftig wirt. Welcher mensch sich durch den glauben in Jesum Christum / in das mitleiden unter Gottes handt unnd zucht gibt / der wirt auch dess leidens oder versünung Christi tailhafftig / unnd uber den selben wirt auch Gottes geist aussgossen / Pro. i. durch den glauben / Galat.iii. Johann. vii. Nemlich der reich geist der verklerung oder erkantnuss Christi inn unsern hertzen.« See Blough, *Christologie Anabaptiste*, 51.

45 *Confession*, 423.12-13, 440.4-6. Cf. *TD*, 27/55.16-21; and Schlaffer, chapter 2.

the first time to pray in the Spirit and truth.«[46] This painful confrontation with the limitations of one's own finitude (that is, the hand and discipline of God) explodes the delusion of mastery and exposes the hopelessness of that self–absorbed and self–sufficient mode of existence (*aigen ticht und annemen*). It jars one to an awareness of the need for resources beyond the self; it opens one to receptivity to the Spirit. Marpeck says the Law, the first grace, reinforces and informs this acknowledgment of sin.[47]

Following Schiemer and Schlaffer, Marpeck twice uses the notion of the »gospel of all creatures« to illustrate this role of suffering.[48] In the first context, he quotes Mark 16:15, reading the genitive »of all creatures,« in order to stress the importance of the physical words of Jesus and his use of parables.[49] In another place he employs this gospel proclaimed in the simplest creatures as a two–pronged polemic against the presumption of spiritual authority based on esoteric knowledge (the *Geister*) or on learning and civil power (the magisterial Reformers): »Indeed, if a dog or cat proclaimed the gospel through the unbelieving world unto its repentance, improvement and witness, who could judge it wrong?... For all visible creatures are put in the world as apostles and teachers (Job 12). It was not necessary that they could speak, for Christ sent the apostles to announce or preach the gospel in such dumb creatures.«[50] From the scriptural context (Job 12:1f.), it appears that Marpeck brings the same indictment against the Spiritualists and magisterial Reformers, as that brought by Job against Zophar, the Naamathite. To Zophar's claim that his sin caused his suffering, Job retorted that even the beasts and birds could tell Zophar that »the hand of the Lord« was in Job's suffering. They knew that hand which reveals human contingency and looses the bonds of kings, leads priests away stripped, overthrows the mighty, and takes away understanding (Job 12:18-19, 24).

For Marpeck, suffering challenges the conventional wisdom of self–sufficiency, based upon the self–absorbed *aigner vernunfft*, and its claim to authority. The simplest creatures know from daily experience what the

---

[46] *KU*, Diiii^r-Diiii^v: »sein geist kann die uberschung dess geists nit empfinden / biss es sich unnder die zucht dess geistes ergibt / da get dann der kampff an / zwischen geist und fleisch / Gal.5. Da werden erst all mangel und gebrechen eroffent und erkennt / da lernt mann erst recht betten im geist und warhait / das ist nit ein soch gebet wie diese Propheten lernen.« Cf. *TD*, 2/10.3-7.

[47] *Confession*, 441.6-15, 445.5-6. Cf. *TD*, 24/49.21-23, for the role of suffering in human self–recognition.

[48] Cf. chapter 2 for Schiemer and Schlaffer.

[49] *KU*, Biiii^r: »da er sagt / Predigt das Evangeli aller / Mar. 16. Dann die gehimnuss und Reich Christi kann creatur on gleichnussen weder auss gesprochen noch verstanden werden.« Blough, *Christologie Anabaptiste*, 48-49, observes the similarities between Marpeck and Hut's use of the »gospel of all creatures,« but notes that its use to emphasize the external is new in Marpeck.

[50] *CV*, biiii^r-biiii^v: »Ja wann ein hundt odder katze das EVANGELIUM durch die unglaubig wellt predigte zur buss / besserung and zeucknuss / wer kunnte es unrecht sprechen? Dann alles das da zur gotseligkait laittet ist gut und nit böss / dann alle sichtbarlichen creaturn seint inn die wellt gestelt zu Aposteln unnd leren / Job.xii. Wo sy reden kunnten were unnot gewesst / das Christus die Aposteln gesendet hett das Evangeli inn solchen stummenden creaturn anzuzeygen odder predigen.«

Spiritualists and Reformers apparently do not – every human ability, possession, or position on which that claim rests can vanish in one unfortunate and unmanageable instant. For Marpeck, the only secure basis of authority or hope is that Spirit of power and strength for which this gospel of all creatures prepares one. Suffering brings a change of will. One desires that Spirit which forces itself upon no one.

After suffering »under the hand and discipline of God,« the next stage of the process is the inpouring of the Spirit through faith or the second grace. According to Marpeck, suffering, or the »gospel of all creatures,« and the law destroy, prune, and break the human and »simply point out sin and incapacity« (*unvermugen*).[51] For those whose hearts are yielded (*gelasen*) or circumcised with the »circumcision without hands,« Christ is their physician.[52] For Marpeck, faith denotes a new receptivity through which the Spirit of power and strength enters the human. He writes, »So now such a transfer happens through faith, for the Spirit of Christ, in the pure flesh, only reaches into and secures my spirit through faith.«[53] By receiving the divine Spirit, the human being participates in the very nature of God. The believer experiences a renewal in the heart, so that the natural (human) and supernatural (divine) may exist together.[54] In another passage, Marpeck says that, through the »knowledge of Christ [granted by the indwelling Spirit] one comes to the knowledge of God (John 8[:47] and 14[:18-20]; II Cor.4 [:7f.]) and becomes part of the divine nature.«[55] Echoing the language of the »*vergottet mensch*« in the *Theologia Deutsch* and Schiemer, Marpeck's biblical references reveal the Johannine theme of coinherence at the foundation of his notion of participation.[56]

To this participation in the divine imparted by the Spirit through faith, Marpeck ascribes justness (*gerechtigkeyt*), justification (*rechtfertigung*), forgiveness (*verzeihung*) and remission (*vergebung*) of sins.[57] The Spirit brings to the believing person the pure order of Christ (*rainen ordenung Christi*). This new order has also a social aspect. Rather than being bent and directed toward the self (*aigen annemen*), the believer is directed outward toward Christ (*annemen Christum*),

---

51 *Confession*, 449.1-450.2.

52 *KU*, Aii^r; and *Confession*, 432.3-6. Cf. *TD*, 21/44.9-11, for a similar notion of Gelassenheit.

53 *KU*, Biiii^r: »Unnd das heisst Johan. 6. fleisch und blut Christi gessen und truncken / das mein geist erst inn dem rainen fleisch und blut Christi erledigt ist. So nun solche ubergab beschiecht durch den glauben / da mag erst der geist CHRISTI in dem rainen fleisch / durch den glauben / zu meinem geist raichen / unnd den versicheren.« Cf. *TD*, 55/99.16-17.

54 *KU*, Cvii^r: »Warumb wolten dann die Christen (so sich wider durch ernewerung ihres lebens / Christo ihrem herren geschenckt / und ergeben haben.«

55 *CV*, cii^v: »Durch welch erkantnuss Christi kompt mann auch zur erkanntnuss Gottes / Johan. viii.xiiii.II. Corinth.iiii. wirt göttlicher natur / so wir anderst fliehen die zergencklichen luste der welt.«

56 Marpeck's later exchanges with Schwenckfeld make it clear that, by participation in the divine nature, Marpeck does not mean substantial divinization of the human being.

57 *KU*, Bvii^r, Dvi^r, Bviii^v.

who is experienced in the members of the body.[58] This justness from faith involves, then, intensely personal and communal experiences. In the new creature or being (*neues wesen*), the spiritual, or internal, and the corporeal, or external, are integrated. In his later debate with Schwenckfeld (chapter five), Marpeck further refines his notion of participation with an innovative use of the term *wesen*.

While he insists that the Spirit comes in to reorder the human being and therefore tends to conjoin justification and sanctification,[59] Marpeck has a strong sense of the *extra nos* character of grace and the work of Christ. As we have seen, he develops the »gospel of all creatures,« which prepares the human to receive the »gospel to all creatures« – the Spirit made available to the human through the life, the suffering, and most radically, through the death of Christ.[60] Without the firm, historical reality of the latter, the former would serve only to crush the conscience and leave the human being without hope.[61] As we shall see, this was the foundation of Marpeck's critique of the *Geister* and particularly of their »lofty« Christologies.

With the inpouring of the Spirit comes the »true knowledge of Christ,« displacing the self – enclosed reason (*aigen vernunfft*), which justifies itself on the basis of the knowledge of good and evil.[62] In the crucible of suffering and the confrontation with death, one acknowledges one's finitude and the need for

---

58 Ibid., Av[V]: »dann Christus ist keinem unglaubigen gesandt... nit das es an Christo mangel / sonder an dem der ihn nitt annimpt.«

59 Williams, *Popularized German Mysticism*, 310, describes this coordination, in certain radicals, of justification and sanctification through a *theologia crucis*. However, Blough, *Christologie Anabaptiste*, 88f., argues against Williams's assertion (p. 294, that the Anabaptists coined the terms gerechtmachung and frommachung. Noting Luther's own use of the terms, Blough insists that the terms themselves are not significant in differentiating the positions of Marpeck and Luther. See chapter 2 for the use of these terms by Schlaffer.

60 In comparing the theologies of suffering of certain radicals and Luther, Williams, »Sanctification,« 20-22, notes the shift from Luther's early identification of the suffering of Christ with God's *opus alienum* and Christ's resurrection and justification of the human with God's *opus proprium* to the later identification of the suffering of the viator with God's strange work and the suffering and resurrection of Christ and the human's justification with God's proper work. He observes that the Anabaptists did not follow this refinement and that, for them, God's strange work »ever remained the bitter Christ, the gospel of all creatures, while the *opus proprium*, the gospel to all creatures was the perception of this suffering incurred in, and because of this world.« See George H. Williams, *German Mysticism in the Polarization of Ethical Behavior in Luther and the Anabaptists*, 301-2. Marpeck seems more in agreement with Luther. For him, the entire reality of Christ, including the incarnation, suffering, and death, constitutes the gospel to all creatures, or God's *opus proprium*, in that it makes available the Spirit which introduces justness in the human sphere.

61 Williams, *German Mysticism in the Polarization of Ethical Behavior*, 295-99, identifies the *Theologia Deutsch* as a source, among the Anabaptists, for a »second at – one – ment,« that is the experiential reconciliation of the human in addition to that achieved in Christ. Here we draw attention to Marpeck's Christological development of the Frankfurter's thought. With his sacramental notion of the body of Christ, (i.e., Christ walks and acts through his members), Marpeck conceives of the reconciliation in Christ and in humans as parts of one historical continuum, initiated decisively by the life, suffering, and death of Jesus.

62 *CV*, avii[V]: »das warhafftig erkanntnuss Christi.«

resources beyond the self. One recognizes, in the suffering and death of Christ, the decisive outpouring of the life–giving Spirit of power and strength, which empowers even this recognition. Because they denied this concrete, historical work of Christ, Marpeck criticized the *Geister* for a lack of the »true knowledge of Christ.« Therefore, they also ignored the necessity of submitting to the contemporary, concrete body of Christ to learn of him.

For Marpeck, baptism involved both of these individual and communal aspects. It required this personal knowledge, that the suffering and death of Christ is the solution to the profound question of human suffering. On this ground Marpeck argued against Bucer and infant baptism. Further, baptism represented one's subjection to the feet of Christ (*zu seinen fussen werffen*), that is to the needs and gifts of the community.[63] Therefore, he argued against the suspension of the ceremony advocated by the Spiritualists.

REALM OF CHRIST

Through the outpouring of the Spirit in his suffering and death, Christ initiated a new kingdom or realm (*reich Crissti*), which Marpeck carefully distinguishes from the realm of the world (*weltliches reich*).

Characterized by the self–absorbed, grasping mode of existence, the worldly realm is ruled by what Marpeck terms variously: coercion, physical force, external authority, fleshly compulsion and force, or the power (*gewalt*) of domination and mastery.[64] Here the political power–holders (*gewalt–habern*) and ecclesiastical antichrists seek only themselves and their own advantage (*eygen nutz*) and can pass their power externally to others.[65]

In the realm of Christ, the nature and exercise of power is quite different: »Here there is no coercion, but spontaneous spirit in Christ Jesus our Lord.« Neither may external power (*eusserliche gwallt*) »dominate, be used, or rule.«[66] When referring to power in the realm of Christ, Marpeck tends to use the word *krafft* in opposition to *gewalt* exercised in the worldly realm.[67] This distinction in

---

[63] *KU*, Biiii[r]: »So wir unns zuvor dem rechten maister mitt aller unnser vernunnfft / krefften / thaten / kunst unnd weisshait aller wasser... durch den waren glauben in ihm gefangen geben / und alles das so wir haben /... zu seinen füssen werffen / und bezeugen auch solchs durch die furgestelt zeucknuss dess Tauffs.«

[64] *Confession*, 424.10f.: »zwang«; *CV*, ciiiv: »eusserlichen zwang«; *Confession*, 506.4: »leiblichen gwallts, herschung noch regierung«; *Confession*, 507.1: »eusserlich obrigkhait«; *CV*, aviiv: »fleischlichem zusamen nötten oder treiben«; and *CV*, biiii[r]: »gewalt der herrschung / odder maisterschafft.«

[65] *CV*, biiii[r]-biiii[v]: »Im weltlichen reich mögen die gewalt haber ihrn gewalt wol andern eusserlich ubergeben / aber im geistlichen reich nit... anndersst ich würde nur mich und meinen eygen nutz mitt allen weltlichen unnd Antichristischen gewalthabern suchen.«

[66] *Confession*, 424.10-11, 425.1-2. See also *Aufdeckung*, C[r] (Hillerbrand, *An Early Anabaptist Treatise*, 43).

[67] Marpeck speaks variously of the krafft of the Spirit (*Confession*, 439.15-16, 481.6-7, 487.3; *CV*, avi[v], cii[r], cv[v]), of Christ (*Confession*, 448.11-12, 449.2-3, 511.14f.) and of God (*Confession*,

terminology reflects the qualitative difference between the dynamics of power, which constitute the two realms. *Krafft* denotes a strength, which empowers and elicits the response of another, while *gewalt* indicates an external force and implies an unwilling coercion or domination.

As we have observed, the Spirit of power (*krafft*) and strength imposes itself upon no one, but pours into those whose willing hearts have been prepared by the first grace of suffering and the law. This Spirit empowers or imparts a capacity (*vermugen*) to the human to participate in the heavenly or divine life, thereby providing the basis for a new being (*neues wesen*) in the human and a new basis for human relationships. In the new nature, the human, through the Spirit, receives resources from beyond the self. Therefore, one is no longer constrained to provide everything necessary for existence: »They [in this new nature] are no longer born into slavery but as free children without humiliation, compulsion, or a guardian, as lords over all things.«[68] The dependence on others, resulting from human nature as material existence, no longer fuels that compulsive necessity of self–sufficiency and domination. In the Spirit it is no longer necessary to experience that partialness and dependence as restrictive and therefore to deny one's bodily nature. Others are not necessarily competitors for those resources by which existence is secured. Rather, one is enabled to embrace one's own incompleteness and others, in whose community completeness is found: »The health [hail] of the soul consists of the love of the neighbor. Whoever does not love him, does not love his own soul and seeks, with ignorance, his own advantage to his own greatest disadvantage.«[69] Therefore, in the justness or reordering of the Spirit of Christ, »believers are set in the freedom of the spirit,« by which they are »resolved to be diligent in all things (II Corinthians 2 [:9]) unto the fulfillment of all justice [*gerechtigkeyt*] Matthew 3 [:15]), not only internally before God, but also externally before humanity (2 Corinthians 8 [:21], Titus 2 [:8]).«[70] The believer, then, is freed from the self–absorbed mode of existence, which grasps what is needed from the neighbor, and desires no

448.11-12; *KU*, Dii[r]). There are exceptions to this distinction in terminology as he occasionally refers to the gewalt aus glauben (*KU*, Cv[r]) or the gewalt Christi (*KU*, Avii[v]). But the latter carries the polemical intent of radically subordinating all worldly power to that of Christ. Further, the preponderance of the use of krafft in the *Confession* may indicate that Marpeck refined this distinctive terminology against Bucer. For the following definitions, I am indebted to the helpful insights of Professor Williams.

68 *Confession*, 439.4-7.

69 Ibid., bii[v]: »Das hail der seel liegt an der lieb dess nechsten. Wer ihn nit liebt / der liebet sein seel nit / sucht sein eygen nutz mit unverstanndt zu seinem höchsten unnutz. Damit bzeugt sich kain wachen oder nüchterkait / weder uber sein noch anndere sele / sonnder lauter schlaff unnd trunckenhait.«

70 Ibid., ci[v]: »Der glaubig wirt sich... befleissen bewert zu sein in allen stucken / ii Cor.ii. zur erfullung aller gerechtigkeyt / Matth. iii. nit alleyn vor God / sunder auch eusserlich vor den menschen.«

domination, but gives the self »in service of the body of Christ and the whole world.«[71]

Here Marpeck formulates most clearly his integration of the two concerns of the Strassburg radicals – personal experience of a change of life and significant participation in the religious community with the concern for social responsibility. Marpeck uses Paul's concern for the collection for the poor in Jerusalem (2 Corinthians 8:21, and Titus 2:8) as an example of the external fulfillment of justice before humanity. This carries the implicit indictment of those who, as Fridolin Meyger had said, considered »themselves good evangelicals and hear[d] sermons daily,« yet who lent money at usurious rates with no regard for the weak or vulnerable (widows and orphans). From Marpeck's perspective, the so-called evangelicals had not come to terms with their own contingency and weakness, and therefore had not received the Spirit freeing them from their anxious grasping. By seeking »his own advantage,« the usurer wounded not only his neighbor but his own soul »to his own greatest disadvantage.«

However, the Spirit poured out in the suffering and death of Christ constitutes a new community (gemeinschaft), characterized by this new capacity for mutuality. The Spirit is granted »according to the measure of the body of Christ,« that is, it is given to the whole interdependent community of persons receiving it. Since receptivity to the Spirit is free and unconstrained, so also is participation in the community. Therefore, according to Marpeck, the true community must be, in this sense, a voluntary community. But because »the gifts of the Spirit express themselves for the common good,« one submits all of one's »reason, powers, deeds, skill and wisdom« to the body.[72] For Marpeck, the realm of Christ entails a bringing to order or justice (gerechtigkeyt) the relationship of the human to God, to the self, and to others through the divine Spirit poured out through the suffering and death of Christ.

Further, the lives of those receiving that Spirit serve as mediators of the extension of that justice or realm in the world:

let the water, which comes from that eternal life, flow from their body, for they have drunk from the fountain of life through faith in Christ (John 4:7).... For the members of the body of Christ give to their fellow members as well as to the world in its deprivation and deficiency with the prescribed medicine and means – the teaching, wisdom and instruction of the Master.[73]

---

71 *Confession*, 498.17-18. See also *Aufdeckung*, Aii[v]: »Allain durch seinen gaist in den seinigen leiblicher weiß regiert« (Hillerbrand, *An Early Anabaptist Treatise*, 36).

72 *KU*, Biiii[r].

73 Ibid., Bvii[v]: »Unnd wasserquellen fliessen lassen auss ihrem leip / die quellen inn das ewig leben / dann sie haben truncken vom prunnen dess lebens durch den glauben inn Christo / Johan.4.7... so die glieder dess leibs Christi / ihren mitgliedern / auch der welt inn ihrer prechlicheyt und mangel / mit der fürgestelten ärtznei und mittel dess waren maisters / lernung / weisung unnd anzeygung geben.«

The Christian receives and shares the Spirit of Christ through concrete acts, words, and gifts, for Christ »was not here for spirits and angels, but for humanity which has flesh and blood and natural receptivity.«[74] In Marpeck's thought the two concerns for social justice and for personal transformation were inextricably bound together. Without personal transformation, people's self–obsession leads to all manner of injustice; without a new, more justly ordered community personal transformation is not possible.

CROSS OF THE CHRISTIAN

Marpeck recognized that the resolution to work diligently for justice »not only internally before God, but also externally before humanity,« brought the believer into conflict with those »power–holders and antichrists,« who exercised *gewalt* »for themselves and their own advantage.« His graphic reports of the persecution, torture, and death of »brothers and sisters in Christ« reflect his personal knowledge, in Rattenberg and perhaps elsewhere, of those who suffered this fate.[75] He considered those experiencing this persecution to be followers of Christ in the cross and participants in »his reconciliation and suffering.«[76] Until the Lamb of God conquers through them, »much deprivation, in the form of anguish, fear, distress, suffering, temptation, conflict, and persecution« is to be expected.[77] But the Christian, having received the knowledge of Christ in the heart, »finally jumps willingly into the sea of affliction with Peter (John 21).«[78]

For Marpeck, as for Schiemer and Schlaffer, the embracing of this cross characterizes the fullest earthly stage in the process of the believer's coming to justness. However, for him, the Christian takes on this cross, not primarily for the sake of continued self–purification, but for the sake of bringing the justice and reconciliation of Christ to the world.[79] As had Christ, the Christian extends, voluntarily and patiently, the offer of the »Spirit of power and strength« to the »deprivation and deficiency« of the world in the face of opposition, coercion, and rejection. As we have noted, this willingness to suffer for the sake of the justice of Christ was impossible without empowerment by the Spirit – the apostles refused to follow Christ in his passion and death before the Spirit was poured

74 Ibid., Bvi[v]: »Darumb hat der Herr Christus in allen seinen wercken der uber natürlichen wunderthaten von ihm beschehen die naturlichen und eusserlichen ding vor lassen gehn / dann er was nit hie von geist und engel wegen / sonnder umb der menschen willen / so gleisch und blut und naturliche empfintligkait haben.«

75 *CV*, avi[v].

76 Ibid., bviii[v].

77 *KU*, Bvii[r]: »Als die auss erwelten Gottes / so erkaufft sein durch viel mangel / durch trübsal / angst / not leiden / anfechtung / streit / verfolgung / biss auff den sig und uberwindung dess lämblin Gottes / so erst zum endt der welt inn den seinigen gar uberwindt.«

78 *CV*, cii[v]: »Je mer ihn nu eyner erkennt / und geistlich siecht /... je bass er ihm gfellt / wirt ihm freundtlich / lieblich / empfecht ihn durch solch erkanntnuss in sein hertz / wachsst also drinn... sprinngt zuletst mit Petro selbs frei / willig / Johan. xxi.in das mär der trübsalen.«

79 Cf. chapter 2 for Schiemer and Schlaffer.

out. Therefore, the experiential cross of the Christian is grounded in and made possible by the historical cross of Christ.

In these first theological writings, Marpeck shares Schlaffer's reticence concerning eschatological speculation. While the integration of the natural and supernatural begins in this »physical life,« he says that the translation is not complete until after this corruptible and changeable time when the »eternal and unchangeable nature appears and is revealed.«[80] He did have the sense that he was living in the last, dangerous days.[81]

For Marpeck, the realm of Christ incorporated both the personal, or individual (internal, spiritual), aspect, as well as the social, or communal (external, fleshly), aspect of human life. Therefore, Marpeck objected: »But these spirits went too far to one extreme to make the realm of Christ, here and now, too spiritual, just as the antichrist [the pope], in contrast, made it too fleshly.«[82] Marpeck developed his position on these two fronts, that is, against the Spiritualists, who, he felt, ignored its social aspect and made the realm of Christ too spiritual, and against the magisterial Reformers, who, like the papacy, lacked respect for the individual and made Christ's realm too fleshly.

»TOO SPIRITUAL«: CRITIQUE OF RADICAL INDIVIDUALISM

In his two 1531 tracts Marpeck focused on the status of communal ceremonies and opposed the tendency of Johannes Bünderlin and Christian Entfelder to stress the internal to the neglect of the external, and thereby the individual to the neglect of the community.[83] Their argument, as it was understood by Marpeck, will be summarized, followed by an examination of his response.

The Spiritualists, Marpeck observes, claim that the ceremonies have been misused since apostolic times and are to be blamed for the hypocrisy in the

---

[80] *KU*, Bvi^v: »dieweil der mensch hie in leiplichem leben ist / untz das die ubersetzung auss dem natürlichen leben in das ubernaturlich / volkommenlich beschiecht. Das aber erst nach dieser zerstorlichen und zergencklichen zeit zu dem ewigen / unveränderlichen wesen erscheint und eröffent wirt. Da hörn als dann erst all naturlich und ubernaturlich mittel auff uns zudienen.«

[81] Ibid., Bvii^r : »dieser geferlichen letsten zeit«; and *CV*, av^r, avi^r. See Schlaffer in Lydia Müller, *Glaubenszeugnisse*, 84: »diser letsten gefärlichen zeit«; and Christian Entfelder, *Von den manigfaltigen im glauben zerspaltungen...* (hereinafter listed as *MZ*), Cv^r, for a similar expression.

[82] *CV*, aviii^v: »Aber diese geister / wolten das reich Christi hie in dieser zeit gar zu geistlich machen / undeynen zuweiten ubersprung thun / wie es der Antichrist im gegentail gar zu fleischlich hat gemacht.«

[83] Helmut Claus, director of the Forschungsbibliothek Gotha, studied the typography of these two tracts and the Stuttgart edition of the *Aufdeckung* and believes that all three were published by the Strassburg printer, Jakob Cammerlander (personal correspondence, May 30, 1988). According to the account of the Strasbourg censors, Christian Herlin and Jacob Bedrot, Marpeck's books, along with Bünderlin's *Explanation*, were sold for a time in Wendelin Rihel's bookstore located in the basement of the Rathaus. See KR, 1:335. Besides Bünderlin, it is clear that Marpeck directed his *KU* against Entfelder's *On the Many Divisions in the Faith (MZ)*. See the following discussion of the epigram: »Nit was / sonder das.«

churches.[84] Since the apostles had no power or command from Christ to transfer their office to another, an external, miraculous command of God through a new prophet is required to restore these and other external ceremonies. Until that prophetic time, the Spiritualists argue, all external order and work of God should be suspended. Their objection to even the election of a *Vorsteher* is based on »the preaching of the Gospel of all creatures« (Mark 16:20), or the conviction that »all are taught [spiritually] by God« (John 6:45), without any external mediation.[85] For Marpeck, their suspension (*stillstandt*)[86] of all other ceremonies reflects the Spiritualists opinion that external ceremonies, such as baptism, the Supper, and the election of a *Vorsteher*, are unnecessary for the spiritual life of faith.[87]

From Marpeck's perspective, this rejection of external ceremonies was tantamount to a denial of the *extra nos* character of grace mediated by the community. His objection to their position began as a pastoral concern because they denied »the gifts of the Spirit for the common good« (1 Corinthians 12), and said that there was no command to use their spiritual gifts for others.[88] In Marpeck's view, such an abandonment of others in spiritual and temporal things betrayed an ignorance on the part of these »drunken prophets« who »want to protect their own interests.«[89] He said that they avoided the discipline of God and the concrete body of Christ.

By these harsh words, Marpeck evidently meant that, by rejecting the ceremonies, like baptism, through which the congregation was gathered and committed themselves to the needs of others, the *Geister* felt no obligation to meet the needs of others. Since for Marpeck, spiritual gifts include things like contributions to the poor, he may have been referring to a reluctance of his opponents to care for the needs of Strassburg's refugees or a lack of concern for the other disadvantaged groups within Strassburg. In this he sensed an absence of faith in the *krafft* of Jesus Christ in the believing community and therefore a »lack of the Holy Spirit among them.« They wounded the neighbor, by withholding what was needed, and remained in the self–obsessed mode of existence of the natural human being, »imprisoned in their own conscience

---

84 *CV*, Aii[r]; and *KU*, Avi[r]. Entfelder, *MZ*,C[r], argues that Lutherans, Zwinglians, and Anabaptists have fled the inner baptism and set up baptism and the Supper as a dividing wall among them. Johannes Bünderlin, *Erklerung durch vergleichung der Biblischen...* (hereinafter listed as *E*), 10[v], makes a similar claim with respect to those ceremonies in the Old Testament. Franck, in his letter to Campanus, KR, 1:303.19f., 309.2f., believes that the fall of the church occurred even before Constantine; for him the external church of Christ, with its gifts and sacraments, ascended into heaven at the end of the apostolic period.

85 *KU*, Cviii[r]; and *CV*, biii[v]. Cf. Caspar Schwenckfeld von Ossig, *Corpus Schwenckfeldianorum* (hereinafter listed as *CS*), 4:422.24-26: »Es gehoret dazu ein Newer schulmaister und ein New lehre davon geschrieben steher. Sie werden alle von Gott geleert.« Also *CS*, 4:753.30-36.

86 *KU*, Aii[r], Diiii[r]. For their notions of Stillstandt, see Entfelder, *MZ*, Bii[v] and Civ[r]; Bünderlin, *E*, 16[v]; and Schwenckfeld, *CS*, 4:818.12f.

87 *CV*, biv[r]; and *KU*, B[r]. Cf. Entfelder, *MZ*, Bii[v], Cvii[v], Diiii[r–v], Fiiii[r]; Bünderlin, *E*, 51[v], 4[r], 5[v], 12[r], 14[r], 20[v]; Franck, KR, 1:316.3-8, 314.9f; and Schwenckfeld, *CS*, 4:422.36-423.1, 490.5-12.

88 *CV*, b[r]; and *KU*, Aiiii[r].

89 *CV*, bii[r].

through a fickle and deluded faith (*wonglauben*).«[90] It was a deluded faith because, at the foundation of their position, Marpeck perceived an almost dualistic rejection of the material: »I can easily believe that they do not feel [*empfinden*] in their hearts such ceremonies and things, which makes them, therefore, strange, frightening and suspect to them, as indeed they are suspicious of the whole [natural] world according to its correct and pure use. They are for them suspect and an abomination because of their ignorance of God's discipline.«[91] And, »How should they want to know and grasp the supernatural when they have not yet known the natural? Indeed when they despise the external word, who will believe them concerning the internal?«[92]

By rejecting the natural, Marpeck felt that the *Geister* closed themselves off from the »Spirit of power and strength« made available in the incarnation and death of Christ and mediated through the life of the gathered community. Standing in self–chosen isolation from resources beyond themselves, they suffered the pain of an imprisoned conscience, unable to help themselves or anyone else. Because they had not experienced a reorientation to the material, they remained incapable of its proper use and enjoyment. What had started as a pastoral concern for the Spiritualists' indifference to the physical and spiritual existence of others, led Marpeck into deeper theological waters. He began to recognize a radically different worldview, which presupposed an unbridgeable dichotomy between matter and spirit. Therefore, they did not seem to share his allegiance to the justice established by Christ, which integrated the internal relationship to God and the external relationship to humanity. According to Marpeck, the proper ordering of the former is impossible except through the Spirit received through the latter.[93]

The purpose of Marpeck's two tracts was to secure the consciences of believers in something concrete and outside themselves, that is, in the *extra nos*, historical reality of the incarnation and cross of Christ through which the Spirit was poured out and, in the *extra me*, reality of the community, organized and regulated by external ceremonies. This intent is reflected in the titles: *A Clear*

---

90 *KU*, Bv[v]: »Wie wollen sie das ubernaturlich erkennen oder begreiffen / weil sie das naturlich noch nit erkennen? ja weil sie das eusserlich wort verachten / wer will ihn das innerlich glauben?... Sie sint gefangen inn ihren gewissen durch ein wanckel mutigen und schweren wonglauben.«

91 *CV*, aviii[v]: »Ich glaub ihnen auch gern / das sie solch ceremonien und sachen im hertzen nit empfinden das macht ihn die auch also frembd / scheulich / und verdechtlich / wie sy auch der gantzen welt nach rechtem rainen brauch zehalten / verdechtlich / unnd ein grewel seien auss ursach ihrer unerkanntnuss unnd scheuhung der züchtigung Gottes.«

92 *KU*, Bv[v]. See n. 87 above. Bünderlin and Entfelder did not reject the reading of Scripture (external word) but became increasingly dubious about the insistence on baptism on faith and the power exercised by elected *Vorsteher*. Marpeck read this reticence as their refusal to submit themselves and their gifts to the needs of the community. He, then, unfairly extended that reticence to a rejection of all natural needs and gifts. It could be argued that this deemphasis on external ceremonies manifested a pastoral concern, on the part of Bünderlin, Entfelder, and Schwenckfeld, for those Anabaptists weary of persecution by affording them a theological justification for avoiding it. This perspective was suggested by Neal Blough.

93 Blough, *Christologie Anabaptiste*, 65f., notes a similar stress in Luther.

Refutation of Several Articles disseminated... by certain spirits concerning the ceremonies of the New Testament (i.e. preaching, baptism, the Supper and the Scripture) for the comfort and encouragement of true Christians, and *A Clear and Quite Useful Instruction against certain deceitful and disgraceful spirits... through whom many pious hearts have erred and been tempted.*[94] To the latter, Marpeck adds an interesting phrase, which appears to be an intentional response to one included by Entfelder on the title page of his *On the Many Divisions in the Faith.* Entfelder wrote »not who, but what« (*Nicht wer, sondern was*), while Marpeck asserted »not what, but that« (*Nit was, sonder das*).[95] The meaning of Entfelder's phrase is clear from the content of his tract. One should give attention not to who says it, but to what is said. Truth rests not on position or power which can be passed on externally, but on a knowledge (*erkantnuss*) which is gained apart from any external thing. Marpeck counters that it is not important what one knows from oneself (*aigner vernufft*), but that Christ has established a justice, which includes the spiritual and material, the internal and external, and the individual and the community. Just before this phrase, Marpeck quotes Proverbs 21: »To the just it is a pleasure to do justice, but to the evil–doer it is humiliating.«

Consistent with his stress on the integration of the natural, including the material, and the supernatural in the incarnation of Christ, Marpeck rejects two spiritualistic Christologies. One »absolutely repudiates the incarnation of Christ and preaches blessedness outside of the same.«[96] Marpeck probably attributed this position to Bünderlin, Entfelder, and perhaps Franck. The other Christology begins with »lofty things about the divinity of Christ and his brilliant majesty.«

But then those prophets capture the consciences of others by speaking of and dealing with the lowliness of Christ, beginning with his teaching, baptism (on and from faith), and also the supper, the laying on of hands, the ban, punishment and similar services of Christ (which should serve us and not we, them). It follows from this that the humanity of Christ is raised and considered as higher

---

[94] See the full titles in the bibliography.

[95] Heinold Fast, »'Nicht was, sondern das'. Marpeckhs Motto wider den Spiritualismus,« 66-74, has also noticed this juxtaposition. He notes that this was/das pair appears in an Anabaptist tract, *Wie die gschrifft verstendigklich soll undershjden und erklart werden.* Cii[r] (Amsterdam University Library) and in *Das Kunstbuch,* xii[v]: »Es ist nit was, sonnder das.« In the two contexts, Fast sees similarities to Marpeck's stress on the radical difference between the Old and New Testaments.

[96] *KU,* Bii[v]: »Die andern geister verwerffen die mensch werdung Christi gar / predigen jtzt die seligkeit ausserhalb der selbigen.« Both Bünderlin and Entfelder would have objected that Marpeck misrepresented their christological positions. A close reading of Bünderlin reveals that the incarnation was important as a Vorbild for the rectifying of the human heart. Although he, too, had a strong imitatio stress, Entfelder spoke of the importance of the »objective body of Jesus Christ.«

than his divinity and, thereby, a reversal of the highest to the lowest and the lowest to the highest takes place.[97]

It is possible that Marpeck is referring here to Melchior Hofmann's monophysite Christology. According to Hofmann, Christ had no human body or flesh at all. Rather, Christ brought his body with him from heaven, passing through Mary, but taking nothing from her except nutriment. Revealing his underlying understanding of the Supper, Hofmann insists that »the external Word of God did not take our nature and flesh from the virgin Mary but himself became flesh (John 1:14), that is, our Lord Christ has not two but only one nature,« otherwise he could not »save us« or »serve as food for eternal life.«[98] For Marpeck »the humanity of Christ is the human being's mediator to the divinity, and not the divinity to the humanity.«[99] However, Hofmann demands an *imitatio Christi* without access to the Spirit of power and strength given through the human nature of Christ and poured out through his death. Therefore, the concrete exchanges facilitated by the ceremonies within the community become an effort at self–justification rather than conveyors of the grace of the Spirit poured out by Christ. The result, in Marpeck's view, is the same as among the Spiritualists – imprisoned consciences.

To underscore the unique possibilities initiated by Christ's life and death, Marpeck stresses the qualitative difference between the Old and New Covenants. Here he is probably dependent on the work of Franck and Schwenckfeld, as he later reports that one in his group copied Schwenckfeld's book against Bucer.[100] In this work Schwenckfeld stressed the importance of the flesh of Christ, his suffering, and the difference between the covenants.[101] He also took a mediating position on externals by allowing for the »external church, teaching, word, sacrament, ceremonies, and service« in the New Covenant. For these reasons, Marpeck later testified that he and Schwenckfeld were in agreement during this

97 *KU*, Bii^V: »Die ersten heben an von der gottheit Christi / und seiner herrlichen maiestat / hohe ding zureden, nemmen ihnen / und machen andern gwissen von der nidrigkait Christi / als von anfang seiner lere / Tauff (auff und auss dem glauben) auch vom Abendtmal / handeauflegen / pann / straff / und der gleichen dienstbarckeyt Christi (so uns und nit wir ihnen dienen) zereden / handeln / und die selben anzururn / darauss folgt das die menschait Christi höher weder sein gottheyt geacht erhebt / und also das obrist zeundrist / und das nidrist zu höchst gekert wirt.« When seen with reference to Hofmann's position, this statement is not a non sequitor. See William Klassen and Walter Klaassen, *Writings of Pilgram Marpeck* (hereinafter listed as *WPM*), 571 n. 11.

98 George H. Williams, *The Radical Reformation*, 328-31.

99 *KU*, Biii^V. See n. 11 above. Cf. *Antwort*, 540-41, where Marpeck mentions his objections to Hofmann's christology.

100 See *Antwort*, 409.7-14. Blough, *Christologie Anabaptiste*, 80f., argues that this work is not Schwenckfeld's »Der viredte Sendbrief,« but a work which appears to have been lost.

101 Blough, *Christologie Anabaptiste*, 78-83, notes the similarities between the positions of Schwenckfeld and Marpeck. He concludes that Marpeck was dependent on Schwenckfeld and questions Klassen and Klaassen, *WPM*, 69, in the assertion that the *KU* was directed against Schwenckfeld. I concur that Marpeck, based on his own testimony, was unaware of any major disagreement with Schwenckfeld. However, as will be shown below, the seeds of that difference were already present.

period. However, the differences in their positions, which became evident to him later, are perceptible even here, for both men were in the process of developing their Christologies. Even though they are allowed to exist, Schwenckfeld states in an unpublished work that »all externals are obsolete« and do not inherently belong to the substance, nature, or essence *(wesen)* of the New Covenant and the realm of Christ.[102] For him the distinction of the covenants corresponds to the distinction between the internal and external, or spirit and matter. For Marpeck, the difference between the covenants is a new possibility of a being *(neues wesen)* which integrates the internal and external, or the spiritual and the material.

Correspondingly, Marpeck rejects any appeal to the »gospel of all creatures« to justify the suspension of »all external order and measures of God.« Without the incarnation and death of Christ and outpouring of the Spirit (that is, the gospel to all creatures), as well as the concrete mediation of the Spirit by the community, there is no gospel of all creatures, but only anxiety, fear, and dread in the face of suffering and death, which strips one of the resources on which one relies.

At the center of the disagreement between Marpeck and the *Geister* was a difference in the evaluation of the place of the natural, material reality as a mediator of the Spirit. For him, unless Christ shared full humanity, including natural materiality, the salvation of the natural was impossible. This difference played a key role in the varying interpretations and uses of the mystical tradition and had several important systematic implications.[103]

Because of the influence of Denck, Hätzer, and Kautz, mystical texts, and especially the *Theologia Deutsch*, constituted an important theological source for Strassburg's radicals. At the time that Marpeck probably first read the tract for himself he had already felt its influence through the theologies of Schiemer and Schlaffer and had developed his own theological concerns in the socio–political contexts of Rattenberg and Strassburg.[104] Marpeck, Bünderlin, and Entfelder shared certain views, such as the nature of sin, as inwardly turned isolation, and the importance of suffering as a preparation for the reception of the Spirit – both characteristic of the *Theologia Deutsch*. However, because of their different philosophical commitments, they read the same text with different eyes and therefore came to different conclusions. For example, Marpeck, with his concern for material reality and social responsibility, and influenced by Schiemer and Schlaffer, understood the Frankfurter's pivotal *leben Christi* in terms of the social reality of the community of believers. Bünderlin and, to a lesser extent, Entfelder

---

102 *CS*, 4:422.36-423.1.

103 The mediation of the mystical tradition by Denck, Hätzer, and Kautz and its varying appropriations by Marpeck, Bünderlin, and Entfelder deserves more systematic and detailed analysis than is possible here. This would provide a more accurate definition and delimitation of the terms spiritualism and mysticism as used to describe and differentiate theological and ethical positions among sixteenth century radicals.

104 The *Theologia Deutsch* was reprinted five times (1519, 1520, 1526, and 1531) in the time preceding and during Marpeck's residence in Strassburg. See Georg Baring, *Bibliographie der Ausgaben der Theologia Deutsch (1516-1961): Ein Beitrag zur Lutherbibliographie*, 35-36, 44, 48.

interpreted that same life of Christ as a guide which directs one's attention away from the external, or physical, to the internal, or spiritual.

»TOO FLESHLY«: CRITIQUE OF COLLECTIVISM

On January 19, 1531, Bucer wrote Ambrosius Blaurer a rather detailed account of his second and third discussions with Marpeck.[105] In this letter Bucer reports that Marpeck: 1, accused the reformers of preaching under the protection of the magistracy and the common man and not under the vulnerability of the cross of Christ; 2, objected that the reformers did not sufficiently distinguish the New Covenant from the Old, with which they justified the use of coercion in their reform program; and 3, claimed that he, not Bucer, had the key to the Scriptures. This exposition of Marpeck's critique of those he felt made the realm of Christ »too fleshly« will be ordered by an examination of these objections, their relation to Marpeck's theological position, and to the socio–political aspects of the reform of Strassburg's religious life.

First, Marpeck claimed that, because the reformers preached under the protection of the magistracy or common man, the result was an inability to produce the fruits of the gospel. Evidently Marpeck meant that Bucer had earlier traded on the interests and power of the common man which made it possible for him not only to stay in Strassburg in 1524, but also to receive his position in the reform at St. Aurelian's.[106] Now he manipulated the interests and power of the Magistrat to enforce church attendance and catechetical instruction and to eliminate his theological opponents. In the *Aufdeckung*, Marpeck says that the »new evangelical preachers« do not wish to come through the narrow door, but earlier encouraged the common man to take the sword and now hide behind the »princes, cities, and lords.« Probably referring to the newly formed Schmalkaldic League, Marpeck predicts that its conflict with the emperor will lead to more casualties than those of the Peasant War.[107] While the marriage of the papacy with temporal power produced the first antichrist, this wedding of the evangelical cause to the power of the »princes, cities, and Lords« constitutes the »new Antichrist.«[108]

Marpeck said that those advocating the use of coercion in matters of faith, »confess only the mortal and physical Christ, but they confess very little of the resurrected Christ, as seen in their lives.«[109] Rather than the justice (*Gerechtigkait* or *fürgestellte Ordnung*) of Christ and his cross, Bucer relied on the coercive power of the sword. He would be, then, one of those »Petrine or Iscariot

---

[105] Traugott Schiess, *Briefwechsel der Brüder Ambrosius und Thomas Blaurer*, 1:314f.
[106] See chapter 3.
[107] *Aufdeckung*, Aiiii[r]. (Hillerbrand, *An Early Anabaptist Treatise*, 37).
[108] *Aufdeckung*, Ciii[r-v] (Hillerbrand, *An Early Anabaptist Treatise*, 44-45).
[109] *KU*, Cii[v]: »Solch Petrisch und Iscariotisch Christen / bekennen nur den todlichen / sterblichen unnd leiplichen Christum / Aber den aufferstandnen Christum glauben und bekennen gar wenig / durch zeugnuss ihres lebens.«

Christians,« who confess only the mortal, physical Christ, denying the resurrected Christ. By focusing on the physical Christ, Marpeck says that those Christians deny the gospel to all creatures, which is the suffering and death of Christ through which the Spirit was poured out and made available in the resurrection. Relying on the human power of coercion, the preachers must view the weakness and vulnerability (cross) of Christ only as a »stubbornness and punishment of God,« but not of any intrinsic value. Therefore, salvific function of the weakness and vulnerability of the human being must be denied and replaced by the exercise of force.

Far from being a »stubbornness and punishment of God,« the cross of Christ, for Marpeck, is the most profound grace of God, that is, the means by which the Spirit was poured out and offered to the human being. And the cross of the Christian is embraced as the means by which that Spirit is received. According to Marpeck, without the personal justness achieved through the »unconstraining Spirit« poured out by Christ, there could be no fruit (that is, brotherly love expressed in a voluntary sharing with the disadvantaged and a refusal to coerce the conscience of another). Making a distinction between the force of the world (gewalt der welt) and strength of the Spirit (krafft des Geistes), he asserts that only the latter is able to create a true community (Gemeinschaft).

Marpeck, therefore, contends that one must be allowed to receive that Spirit consciously and willingly. For him, »fleshly« coercion in matters of faith is a »blasphemy of the Holy Spirit« and denigrates both the suffering, which brings the human to a willing receptivity to the Spirit, and the cross encountered when the Christian patiently offers that Spirit of justness to others. The true community is constituted by that Spirit voluntarily received by its participants. In response to Bucer's accusation that the radicals destroyed the love and unity of the corpus Christianum, Marpeck's position might lead him to reply that love must include a refusal to violate another's conscience and that unity must not be construed as an enforced uniformity. For Marpeck, then, there can be no justice without justness.

This denial of the cross and resurrection has, in Marpeck's view, several important implications. First, this position leads to an insecurity of conscience in that it encourages a reliance strictly on humanity's own resources. That is to say, one is not grounded in the power and strength of the divine Spirit, which comes from extra nos. It is possible that Marpeck includes Hofmann's apocalyptic visions in this indictment. Second, there is no affirmation of the new being (neues wesen) initiated in and through the Spirit of Christ, which integrates the spiritual and the temporal. Here, Marpeck rejects a latent spiritualism in Bucer's position, reflected in the latter's insistence on the continuity of the Old and New Testaments and his development of the notion that Christ is an eternal savior (ewiger heyland).[110]

---

110 KR, 1:417: »Dan Christus ist ein einiger unnd ewiger heyland, der auch vor seiner menschwerdung verzeyhung der sundern und alles guts in den seinen gewurcket hat.« It is possible that the seeds of Calvin's position of Christ as eternal mediator can be traced to this

This leads to the second area of Marpeck's protest – Bucer's failure to distinguish the covenants, allowing him to justify the use of coercion to »protect piety.« Bucer reported that Marpeck held that the faith of the ancients (people of the Old Testament) was to be separated from the remission of sins and true justness (*vera iustitia*). Marpeck stressed the centrality of the incarnation and life of Christ, saying that the Spirit, poured out uniquely in the life and death of Christ, mediated a new order and capacity (*vermugen*) to humanity. This new reality, therefore, distinguished the New from the Old Covenant.[111] According to Marpeck this Spirit was a voluntary or unconstraining Spirit (*freiwilliger Geist*). Therefore, Bucer testified that Marpeck objected that the gospel not be forced willy–nilly on all. Finally the response of the individual, strengthened and enabled by the power of this Spirit, found appropriate expression in the commitment and submission to the body of Christ in the believer's baptism. According to Bucer, Marpeck even called infant baptism a crime.

The stress Marpeck placed on the participatory role of the individual within the community is seen most clearly in his understanding of baptism. The outpouring of the Spirit through the cross of Christ makes possible a new kind of covenant between God and the human being. The Old Covenant of God was constituted totally by the promise of God, because the human being (without the Spirit) had no capacity (*vermugen*) to respond to that promise. Circumcision, the sign (*zaichen*) of this unilateral covenant was therefore received by all. However, the Spirit empowers the human to respond personally in a »new covenant of good conscience«: »But our covenant, which we made with God, belongs only to one who binds himself to God and vows from the power of the Holy Spirit in faith, of which water is a witness [*zeug*] and not a sign [*zaichen*].«[112] The Spirit, therefore, provides a new relationship of mutuality between the individual and God and the individual and the community. In baptism one freely submits oneself in receptivity and service to the new community.[113] There are, then, two aspects or movements in baptism, for which the water is the witness, or even the medium. One receives the Spirit from God through the community, in part through the administration of the water by the *Vorsteher*. One also gives or bears witness to that Spirit to those persons present.[114] The personal experience of faith requires the community, but the community also requires the personal experience of faith.[115] Here, Marpeck's affirmation that the new being (*neues*

confrontation between Bucer and Marpeck. See George H. Williams, *Francis Stancaro's Schismatic Reformed Church, Centered in Dubets'ko in Ruthenia, 1559/61-1570*, 931-57.

[111] As we have noted in chapter 3, Capito seems to have been attracted to this notion.

[112] *Confession*, 487.2-4. Marpeck may have developed this terminology from Schiemer and goes beyond Schlaffer, who calls water baptism a zaichen.

[113] Ibid., 352.22-24. Cf. chapter 2 for Schlaffer.

[114] *Confession*, 481.1f., 482.7-10, 424.10-12, 513.13f. Marpeck uses Schiemer's threefold scheme of baptism including water, spirit, and blood. Cf. *Confession*, 479.9f., 480.7f. Marpeck further develops his notion of ceremonies as a means of grace in chapter 5.

[115] Karl–Heinz zur Mühlen, *Luther's Tauflehre und seine Stellung zu den Täufern*, 126f., has a helpful survey of four distinct notions of baptism among the Anabaptists. He notes that Luther stressed, against the Spiritualists and Zwingli, the unity of the inner and outer aspects of the

wesen) integrates the spiritual and material leads him to a radical ecclesiology, which implicitly rejects Luther's distinction between the visible and invisible churches. For him, the new nature incorporates individual and communal reality.

Finally, Bucer complained that Marpeck took the »keys to the Scriptures« away from him and claimed them for himself. Indeed, Marpeck objected to Bucer's increasing tendency, not only to arrogate authority in matters of faith to the parish pastors, but also to allow the magistrate to construe itself as the final court of appeal.[116] Marpeck challenged the claim of the preachers or the councillors to arbitrate the dispute about the Scriptures, insisting that only the whole body of Christ in Strassburg had that right.[117]

Although he rejected any claim that they should rule over matters of faith, Marpeck acknowledged the role of civil power and authority, endorsing »worldly, bodily and earthly rulers as servants of God in the earthly realm but not in the realm of Christ. All bodily honor, fear, obedience, tax, toll and tribute belongs to them according to the words of Paul.«[118] Marpeck envisioned both negative and positive aspects of the state's task. He affirmed the role of civil power as the protector of the just and punisher of the civilly unjust, as he had done earlier as mining magistrate.[119] Marpeck admits that civil authority is necessary to protect property and keep the temporal peace, and says that Christians« owe obedience to this »external *gewalt*« unto death.[120] Further, his work in the city's forest and with the poor relief suggests that he recognized and supported the positive social contributions the state could make to the common good. Consistent with this appreciation and respect for the role of civil government, Marpeck addressed the councilmen with their honorific titles.[121] As for the oath, there is also no conclusive evidence that Marpeck ever rejected the civil oath. He swore it upon becoming a citizen in 1528 and upon his entrance into his office as *Holzmeister*. In addition, he swore lesser oaths in the course of transacting daily business. Martin Bucer and Jakob Sturm reported that Marpeck argued against »swearing and defending.« While it is true that Marpeck

---

sacrament, arguing that faith should be grounded in baptism and not baptism in faith. As we have shown, Marpeck would agree with the unity of the inner and outer. He would argue that one's faith is grounded in the death and resurrection of Christ, not in baptism. For him, baptism served a different function than it did for Luther.

116 See chapter 3.

117 See chapter 5 for the way he develops this democratizing notion of spiritual authority by asserting that the proclamation of the gospel is within the province of the most common person in Christ's body.

118 *Confession*, 505.10-506.6. Clarence Baumen, *Gewaltlosigkeit im Täufertum*, 279, observes that the identification of the state with the world often led to a *Staatsfeindlichkeit or Dämonisierung* among the Anabaptists. This is not the case with Marpeck.

119 *Confession*, 530.2f. Marpeck encourages the council to protect »those distressed people, who have no place on earth to go and have fled to you.« His associate, Leupold Scharnschlager, states this explicitly in his letter to the council, Manfred Krebs and Hans Georg Rott, *Quellen zur Geschichte der Täufer* (hereafter KR), 2:351.

120 *Aufdeckung*, Biiʳ (Hillerbrand, »An Early Anabaptist Treatise,« 39).

121 *Confession*, 530.6-7.

encouraged fellow prisoners not to swear an oath to desist from Anabaptist meetings, there is no evidence that he rejected the civil oath.[122]

Marpeck's quarrel was with those magistrates who wanted to »use such bodily force to reign or rule in the realm of Christ,« for when that happens, »Christ is forgotten.«[123] He did not say that magistrates could not be Christians, nor that civil power did not maintain a certain needed order; he only objected to those Christian magistrates exercising coercive power in matters of religious conscience and church reform.[124]

Although a theoretical possibility, a Christian magistrate was virtually a practical impossibility, for Marpeck deemed vengeance and armed assault inconsistent with the cross of Christ: »Therefore also revenge against the enemy is suspended in the New Testament, because the spirit is more powerful to overcome through patience than in the Old. Therefore Christ forbade such vengeance and defensive assault... and commanded us to love and bless the persecutor and opponent even more and to overcome through patience (Matthew 5, Luke 6).«[125] Although he quotes the Sermon on the Mount, Marpeck's reasons for rejecting deadly force do not reflect a biblical – literalism concerned with a strict notion of obedience and the purity of the Christian. Rather, Marpeck believes that, since the outpouring of the Spirit of power and strength, there is finally a possibility for overcoming the violations of justice perpetrated by the unjust.[126] This rejection of deadly force may be viewed, then, as a manifestation of Marpeck's concern for, rather than indifference to, injustice and its victims.[127]

---

[122] Ibid., 350.8-10, 352.3f.

[123] Ibid., 506.1f.; and *Aufdeckung*, Aiiii[r] (Biiii[r]) (Hillerbrand, *An Early Anabaptist Treatise*, 41).

[124] Scharnschlager extends this argument in his letter, KR, 2:348-49. He asks the councilmen to examine themselves and admit that they also want voluntary access to God without coercion. If they had not wanted to be free of the coercive strictures of the pope, they would not have expelled the bishop. He then appeals to them to grant the Anabaptists the same right which they demanded for themselves.

[125] *CV*, cii[r]-cii[v]: »Daher auch die rach wider die feinde im newen Testament ist auff gehebt / weil jtzt der geist krefftiger ist / durch gedult zuuberwinden wedder im alten. Darumb hat CHRISTUS solche rach unnd gegenwer den kinderen dess geystes news Testaments verbotten / Luce.ix.xxi.Mat.v. und befolhen die feindt / verfolger und widersacher vil mer zuliben / benedeien / unnd durch gedult zu uberwiden / Matth.v.Luce vi.« Marpeck believed that the sword was used most often to pursue self – interest behind the veil of love of neighbor. Since Christ wants no »help or love through which another might be hurt or hated,« he believed Christians ought to avoid its use, as they did »in the apostolic age up to the time of the emperor Constantine.« See *Aufdeckung*, Biii[v], Ciii[v], Cii[v] (Hillerbrand, *An Early Anabaptist Treatise*, 41, 45, 44).

[126] The Frankfurter's protestation that a Christian would rather die one hundred times than to kill another, may have been one source of Marpeck's refusal to take the life of another. See *TD*, 31/63.4-9.

[127] With respect to Williams's four types of pacifism among the radicals (see chapter 2 n. 108), Marpeck seems to constitute a fifth type, for one suffers in order to bring justice into the world, not primarily to purify oneself or confirm one's own election.

It is possible to see Marpeck's conception of the relation of church and state as a »radicalization« of Luther's two – kingdom doctrine.[128] He did not view the distinction of the two realms as that between the internal and the external (Spiritualists) or the private and public person (Luther). Rather he conceived of a voluntary community, which included both individual and communal transformation, within the larger social realm.[129] As we have seen from his activity and testimony, this voluntary community served as a medium for the extension of the justice of Christ in the world.[130]

Marpeck developed a notion of religious community *(Gemeinschaft)* which held individual and communal aspects in dynamic tension. Against those with spiritualist, separatist, and apocalyptic tendencies, Marpeck stressed the corporate nature of human life with its physical interdependence and consequent social responsibility. In opposition to the few exercising power based on an appeal to the collective good, Marpeck emphasized the importance of the individual by challenging the exclusive claims of the Reformers and *Magistrat* to spiritual authority and by insisting on believer's baptism. This notion of religious community constituted a unique alternative for the actors in Strassburg's Reformation drama and had the potential for a broad base of support among the city's radicals. Indeed, Bucer reported that some »esteemed and honored him as a star.«

The *Magistrat* probably viewed this esteem and Marpeck's potential for mobilizing the powerful common man as a possible source of political instability. The council responded by removing him from the scene with as little fanfare as possible. However, it was to Bucer that Marpeck posed the greatest threat. His presence and protests touched the most vulnerable points in the Reformer's program – the disunity among the evangelical preachers and the lack of moral

---

128 Blough, *Christologie Anabaptiste*, 106, suggests this view. Luther included the visible church and the state under God's left hand, while only the invisible church represents God's right hand or *opus proprium*. Marpeck's radicalization involves the inclusion of the whole external, gathered community under God's right hand. In other words, he broadened Luther's notion of the externality of God's proper work beyond the sacraments – baptism and the Supper – to the whole, concrete life of the community.

129 William Klassen, *The Limits of Political Authority as Seen by Pilgram Marpeck*, 345f., 359, shows his interpretation of Marpeck's position approaches my own: »He [Marpeck] was not anti – political or apolitical, but remained committed to a view of politics which allows freedom of expression for a minority position.« He also points out that Baumen's label of »apoliticism« is inaccurate. James Stayer, *Anabaptists and the Sword*, 180-81, notes that Marpeck later objects to Schwenckfeld's claim that he rejected the civil magistracy out of hand.

130 We recall here Marpeck's organization of a contribution to the city's poor relief for the use of all of the city's disadvantaged, as well as his affirmation that members of Christ's body give not only to their fellow members, but also to the world. Before the council, Marpeck pleaded that the council not persecute the Anabaptists for its own sake (*Confession*, 530.2f.), and claimed that he acted because »such things involve the salvation of all humanity« (*Confession*, 529.31). George H. Williams, *Sectarian Ecumenicity: Reflections on a Little Noticed Aspect of the Radical Reformation*, 146, 159f., has developed this »universalizing intention of Anabaptism« and suggested that »Anabaptism involved its proponents in a political metaphor more exacting than that of the Magisterial Reformation.« This could be said of Marpeck.

reform in the city. In his 1531 encounter with Marpeck and in the synod beginning a year and one – half later, Bucer succeeded in disposing of many of the troublesome radical leaders and unifying the clergy.[131]

Although brief, Marpeck's residence in Strassburg was an important, formative period. Here he developed a notion of the true community, which combined both individual and social aspects. Against the individualistic Spiritualists, he argued that there could be no individual justness without social justice. Against the collectivistic Reformers, he insisted that there would be no social justice without individual justness. From Marpeck's perspective, coercion (*weltliche gewalt*) can neither secure the individual conscience, nor constitute a true community (*gemeinschaft*).[132] These are accomplished only by the reordering Spirit poured out by Christ, by means of which the individual moves out of the self – obsessed mode of existence into participation in the divine through the transformed community.[133] Because it must be voluntary, that true community was the conventicular *Gemeinde* of those who gave and received the Spirit. However, as each believer extended, voluntarily and patiently, that »Spirit of power and strength« to the »deprivation and deficiency« of the world, Marpeck may have expected that true community to grow to include the whole of Strassburg. Indeed, that may have been his vision as he viewed the imperial city in its entirety, inside and outside its walls, from the lumber yard at Kehl. However, his arguments with Bucer reveal that, while the true community might grow from the bottom up to include the whole city, it could never be imposed by coercion from the top down.

[131] One of the results of the synod was somewhat ironic. Although rid of many of the Anabaptist leaders, the magisterial Reformers emerged from the closed synod with less control of the parishes than they anticipated. The lay *Kirchenpfleger*, who had complete responsibility for parish discipline, were not selected by the preachers nor the congregation but by the council. A decade later, Bucer, frustrated by a lack of moral improvement in the parishes and dissatisfied with the discipline controlled by the council, began to gather small, voluntary groups for mutual correction. This attempt to establish a *christliche Gemeinschaft*, brought quick opposition from the council and led ultimately to Bucer's own expulsion. See Miriam U. Chrisman, *Strasbourg and the Reform*, 229f.; and Werner Bellardi, *Die Geschichte der »christlichen gemeinschaft« in Strassburg (1546-1550)*.

[132] *Confession*, 509.8-510.9. Marpeck claims that the historical record (i.e., the Old Testament) shows that the civil authorities always punish true prophets and not false ones so that justice does not follow. In a polemic against the magisterial preachers, Marpeck points out that it was given to »the women, as the weak and afflicted members of the body of Christ« to proclaim to the apostles the resurrection of Christ. Although women such as Anna Marpeck, Helena von Freyberg, Magdalena Marschalk, Kunigunda Schneider, and Anna Schmidt (see chapters 6 and 7) took active roles in the Marpeck groups, he never spoke explicitly of the status of women in the fellowships.

[133] Marpeck later (chapter 5) develops and refines his understanding of this participation on various levels.

Chapter 5

INTERIM YEARS: STRUGGLE FOR UNITY AND INSTITUTIONAL IDENTITY

The paucity of information concerning the period between Marpeck's departure from Strassburg in January 1532 and his appearance in Augsburg's city records in February 1544 prompted John C. Wenger to call these the »obscure years.«[1] The absence of Marpeck's name from official documents must be due, in part, to the far – reaching effects of the Münster debacle.[2] Throughout the empire, civil authorities increased restrictive measures to suppress the Anabaptists, who were often considered politically subversive.[3] Therefore, Marpeck probably resided outside the cities and towns which he visited during this time.

However, the discovery of *Das Kunstbuch*, the clarification of Marpeck's editorial changes to Bernhard Rothmann's *Bekentnisse* in the *Vermahnung*, and the identification of the *Bekenntnis an Jan von Pernstain* as the work of Marpeck, provide considerable data concerning the development of his theological position.[4] The focus of that position remained the integration of the internal (spiritual) and external (material) aspects of the human being, and therefore of the individual and the community in the realm of Christ.

In this chapter I trace Marpeck's movements and concerns in these years and then describe the developments in his thought in the context of his exchanges with those whom he felt made the Christ's realm too fleshly (Münsterites, magisterial Reformers, Swiss Brethren, and Hutterites) or too spiritual (Caspar Schwenckfeld).

---

1 J. C. Wenger, *The Life and Work of Pilgram Marpeck*, 155, is followed by Klassen and Klaassen, *WPM*, 36.

2 Inquiries to the Kantonsbibliothek and Landesarchiv in Appenzell, the Stiftsarchiv and Staatsarchiv in St. Gallen, and the Ulm Stadtarchiv and the Staatsarchiv for Graubünden in Chur uncovered no mention of Marpeck in the pertinent registers.

3 Local histories document increased persecution during this time in St. Gallen, Appenzell, Chur, Moravia, and Ulm. In a letter to Marpeck dated September 1542, Schwenckfeld bemoans the danger he and his sympathizers face in and around Ulm, thereby making a personal meeting with Marpeck difficult.

4 See Heinold Fast, *Pilgram Marbeck und das oberdeutsche Täufertum. Ein neuer Hand-schriftenfund*, 212-42; and Frank Wray, *The 'Vermanung' of 1542 and Rothmann's 'Bekenntnisse'*, 243-51. Hans Hillerbrand, *Ein Täufer Bekenntnis aus dem 16. Jahrhundert*, 40-50, published this anonymous confession preserved in the Regensburg Stadtarchiv (Signatur Eccl. I, 52, 74), associating it with the Marpeck/Schwenckfeld controversy.

TRAVEL AND CONCERNS (1532-44)

1533-40: Switzerland, Moravia, and the Bekenntnis an Jan von Pernstain

After leaving Strassburg, Marpeck probably travelled up the Rhine and settled in the vicinity of St. Gallen.[5] Jörg Maler, later an associate in Augsburg and editor of *Das Kunstbuch*, reported that he had heard of the »khostlichs werckh zur walckh« built by Marpeck in St. Gallen.[6] He probably referred to a system of water flumes constructed for the city's weaving industry in 1535. Johannes Kessler, chronicler of the canton, reports that the city council converted a house and barn into a bleacher. The water flumes conducted water around a nearby mountain to service not only the bleacher but also the city's needs for drinking water.[7] Because Marpeck's name does not appear in any of the St. Gallen archives, he probably lived outside the town, perhaps between St. Gallen and Appenzell, while working on the project.[8]

During this period Marpeck apparently returned, periodically, to the Tirol.[9] In a 1535 letter, Anna Scharnschlager instructs her brother–in–law, a lawyer in Kitzbühel, to send his reply by Marpeck.[10] Therefore, Leupold and Anna Scharnschlager may have joined Marpeck in the St. Gallen area after their own expulsion from Strassburg in June 1534.

An anonymously written *Bekenntnis* submitted to the Oberster Landeshauptmann of Moravia, Jan von Pernstain, reflects the involvement of Marpeck in an Anabaptist congregation there in the mid–to–late 1530s.[11] After

---

[5] The fact that Bucer warned Ambrosius Blaurer about Marpeck after his departure may indicate that Marpeck stopped in the Constance area on his way to St. Gallen. Helena von Freyberg, formerly von Münchinau, then living in Constance, may have encouraged his move to Switzerland.

[6] St–A.A., Urgichten, April 28, 1550. See Heinold Fast, *Ostschweiz*, vol. 2, *Quellen zur Geschichte der Täufer in der Schweiz*, 237.

[7] Johannes Kessler, *Sabbata Mit kleineren Schriften und Briefen*, 434. Based on Maler's testimony William Klassen, *CC*, 33, says Marpeck also built a fulling mill. Fast, *Ostschweiz*, 237-38 n. 5, points out that Kessler makes no mention of the mill.

[8] In the Stadtarchiv in St. Gallen, Marpeck's name does not appear in the Ratsprotokolle, 1533-41, the Steuerbücher, vol. 283 (1535), the Buch der Amtleute der Stadt St. Gallen, 1510-76, or the Rechnungen über Büssen, Einkauf in the Burgerrecht, Abzüge, 1529-36.

[9] In a 1533 letter to the congregation in Rattenberg from a Ludwig Fest, an Anabaptist imprisoned in Schwaz, he sends greetings to »die Marbeckin.« See Josef Beck, *Die Geschichts–Bücher der Wiedertäufer in Österreich–Ungarn (1526 bis 1785)*, 107; and A. J. F. Zieglschmid, *Die Älteste Chronik der Hutterischen Brüder*, 138. Based on this and the Anna Scharnschlager letter, Wenger, *The Life and Work of Pilgram Marpeck*, 156, concludes that Marpeck went directly back to the Tirol from Strassburg. Jan J. Kiwiet, *Pilgram Marbeck*, 35, comes to the same conclusion with the added reference to »Marbeckin« in a 1534 letter from Jakob Hutter to the congregation in Etschland. Klassen in *CC*, 32 n. 80, conjectures that the »Marpeckin« is probably not Pilgram's wife, Anna, but the wife of Gilg Marpeck.

[10] Fast, *Ostschweiz*, no. 628a, 511-12.

[11] Heinold Fast directed my attention to the *Bekenntnis*, suggested it was Marpeck's and made his typescript of the Regensburg manuscript available to me. The *Bekenntnis* carries the signature,

being called before a local representative of Pernstain to defend himself against charges of denying Christ, the author is asked to submit a written summary of his position. External and internal evidence point to Marpeck as the author of that *Bekenntnis*.

Although the *Bekenntnis* is undated, circumstantial evidence suggests the period 1535 to 1539. On December 17, 1539, the Regensburg city council reported to Ferdinand I the activity in that city of two Austerlitz Anabaptists. With the letter they sent »two copies of some writings which are sent from time to time from Moravia.«A modern scholar suspects that the *Bekenntnis* was among these.[12] If he is correct, the confession received a wide circulation and was written before December 1539. Its *terminus post quem* must be the 1531 publication date of Sebastian Franck's *Chronica*, which is cited on folio 164 of the *Bekenntnis*, and could be the onset in 1535 of intense persecution ordered by Ferdinand throughout Moravia.[13]

As to the location of the interrogation leading to the writing of the *Bekenntnis*, Austerlitz (Slavkov), Znaim (Znojmo), and Eibenschitz (Ivancice) seem to be likely possibilities.

Marpeck's relations to a group in Austerlitz date from before the 1531 letter of Wilhelm Reublin.[14] We have already noted that the two missionaries carrying the *Bekenntnis* to Regensburg came from there. Further, a 1538 letter from Hans Felix to his father–in–law, Leupold Scharnschlager, indicates the existence of an Austerlitz congregation open to the leadership of Marpeck.[15] A »Pilgramite« group in the small free city of Znaim in Moravia could have had its origin as early as 1535 with the arrival of Reublin. Eibenschitz, which belonged to the domain of the husband of Jan von Pernstain's sister, Bohunka, had been the scene of Christian Entfelder's ministry before his departure for Strassburg and was probably visited by him in the mid–1530s on his way to ducal Prussia.[16] It is

Regensburg Stadtarchiv, Eccl. I, 52, 74. I shall refer to this manuscript hereafter as *Bekenntnis*. Perstain, a neo–Utraquist to whom Hubmaier dedicated his *Grund und Ursach* (Nicolsburg, 1527), was sympathetic to the radical movement and probably encouraged the 1528 discussion between the Anabaptists and the Unity of Brethren. See Jarold Knox Zeman, *The Anabaptists and the Czech Brethren in Moravia 1526-1628*, 80, 221ff.

12 Karl Schornbaum, ed., *Bayern II Abteilung*, vol. 5 of *Quellen zur Geschichte der Täufer*, 95f., and especially 97.26f. Consequently, the *Bekenntnis* was preserved in Regensburg.

13 In 1535 Jakob Hutter was called upon to write a similar defense for the Hutterites living on the Liechtenstein lands. See Ziegleschmid, *Chronik*, 148-54.

14 In his letter Reublin wanted to defend himself against charges Marpeck may have heard from others in Austerlitz. See C. A. Cornelius, *Geschichte des Münsterischen Aufruhrs*, 2:253-59. Some among the Austerlitz group knew Marpeck from his 1528 stay in Bohemian Krumau, for a group of 80-90 of them moved to Austerlitz in 1529. Zieglschmid, *Chronik*, 91.

15 Fast, *Ostschweiz*, 513f., October 29, 1538. This group, which received Felix and his wife, Ursula in 1534/35, may have been a part of the Reublin/Zaunrig group who went to Auspitz in 1531 but returned to Austerlitz in 1534, dissatisfied with Hutter's leadership.

16 KB, no. 17, 170. See also Jarold Knox Zeman, *Historical Topography of Moravian Anabaptism*, 149.

possible that a group sympathetic to Marpeck was one of the several opposing Anabaptist congregations there at the time.[17]

Although contact between Marpeck and these groups can be established, there is no archival evidence documenting his presence in Moravia during these years. However, his visits to Austerlitz in 1540 and to Schakwitz in 1541 suggest that an earlier visit or stay might have been possible. Indeed, in his 1544 letter to the Moravians, he greets Cornelius Veh as »mein geliebter und geschenckter sun nach dem glouben.«[18] Apparently, Marpeck had been instrumental in Veh's entrance into the Austerlitz congregation sometime before 1544 and perhaps during the period in question.

While external evidence provides only the possibility of Marpeck's authorship, the terminology and argumentation of the *Bekenntnis* are clearly his, and appear to constitute a bridge in the development of his thought between his early work (the 1531 tracts and the Strassburg *Confession*) and his later controversy with Schwenckfeld.

The *Bekenntnis* is replete with words and phrases characteristic of Marpeck: »Verhaissung um gmaines hails wegen der gantzen welt; Verklärt nach dem fleisch ynss himlisch vesen; den val des fleisches Adae wider zu recht pracht; krafft seines geistes... krafft Christi... Gotliche krafft; erkanntnuss gottlicher warhait; gelassen seiner seelen; mitzeugnus gotlicher warhait; disen lesten bösen tagen.«[19]

The polemic in the *Bekenntnis* against »many who envy us« and »describe, twist, and falsify our simplicity to their own opinion« reproduces many of Marpeck's anti–Spiritualist arguments from early works, as well as from his later writings. The author calls his opponents »godless... erring spirits.«[20] Concerning Christology, he accuses some of denying that the Word assumed the seed of Abraham, while others denied its having assumed »our flesh.«[21] Against them, the writer stresses that Christ was born from the seed of woman and that he feared death.[22] Further, he insists that Christ is the savior and the reconciliation according to his human nature and that, perfectly, only in his suffering and

---

[17] Zeman, *Czech Brethren*, 232. Entfelder reprimands the legalism, hard ban, and the rejection of civil authority practiced by some in Eibenschitz, *MZ*, hiii[r]-hvi[v].

[18] *KB*, no. 17, 170[r].

[19] *Bekenntnis*, 161[v], cf. *CV*, bviii[r] (chapter 4 n. 42); 162[r], cf. *KU*, Bvi[v] (chapter 4 n. 17); 162[v], cf. *KU*, Av[r] (chapter 4 n. 16); 163[v], 165[r], 163[v], cf. chapter 5 n. 67; 161[r], cf. *CV*, avii[v] (chapter 4 n. 52); 161[r], cf. *KU*, Aii[r], and *Confession*, 432.3-6 (chapter 4 n. 52); 163[r], cf. *Confession* 487.2-4; and 164[r], cf. *KU*, Bvii[r] (chapter 4 n. 81).

[20] *Bekenntnis*, 165[r]; cf. *CV*, aviii[v] (chapter 4 nn. 82, 91).

[21] *Bekenntnis*, 162[v]; cf. *KU*, Bv[v] (chapter 4 nn. 90, 92).

[22] *Bekenntnis*, 162[r]: »der warlich naturlich sam des weibs«; cf. *KB*, no. 5, 13[r]: »vom weibssomen«; and 162[r]: »Er weinet... er zittert, furcht den tod, wirt geungstiget«; cf. *KB*, no. 7, 34[r]: »wie ouch Christus Jesus der derr, ob wol sein fleisch schwach... aus dem bath er den vater, den kelch von im zenemen.«

death.[23] The sharing (*ausstailung*) of the Spirit requested by Christ plays a central role in the freeing of the conscience, sanctification of the believer, and the gathering of the church.[24] The author also recounts the same arguments of the Spiritualists against the restitution of the ceremonial acts, such as baptism and the Supper, because there is no promise of God to do so and such a command must be accompanied by a miracle.[25] Finally, as we shall see, the position taken on the relation of the believer to civil authority is the same as that taken by Marpeck in the Strassburg *Confession* and letter of farewell to the council in 1532.

Taken together the external and internal evidence provide a strong warrant for the inclusion of the *Bekenntnis* in the Marpeck corpus.[26] Probably written between 1535 and 1539, the *Bekenntnis* clearly contains Marpeck's terminology and argumentation. There is reason to believe that Marpeck travelled in von Pernstain's Moravian domain during this period. Further, since Znaim had a strong »Pilgramite« group from 1535 through the 1570s, this may well have been the scene of his stay and authorship of the *Bekenntnis*.

Marpeck's continued concern to differentiate his position from that of the *Geister* can be explained by developments in Moravia. Based on a careful historical analysis of the relations between the Czech Brethren and the Anabaptists, Jarold Zeman posits the early and continued existence of a spiritualizing group – a third major type within Moravian Anabaptism – alongside the Schwertler and Stäbler.[27] There are several expressions of the vitality of this tendency before and during the period of the *Bekenntnis*. Entfelder's correspondence with and possible visit to Eibenschitz has been mentioned. In Strassburg, Bünderlin expressed a desire to return to Nicolsburg, which he may have done between his 1532 expulsion from ducal Prussia and the last historical trace of him in 1539. With the outbreak of persecution in 1535, the spiritualistic Gabriel Ascherham led many of his followers back to Silesia, where they came into contact with Schwenckfeldians in the country of Glatz, a dominion of Jan von Pernstain.[28] Therefore, the charges against which Marpeck

---

[23] *Bekenntnis*, 162[r]: »nach disem tail bekennen wir in unnsern und aller wellt mittler, versonung... ainigen hailand.... Welcher erst durch leiden gevolkumet ist«; cf. *KU*, Biii[v] (chapter 4 nn. 14, 99).

[24] *Bekenntnis*, 164[r]: »ausstailung des heiligen geistes«; 163[v]: »krafft seines geistes.... Ym gwissen vonn sunden freyet, rainiget, freimmacht, heiliget«; cf. *Confession* 439.15-16.

[25] *Bekenntnis*, 164[r]: »alls habe gott nyrgend verhaissen, die verfallen kirch, durch verwuestung des Antichrist, widerumbaufzurichten«; cf. *KU*, cv[r]; and 164[r]: »ware auch vonnoten gewesen, die mit wunder werckh zu bevestigen«; cf. *CV*, avi[r], av[v], aiii[r].

[26] The *Bekenntnis* begins with a brief introduction in the first person singular recounting the discussions with the local Hauptmann. The *Bekenntnis*, composed in first person plural, follows and constitutes the bulk of the document. It is possible that Marpeck is responsible for the *Bekenntnis*, but someone else delivered it to the Hauptmann. Or, Marpeck could have been present for the discussions and written both parts. Letter received from Heinold Fast, February 8, 1984.

[27] Zeman, *Czech Brethren*, 240.

[28] George H. Williams, *The Radical Reformation*, 413. Fabian Eckel, a close associate of Schwenckfeld's, arrived in Glatz from Liegnitz in April 1538 and mediated a christological dispute between Schwenckfeld and Entfelder. See *CS*, 8:79.

defends himself, could have reached the ear of the *Landeshauptmann* from a variety of sources within his Moravian and Silesian jurisdiction.[29]

1540–Spring 1542: Activity in Graubünden, Alsace, Southern Germany, and Moravia

Sometime between March and June 1540, Marpeck visited both Caspar Schwenckfeld in Justingen and Wolfgang Sailer in Austerlitz.[30] Schwenckfeld's reply to Sailer's letter of June 4 reveals that Marpeck reported that Schwenckfeld had initiated the exchange over christological issues with the Lutheran preachers at Schmalkalden. He might also have visited the Strassburg congregation before or after these stops.[31] By December Marpeck had made his way to Graubünden, perhaps to Ilanz on the Rhine, which seems to have served as his primary residence during this period.[32] Responding to a personal report by Ludwig Hafner, Marpeck wrote a letter on the unity of the bride of Christ to the »elect around Strassburg, in Alsace, in the Kinzig Valley and in the Leber Valley.«[33]

According to the testimony of Schwenckfeld, Marpeck either wrote or collaborated on a letter from Graubünden dated September 26, 1540. He claims that Marpeck asserted that »Christ had a flesh capable of sin, that is a flesh that could sin« and that, as with Adam, »Christ had a free will to sin.«[34] The letter might have been sent to Helena von Freyberg, then living in Augsburg, for the grammarian, Valentin Ickelsamer, wrote a refutation, *Ob Christus hab mogen sündigenn*.[35] Schwenckfeld quoted excerpts from the letter in this booklet. I shall return later to this matter and its role in the controversy between Marpeck and Schwenckfeld.

Early in 1541 Marpeck travelled again to Moravia. Probably stopping first to see Sailer and Veh in Austerlitz, he went on to Schakwitz »in order to bring together and unify all the people who were divided and in conflict concerning things of the faith.«[36] Contemporary sources reveal two groups with which

[29] Werner Packull, *Mysticism and the Early South German–Austrian Anabaptist Movement, 1525-1531*, 227 n. 61, correctly related the anti–Spiritualist content of the *Bekenntnis* to the 1531 controversy between Marpeck and Bünderlin.

[30] *CS*, 7:164-67: Schwenckfeld to Wolfgang Sailer, August 10, 1540. See especially 164.11.

[31] *KB*, no. 32, 254[r]. Scharnschlager in an undated letter wrote that he could not come to Strassburg but hoped that »durch unsern liebsten im herren, den bruder Pilgram und andere eure diener bey euch noturftigelich, ja leiplich besucht und versorget seit worden und noch werden.« Because of the contact between Marpeck and Strassburg in December, Scharnschlager's letter might belong in this time period.

[32] *KB*, no. 5, 14[v]: »inn dem Obern Pundt zu Graubünden.«

[33] Ibid., no. 5. Fast, in his introduction to the undated letter, *KB*, no. 4: »On Love,« suggests that its reference to the Song of Solomon may place it close to *KB*, no. 5.

[34] *CS*, 8:220.14-16, 274.32f., 291.1f.

[35] From 1537 to 1545 Helena von Freyberg appears on the Augsburg tax roles in the district »Vom Schmidhaus.« She died in 1545. Friedwart Uhland, *Täufertum und Obrigkeit in Augsburg im 16. Jahrhundert*, dissertation.

[36] Zieglschmid, *Chronik*, 224.

Marpeck sought unification. In a letter, Cornelius Veh opposed two »pernicious sects« – the Swiss, who forbad the use of certain things, and the Hutterites, who insisted on the community of temporal goods.[37] He probably referred to the group of Swiss Brethren in Znaim, where there was also a group of Cornelians.[38] The Schakwitz congregation of Hutterites, under the leadership of Hans Amon, had moved from Auspitz during the 1535 persecution.[39] The Hutterites refused to hear Marpeck as they had Veh shortly before and, according to the chronicler, »he became bitter and said publicly that he would rather unite with the Turks or Pope than with this congregation and stormed off.«[40] As we shall see, Marpeck opposed what he believed to be a divisive legalism among the Hutterites and was concerned about their effects upon other Anabaptist groups in Moravia.

Later in 1541 or early 1542, Marpeck translated and edited Bernhard Rothmann's low German *Bekenntnisse van beyden Sacramenten* as the *Vermahnung* or *A Clear, Thorough and Incontrovertible Account for a True, Christian and Eternal Covenanted Unity of all the True, Believing, Pious and Sincere.*[41] Marpeck hoped that the *Bundeszeuknus*, as it was also called, would serve to unify the Anabaptists by delineating a position in opposition to both the anti–institutional tendencies of the Spiritualists and the coercive measures of the magisterial Reformers and the Münsterites.[42] As we shall see, Marpeck developed a notion of hypostasis (*wesen*) to stress the integration of the inner and outer against those Geister, whose »obstruction, slander and apostasy« was then »in its twelfth year.«[43] He referred here to the 1531 publications of Entfelder and Bünderlin in Strassburg. Responding to those using coercive force (*Gewalt*) in service of the gospel, he insisted that the believer must fight for »divine justice and truth... with the weapon and sword of the Holy Spirit.«[44] Published sometime in the spring of 1542, the Vermahnung precipitated a heated controver-

---

37 *KB*, no. 24, 222[r]. Cornelius Veh to Appenzell and Zurich, March 8, 1543.

38 Zeman, *Czech Brethren*, 282. See Zieglschmid, *Chronik*, 242-43, for a condemnation of the Swiss Brethren in Pollau (Pavlov) by the Hutterites.

39 Zieglschmid, *Chronik*, 146.

40 Ibid., 224.

41 Cited as *Vermahnung* with the number of the page and line from the edition of Christian Hege in *Gedenkschrift zum 400– jährigen Jubiläum der Mennoniten oder Taufgesinnten 1525-1925*. Based on Schwenckfeld's, *CS*, 8:221.25-26, statement that he believed that »Pilgram unnd sonnst auch ainer« published the *Vermahnung* many have assumed that Leupold Scharnschlager collaborated on this work. (Most recently Neal Blough, *Christologie Anabaptiste*, 114 n. 2). It is possible that Marpeck and Scharnschlager worked together in Graubünden during this time, but Schwenckfeld's statement could also reflect his perception that the detailed historical arguments on the sacraments might have been the work of someone else. Wray, »The 'Vermanung',« 243-51, discovered that the *Vermahnung* was a redaction of Rothmann's earlier work. While Heinold Fast, »Bemerkungen zur Taufanschauung der Täufer,« 140, thinks Scharnschlager »probably« collaborated, Torsten Bergsten, »Pilgram Marbeck und seine Auseinandersetzung mit Caspar Schwenckfeld,« 85, has no doubt that Marpeck was the primary author. See Bernhard Rothmann, *Die Schriften Bernhard Rothmanns*, ed. Robert Stupperich, 138-95, for a modern edition of Rothmann's work.

42 *KB*, no. 16, 167[v]. Marpeck sent twenty copies of the »bundszeuknus« to Moravia in 1553.

43 *Vermahnung*, 187.2-3.

44 Ibid., 187.31-34.

sy between Schwenckfeld and Marpeck which began through the activity of two
of their respective patronesses.

Summer 1542–44

Southern Germany: Controversy with Schwenckfeld

After his expulsion from Ulm, Caspar Schwenckfeld took refuge in the castle
of Jörg Ludwig von Freyberg in Justingen, 1540-47. From there he continued
correspondence and visitation to conventicles of sympathizers throughout
Southern Germany.[45] He maintained particularly close ties with the nearby Ulm
group, centered around the widow, Helena Streicher, her five daughters and son.
Another circle, led by the former Benedictine nun, Lady Magdalena Marschalk
von Pappenheim, expressed an initial interest in the teaching of Schwenckfeld,
but was drawn to Marpeck's position through personal contact and
correspondence.[46]

Perhaps because of her contact with Magdalena, Helena Streicher began
correspondence with Marpeck in an effort to win him to the Spiritualist position
of her teacher.[47] In her second letter she asserted that Christ said his teaching was
»spirit and life« and that his rule in heavenly glory no longer included elemental
reality. She criticized Marpeck saying, »man has had enough of baptism by men«
and that he knew Christ only as a creature and made an idol of the cross.
Marpeck sent a very strong reply to Magdalena, who copied it before passing it
on to Helena. His argumentation reflects that of his earlier polemic against the
Strassburg *Geister*. He insists that the work of the Spirit includes the physical but
is not bound to it, criticizes an idealistic appeal to a pristine church in Jerusalem,
which overlooks its divisions, and chides her for her desire for a »proud, lofty
and arrogant Christ.«[48]

Until this time the relationship between Marpeck and Schwenckfeld had not
yet deteriorated.[49] Marpeck later wrote that he had written Schwenckfeld a
»treues gewarnen und entschuldigen« from Ulm and scolded him for then »going

---

[45] Williams, *The Radical Reformation*, 466, notes other cities with Schwenckfeldian circles:
Speyer, Esslingen, Kaufbeuren, Kempten, and Memmingen.

[46] *CS*, 8:217.16f. Letter of August 21. R. F. Hege, *ME*, 3:115-16, suggests, without documentation, that Magdalena's brother Joachim (d. 1536) first made contact with Marpeck. In addition to
these, Joachim's daughter Walpurga, who preserved one copy of the Verantwurtung and wrote a
hymn, and a Sophie, who married a Baron von Budenhofen, also belonged to the group.

[47] Magdalena Marschalk seems to have relayed the two letters from Streicher and Marpeck's
two replies. See *Antwort*, 180.16f.

[48] Ibid., 180.33f., 185.33f., 184.38-39.

[49] I disagree with the dating of the Streicher letter by Klassen and Klaassen in *WPM*, 581, no. 5
n. 1, who place it as late as 1544 based on the tone and language. I believe it comes at the
beginning of the controversy, spring or early summer 1542.

behind his back« by writing the Juditium and sending it to Magdalena.[50] It is possible that Marpeck had not included Schwenckfeld among the Spiritualists against whom he directed his *Vermahnung* and had not realized that Streicher represented Schwenckfeld's position.[51] On a visit to Ulm, Marpeck may have learned from Streicher of Schwenckfeld's objection to the *Vermahnung* and may have written this first letter clarifying his position against Entfelder and Bünderlin.

From his side, Schwenckfeld received several documents in the spring of 1542 from which he quickly perceived fundamental differences between his position and that of Marpeck. First, as we have noted, Ickelsamer's book came to him with christological excerpts from the alleged Marpeck letter of 1540. Second, Magdalena Marschalk sent Schwenckfeld a copy of Marpeck's letter to Streicher under her own name.[52] And third, he received a copy of the *Vermahnung* from Helena von Freyberg in Augsburg.[53] He responded with his *Juditium*, in which he treated twelve issues: the word sacrament, baptism, whether external baptism is a sign of grace, proof of the Spirit of God and spirit of error, original sin, becoming a child of God, the Word of God, the church, the faith of the patriarchs, the sources of the Anabaptists' errors, the Supper, and the words of the institution.[54] The circulation of *Juditium* manuscripts led to a series of letters and literary exchanges, in which Schwenckfeld and Marpeck clarified and developed their respective positions, leading to an irreversible parting of the ways.[55]

On August 21, 1542, Schwenckfeld responded to Magdalena's letter by identifying the ideas as Marpeck's and sending her copies of the *Juditium* and Ickelsamer's book.[56] Both Magdalena and Marpeck replied. Magdalena defended Marpeck and instructed Schwenckfeld to read the New Testament more closely. Marpeck claimed that Schwenckfeld had misrepresented his position and objected to his doing so to others (that is, to Magdalena, Helena von Freyberg, and others to whom Schwenckfeld had sent the *Juditium*).[57] Schwenckfeld answered both

---

[50] *Antwort*, 58.2-3. This letter must be before the August 21 letter to Magdalena but after the publication of the *Vermahnung*.

[51] Bergsten, *Pilgram Marbeck*, 70, concludes that Marpeck was probably unaware of the shift in Schwenckfeld's Christology which took place around 1538/39.

[52] The excerpts Schwenckfeld quotes from Magdalena's letter have almost verbatim parallels in Marpeck's letter to Streicher. Cf. *CS*, 8:217.22-23, and *Antwort*, 184.38-39; and *CS*, 8:218.11-14, and *Antwort*, 182.40-42. No doubt Streicher had also sent a copy to Schwenckfeld so that he knew that Marpeck had written the letter from Magdalena.

[53] *CS*, 8:618.6-7.

[54] The full title is *Über das new Buechlin der Tauff brueder Im 1542 Jare aussgangen Juditium*; see *CS*, 8:168-214.

[55] Part 2 of this chapter deals with these theological developments. Schwenckfeld, *CS*, 8:618.18-19, says that he sent the Juditium to Helena von Freyberg, Magdalena, and »etliche wenige der unsern.« In a letter to Jörg Straub (April 25, 1546), Schwenckfeld, *CS*, 9:728.26-729.4, says that the »Teuffer Fursteher« prohibited their people from talking with him. This may refer to Marpeck's group.

[56] *CS*, 8:217.16f.

[57] Ibid., 8:281.5f., 271.16f.

letters on September 25. To Marpeck, he listed his reasons for writing the *Juditium*: to accommodate »some brothers« who asked him to reply to the *Vermahnung*, to test Marpeck's sectarian spirit, to show that he was not an Anabaptist, and to defend the faith of the patriarchs. He denied having misrepresented Marpeck's position and told him to recant or clarify his position (especially concerning Jesus's capacity to sin). Because of Marpeck's well-known proclivity for »many long speeches and sharp words,« Schwenckfeld preferred a concise, point-by-point clarification to a personal meeting.[58]

In his letter to Magdalena, he enclosed a newly arrived copy of the alleged Marpeck letter of 1540 and documented twelve errors to which Marpeck should respond.[59] Four days later Schwenckfeld sent Marpeck a copy of the 1540 letter and asked him to respond, with a simple yes or no, to the twelve articles in Magdalena's letter.[60] Shortly thereafter, Marpeck appears to have travelled to Ulm hoping, without success, to speak personally with Schwenckfeld.[61] The controversy subsided as Schwenckfeld made several trips during the fall and winter.[62] By May he had composed a *Summarium* of the *Juditium* and an »excerpt of articles« and sent them to Helena von Freyberg, because he did not know where to find Marpeck or Magdalena.[63]

Abandoning his attempt to engage Schwenckfeld in a personal discussion, Marpeck wrote a detailed response, the *Verantwurtung I*, to the first part of the *Juditium*.[64] It must have been ready by Christmas 1543, for Marpeck sent it to Schwenckfeld with a cover letter on December 31.[65] A note in Walpurga Marschalk's copy of the *Verantwurtung* reads: »The blessed brother Pilgram sent the first part of this judgment to Caspar Schwenckfeld. Schwenckfeld never responded to it.«[66] Although Marpeck had replied only to the first part of Schwenckfeld's critique and another, even longer response was to follow, the

[58] Ibid., 8:271f. Schwenckfeld sent the letter to Augsburg. It must have reached Marpeck, for the group kept it and quoted from it. See *Antwort*, 408.4f.

[59] *CS*, 8:281-85.

[60] Ibid., 8:291-94.

[61] Ibid., 8:292.9-12.

[62] Selena G. Schultz, *Caspar Schwenckfeld von Ossig (1489-1561)*, 277, notes trips to Landau and Eschlingen.

[63] *CS*, 8:618.9f. Schwenckfeld also wrote a *Dialogus*, or a conversation between him and Marpeck. It is no longer extant. His February 21, 1544, letter to Michel Sporer of Stetten near Esslingen indicates that Sporer and his group, led by Jörg Scherer, were admirers of Marpeck.

[64] *Verantwurtung über Casparn Schwenckfelds Judicium*, cited from Loserth's edition as *Antwort*. The first part, or *Verantwurtung I*, deals with Schwenckfeld's *Juditium*; see *CS*, 8:168-89.26.

[65] Marpeck, in *Antwort*, 175.8-10, says that he wrote the first part quickly in order to send it to his associates lest they be led astray by Schwenckfeld. There has been considerable controversy about the date of this letter and, thus, the *terminus ad quem* of the *Verantwurtung I*. Jan J. Kiwiet, *Pilgram Marbeck*, 62, 74, follows Fritz Blanke in interpreting »Newenjarsabent anno 1544« as December 1544. Bergsten, *Pilgram Marbeck*, 54, 58; and Wenger, *The Life of Pilgram Marpeck*, 160, argue for 1543. Klassen in *CC*, 49 nn. 142-44, citing Grotefend and Schmeller, asserts that the proper interpretation is December 1543.

[66] *Antwort*, 49. Leupold Scharnschlager may have helped prepare this part of the *Verantwurtung*, however there is no evidence that he was with Marpeck in Southern Germany at the time. Kiwiet, *Pilgram Marbeck*, 74, argues that Marpeck composed it alone.

controversy effectively ended here. Schwenckfeld's patience had worn thin and he despaired of Marpeck's ever coming to the true recognition of »our glorified Christ and spirit.«[67]

During this controversy, Marpeck seems to have spent most of his time in Southern Germany, particularly Augsburg and in or around Ulm.[68] It is possible that he made contact with and perhaps even stayed in Langenau, northeast of Ulm.[69]

Switzerland: Division

During the time of his controversy with Schwenckfeld, Marpeck concerned himself with developments within the Anabaptist communities of Switzerland. Two of his letters, »An die Schweizer Brüder: Von jähen Gerichten und Urteilen« (1541-43), and »An die Schweizer Brüder in Appenzell: Über die Ursachen des Zwiespalts« (1543), date from this period and address what Marpeck considered to be a coercive legalism within one of the Appenzell congregations.[70] While his contact with the group extended to his activity in the area around 1535, Marpeck admits that they had never been in complete agreement.[71] The issues which elicited his two letters included the Appenzellers' strict exercise of the ban and the poor quality of their leadership.[72] As we shall see, Marpeck's opposition to »hasty judgments and decisions« forced him to clarify his notion of the freedom of the Christian and a practice of penitential discipline consistent with the activity of the »unconstraining Spirit.«

During these itinerant years, Marpeck travelled extensively and sought a theological basis for the unity and institutional identity of widely scattered and,

67 Schwenckfeld probably included Marpeck among the »creaturists,« represented by the Ulm pastor, Martin Frecht, with whom Schwenckfeld engaged in a dispute about Christology. See R. Emmett McLaughlin, *Caspar Schwenckfeld: Reluctant Radical*, 218-20.

68 We have noted that he wrote a letter to Schwenckfeld from Ulm and that Schwenckfeld sent two letters, September 1542, and May 1543, for him to Augsburg.

69 *KB*, no. 5, 158^r-163^v. Marpeck writes a 1555 letter to the congregation in Langenau and exhibited a personal knowledge of some of the members.

70 *KB*, no. 7, 27^r-62^v, and *KB*, no. 8.63^r-66^v. Jörg Maler, the editor of *KB* gave these letters their titles. Although they carry different dates (*KB*, no. 7, 1531, and *KB*, no. 8, 1543), they deal with the same people and issues, and Maler links them with a common introduction. Therefore, Heinold Fast suggests that the 1531 date on no. 7 is probably a writing mistake and that no. 7 precedes no. 8 but in a much closer chronological sequence. I agree with Fast's dating of no. 7 between 1541 and 1543.

71 *KB*, no. 7, 27^r: »des spalts [halben] so sich gehalten hat bisher zwischen uns... das wir dess erkanntnuss und verstands inn Christo Jesu nyee unsern hertzen und gwissen an einander erkennen noch treffen haben mogen.«

72 Among the leaders criticized was Maler, who was an Appenzell Vorsteher 1541-48, when he joined Marpeck in Augsburg. See Fast, *Ostschweiz*, 222 n. 3. This may explain some of Maler's critical glosses to these letters in the *KB*. Maler's later testimony in Augsburg reveals a growing disagreement between the group closer to Marpeck's position, including Maler, and the stricter group, to whom Marpeck writes. Franz Stark, *Das Ungeteilte Land*, 349, distinguishes a rigorous from a laxist group.

in some cases, persecuted Anabaptist groups in Alsace (Strassburg and the Leber Valley), Southern Germany (Ulm, Langenau, Augsburg, and Esslingen), Moravia (Austerlitz, Schakwitz, Znaim, and Eibenschitz) and Switzerland (St. Gallen, Appenzell, Chur, Ilanz, and Zurich).

THEOLOGY OF THE CROSS: BASIS FOR THE UNITY AND IDENTITY OF THE ANABAPTIST MOVEMENT

In his attempt to articulate a foundation for the unity and identity of these groups, Marpeck continued to steer between those who, as he had said in Strassburg, made the realm of Christ »too fleshly« and those who made it »too spiritual.«

»All Coercion Has Ceased«

In Strassburg, Marpeck had argued that Bucer and others who allowed force in matters of faith »confessed only the mortal and physical Christ but they confessed very little of the resurrected Christ.« They substituted human force (*Gewalt*) for the strength (*Krafft*) of the »unconstraining Spirit.« This led, in his view, to a denial of the necessity of one's personal cross, the coercion of the individual, and therefore insecure consciences. The result was the obstruction of individual justness and therefore social justice or the possibility of mutuality and a true community. During the period 1532-44, Marpeck opposed two manifestations of coercion.

»The Physical Sword«

Marpeck continued to criticize those who used force in matters of faith. He says that, unfortunately, almost all teachers »pay more attention to the sharpness of the physical sword and its power... than the sharpness of the Word.«[73] Among these, he says the »Papists and Evangelicals (as they call themselves) use the cities, princes and lords... and all earthly power [*gewalt*].« He extends his critique to others who want to fight with the physical sword in the appearance of the gospel: »As it was done in the Peasants War, and again by the Zwinglians and now, under the appearance of the true baptism of Christ, by the Münsterites in Westphalia.«[74] So, even in the translation of the *Bekenntnisse* of Rothmann, Münster's premier theologian, Marpeck denounced the use of coercive power by that city's radicals.

---

[73] *Vermahnung*, 279.19-23. All quotations from the *Vermahnung* are Marpeck's additions or changes to Rothmann's text unless otherwise noted and are taken from Hege's modern edition.
[74] Ibid., 217.19f.

Consistent with his belief that the outpouring of the Spirit provides a new possibility for overcoming injustice, Marpeck asserts: »[We] destroy aggression and all heights, which raise themselves against the knowledge of God... not from our own strength and power, nor through earthly or physical force and sword, but from the strength and power of the Lord Jesus Christ, who overcame all with patience, as we also overcome through death in Christ our Lord.«[75] That strength and power (*macht und gewalt*) is the power of the Holy Spirit, poured out in the death of Christ, which »does not rise up against, resist, or strive against physical force, but is obedient, in suffering, through patience unto death.«[76] Just as Christ offered the »unconstraining Spirit« even unto death, so the believer is also obligated to fight only with the »weapons and sword of the Holy Spirit.«[77] That is, the believer shares that Spirit, not through coercion or external force but through a vulnerable offer. As long as sin continues in the world, participation in the realm of Christ, ruled by that unconstraining Spirit, necessarily involves one in patient suffering. Therefore, Marpeck begins to sign his letters »servant and companion in the realm and affliction which is in Christ.«[78] The realm of Christ and the cross are inextricably linked. The Münsterites and peasants denied, then, the cross and substituted their own power for that of the Spirit.

As for the role of civil authority, the *Bekenntnis an Jan von Pernstain* reveals that Marpeck's position remained the same in spite of the intense persecutions after the events at Münster. Responding to the charge that his group strove against the *Obrigkeit* with violence, Marpeck writes:

We say that we confess the civil authority as a good order of God, ordained for the peace of human life.... Therefore, everyone should rightly obey both good and evil authorities, help the poor, and help promote its power... with taxes, tolls and interest, so that the pious may be maintained in peace under her and the evil may be punished by her, for she was ordained a servant of God for vengeance.[79]

He even expresses a willingness »to protect your subjects according to your [von Pernstain's] command.« Evidently Marpeck means vengeance against those who unjustly disturb the peace of the just. Because of the uncertainty of the context of the *Bekenntnis*, the precise kind of defensive service to which Marpeck refers remains unclear. However, since he was in Moravia, he may have had in mind defense against the Ottomans. Further, Marpeck affirms the role of the civil

75 Ibid., 188.17-23.
76 Ibid., 280.16f.
77 Ibid., 187.34.
78 *KB*, no. 4, 10ᵛ: »euer diener und mitb[rude]r am reich und am truebsal, des inn Christo ist.«
79 *Bekenntnis*, 165ᵛ: »Sagen derhalben, das wir bekennen die obrigkait, wie die sey ein guete ordnung gottes, verordnet zum frid mennschliches lebens,... dero billichen yederman gehorchen soll, frumm und böss, ja auch hanndraichung thuen und hilff, es sey mit steuer, ränd und zynnss, und wie es genennt mag werden, iren gwalt zu volfieren, damit die frummen unntter yr im frid erhalten, die bösen aber durch sy gezuchtiget werden, dieweil sy ain dienerin gottes, zur rach verordnet, ist.«

authority in maintaining a just order and prays that it might receive the »spirit of justice and truth.«[80] Therefore, he admonishes von Pernstain not to »persecute and crucify the Lord unawares« (that is, those believers who have received and offered that »spirit of justice and truth«).[81]

In spite of this willing obedience, Marpeck asserts that believers do not need the civil authority for themselves. Elsewhere, he states that a true Christian »need not seize, protect or promote city, land or people... for such belongs to earthly and temporal rule.«[82] The sense here is that the believer is freed from the need to secure the self by grasping and controlling temporal things. Further, that obedience reaches only »up to the conscience,« for he says »without reservation« that if that authority goes beyond its sphere and »wants to rule, order and dominate our consciences against God and his truth,« the believer must refuse. Rejecting arguments from the Old Testament for the use of force in matters of faith, Marpeck asserts that »with the free preaching of the gospel of Christ, all coercion has ended.«[83]

»Law, Commands, and Prohibitions«

In Moravia and Switzerland Marpeck encountered what he considered to be another manifestation of the use of external force in matters of faith – the coercive use of the law. In his exchanges with the Swiss Brethren and Hutterites, Marpeck clarified his understanding of sin, the work of Christ, and the rebirth and developed his notions of freedom, love, and a penitential discipline appropriate for a voluntary *Gemeinschaft*, gathered by the unconstraining Spirit.

We have examined Marpeck's notion of sin as a self–enclosed mode of existence (*aigen annemen*) by which the human being isolates the self from external resources, both communal and divine. In his writings to and about the Swiss Brethren, Marpeck further stresses the proclivity to self–rationalization (*aigen vernunfft*) by means of the knowledge of good and evil. According to Marpeck: »[I]nherited sin is first inherited in the knowledge of good and evil, which Adam and Eve bequeathed.... In the legacy of all humanity, it was there before the knowledge [wissen] of the recognition [erkandtnus] of good and evil, but was neither inherited nor reckoned as actual sin before God.«[84] In another place he again calls what preceded this knowledge the »root of sin,« so that one, according to the flesh, abandons the good and does evil as soon as the recognition and knowledge begins.[85] Apparently that root of sin or mode of the flesh is the

---

[80] *KB*, no. 8, 65[v].

[81] *Bekenntnis*, 166[r].

[82] *Vermahnung*, 217.32f.

[83] *Bekenntnis*, 165[v]: »yezund aber zu diser freier predig des evangelii Christi had aller zwang aufgehört.«

[84] *Vermahnung*, 215.30f.

[85] *KB*, no. 7, 44[r]: »Weiter so ist die wuttzl der sund, grundt und anfanng, von unserm ersten vaterr und muter Adam unnd Eva her, namlich im erkanntnus des guten und bösen, das man von

legacy received from humanity's parents, and therefore from one's own parents, grandparents, and neighbors by contagion. That is, the grasping mode of others around him or her encourages the child, entering »wissenheit,« to grasp also for survival. To the extent that one's parents are concerned about securing themselves in the world, they are incapable of providing for the security of the child. Perceiving this and convinced from experience that no one (including God) will provide for him or her, the adolescent sets out to secure himself or herself in reality. Therefore, according to Marpeck, inherited sin is not transmitted physically but through social interaction. The problem, then, does not lie in the recognition of good and evil itself, but rather in the self–enclosed mode (flesh) which employs that recognition for its own purpose. That purpose is to secure blessedness »from our own strength« (*eignen kreften*),[86] apart from any reality outside the self.

At the heart of the Appenzellers' commands and prohibitions, Marpeck believed that he perceived the operation of the fallen reason (*verfallen vernunfft*), which used the law to rationalize, and even justify itself. With respect to their »hasty judgments and decisions« he says, »It happens quickly that one rules more from one's own understanding and knowledge [*eigen verstand und wissen*] than from love.«[87] In doing so, one replaces the power of the Holy Spirit with one's own: »Whoever thinks or holds that the realm of Christ is to be maintained, ruled, and directed through the law, command and prohibition... pushes the unconstraining Spirit of the Lord Jesus Christ, the rightful ruler of the heart, out of the middle and places himself in that place.«[88] Therefore, in the guise of the law of God, one person rules over the conscience of another. However, just as physical force cannot secure the conscience, neither can this legalistic coercion. Marpeck claims, »They throw out the Lord and make sin where there is no sin. They are murderers of souls and thieves and lead weak hearts and consciences into captivity and against themselves.«[89] When one is grounded strictly in one's own strength (*eigen kreften*) or in that of another human being, the dread of death, which can take away every human capacity, wreaks »chaos and disquiet in the heart and conscience.«

Marpeck opposed, then, the strict ban (governed by »hasty judgments and decisions«) of the Swiss congregation. As he said, they destroyed the blossom before it was able to bear fruit. There is both indirect and direct information concerning the issues about which Marpeck and the Appenzellers might have

---

unser natur und geburt (als vom fleisch geborn ist, das ist fleisch) verlasst das gut und thut das böss, sobald nu das erkennen und wissen angeet nach dem fleisch.«

86 Ibid., no. 7, 31ʳ.

87 Ibid., no. 7, 27ᵛ.

88 Ibid., no. 7, 40ᵛ: »Herwider, wer sich understet, das reich Christi durch gsatz, gebot und verbot, ja halt... der stost den freywilligen geist des herren Jesu Christi als den rechten regierer der hertzen uss dem mytel und stelt sich an die stat, do er nit soll.«

89 Ibid., no. 7, 40ᵛ: »[S]o stossen sy den herrn uss unnd machen sundt do kein sundt ist. Solch all send selmorder und dieb, fueren die weibischen hertzen und schwache backennprennte gwissen gfanngen durch gebot und verbot wider sich selbs.«

disagreed. In 1559 Jörg Maler (a close associate of Marpeck's in Augsburg) indicated several positions taken by the rigoristic Appenzell congregation with which Maler disagreed at the time of his departure in 1546: do not carry nor use a sword; do not marry an unbeliever or a person from another confession; do not make bright colored or suggestive clothing; do not punish or strike one's wife; do not go before the civil government with a complaint; and do not, under any circumstances, swear an oath.[90] Although it is uncertain in which cases Marpeck agreed with Maler that the Appenzellers made »sin where there is no sin,« one case is clear. For Marpeck, in 1543, wrote the Appenzellers: »After having received sufficient clarity from you concerning your position on the oath, we cannot bind anyone's conscience to it or put a noose around anyone's neck. Neither can we bind our own conscience to it.«[91] We have already noted that Marpeck, in Strassburg, was willing to swear the civil oath as well as other lesser oaths.

He also considered the Hutterites' strict insistence on the community of goods an inappropriate coercion of conscience. His comments in the Vermahnung probably reflect his perspective concerning his unpleasant 1541 visit to Schakwitz. He argues that the Jerusalem community in Acts 4 shared their possessions not »because there was a law to have all things in common but simply out of unconstrained love.« Peter's question to Ananias, »Could you not have kept something for yourself?« proved that the sharing was voluntary and involved no coercion (zwang). It was not as some coercers (Zwinger) say, »who want to have all things in common more from greed than from love.«[92]

In Marpeck's opinion the Swiss and Hutterite elders, by their radical separatism (secterey) defined by their self-rationalizing (aigen vernunfft) use of the law, replaced the unconstraining Spirit as the ruler of all hearts and thereby threatened to destroy the unity of the body of Christ.[93] As with those employing physical force, these legalists made void the cross of Christ, through which that Spirit was given, and denied the cross of the Christian by which that Spirit is freely received.

---

[90] St-A.A, Urgichten, April 28, 1550. It is significant to note that, although Maler refused to make the swearing of the oath grounds for the ban, he was forced to leave Appenzell because he refused military service.

[91] KB, no. 8, 66ᵛ: »Des eyds halben konnen wir mit eurem verstandt, den wir gnugsam mit ernst von euch verstannden haben niemants gwissen fahen noch binden, ouch niembt kein strickh am halss ze legen, konnen ouch uns undter euren verstandt mit unser gwissen nit verbinden.« Klassen and Klaassen, WPM, 580, suggest two possibilities as to why this page representing Marpeck's position on the oath was torn out: 1, Maler used it in his own discussion of the oath (KB, 157ᵛ); or 2, Maler disagreed and did not wish to represent both positions in the KB. Fast, in his yet unpublished »Introduction to KB, no. 8,« uses Maler's testimony of 1550 to show that Maler had earlier changed his mind. Therefore, Maler may have torn out this page because it no longer applied to him. If that was the case, Maler could have left it out of his original transcription of the letter. It seems more likely that a later heir of the KB, uncomfortable with Marpeck's acceptance of the oath, tore out the page.

[92] Vermahnung, 265.10f.

[93] KB, no. 7, 40ᵛ: »und wirt als nit anders dann secterey und bapstum daruss.«

In this context Marpeck further developed his unique notion of the work of Christ. Focusing on the passion narrative in the Gospel of John (particularly John 19:30), Marpeck expresses more explicitly what had been implicit in his earlier work: »But the perfect love of God only overcomes and achieves the victory in the bodily dread in death, where this bodily life has an end. As the Lord cried 'My God, why have you forsaken me?' and said, 'It is completed!' whereby he gave up the Spirit. But in this, love achieved the victory against bodily dread. But it was not driven out before death.«[94] Christ communicates the Spirit, which alone overcomes the dread of death, only in his death. For the mortal human being, death, which takes away every human capacity, brings with it the dread of extinction, the loss of identity. However, the Spirit, poured out in Christ's own death, grants life from beyond the human being, from the source of all life itself. The perfect love of God, or that willingness to share the divine life, thereby wins the victory in the human being over the dread of death. So, through Christ, life flowed into an isolated and stagnant humanity. Comparing Christ to the sun in Song of Solomon 2:10-14, Marpeck says that human beings first began to bloom at the incarnation, but remained without fruit before the descent (death) of the sun, Jesus Christ. Further until the time of the resurrection and ascension of Christ, there were still only flowers and buds as a foretaste until the brilliance of spring came. Only with the turtledove, the Holy Spirit, did the first early fruits appear.[95] The meaning of his criticism that the Swiss do not wait to examine the fruit but cut off the blossom is clear. They reject the slow, nurturing work of the Spirit and substitute their own »self – rationalizations« (aigen vernunfft).

They have also not yet realized the necessity of the suffering of the Christian, that is, the confrontation with one's own limitation. The proper function of the law is to crush the aigen vernunfft, not to be used by it. As soon as the law is announced: »[O]ur fallen reason finds itself damned and wants very much to keep the law in order to become blessed, but that is impossible for it. In this way, that capacity is taken from it, by which it wanted to be a god and its own lord... that power (which belongs only to God) which it presumed it had to be blessed or

---

94 Ibid., no. 7, 39ᵛ: »Aber die föllig lieb gotes uberwinth und behalt den sig inn diser leiplichenn forcht, aber erst im tod, do das leiplich leben ein end nympt. Wie ouch der herr schrey: 'Mein got, wie hastu mich verlassen!' inndem er den geist ufgab. Aber inn dem allem gehalt di lieb den sig wider die leiplich forcht; wirt aber nit usstribenn vor dem tod.« Blough, Christologie Anabaptiste, 123, notes the Johannine influence concerning the advent of the Holy Spirit after the resurrection.

95 KB, no. 5, 13ʳ: »do haben die menschen erst anfahen zu plueen, die feigenbeum und weinstöckh knöpf und ougen gwunnen, aber noch als on frucht vor undergang diser sonnen Jesu Christi; durch wölchen underganng di hitz des tags, das ist der zorn des vaters ist kuel worden. Und bis auf die zeit der uffersteeung und uffart Christi hat der preutgam sich sambt der prauth nun undern plumen, knöpfen, ougen und rosen geweidet als im forschmackh und schatten bis der glenntz oder frueeling komen ist. So sich die turteltaub horen hat lassen, das ist der h[eili]g geist, do send erst die ersten und frueen frucht worden.«

damned from and out of its own strength.«[96] Therefore, the active, aggressive
mode of the *aigen vernunfft* is stilled; its incapacity revealed. Echoing the
Theologia Deutsch, Marpeck says that thereby one is reborn in »simplicity and
unknowing« (*einfalt und unwissenheit*) through faith and baptism.[97]

Through faith, or the receptivity born of the acknowledgment of incapacity,
one receives the unconstraining Spirit, which is the foundation of freedom and
unity in the bond of love. The Spirit is that »spontaneous life through grace...
[which] frees from death to life.« That is, one is freed from the self–enclosed
mode to serve others. Since resources flow from without, through the Holy
Spirit, and a believer is confident that the love of God will continue that flow,
one is free to channel them to the neighbor. Freedom is, then, only possible in
this relationship of participation in the Spirit of God, so that a person »with the
whole desire of the heart fulfills the whole desire of God.«[98] A Christian is,
therefore, free from all law, commands, or prohibitions and gives oneself freely
to others. Marpeck expresses this notion of unity using the Johannine theme of
mystical coinherence: »And Christ prayed for this unity for his own – to be one
in him, as he is one in the Father and the Father is one in him and he is one in us,
so that we should also have a unity in him among one another. So we may also
be a sacrifice for one another before God the Father as Christ was for us.«[99]
Marpeck believed that the rigoristic tendencies among the Hutterites and some of
the Swiss Brethren threatened to substitute human reason for the unconstraining
Spirit and thereby destroy the unity of the movement. Therefore, he counselled a
more patient approach to penitential discipline. He pointed out that Jesus said,
»You will know them by their fruits« (Matthew 7:20), not by their blossoms or
leaves.[100] Since love always seeks correction, a believer should not judge but warn
and admonish those with early signs of serious sins. One should always wait for

96 Ibid., no. 7, 31ʳ: »Dan sobald unnser verfalline vernunft das gsatz und gut gebot gotes
verkundet wirt, finth sy sich darunterr verdampt sein und wolte das gsatz gern halten darum, das
sy selig wurde des dann unser verfalline eignen vernunft nit muglich ist. Dann deshalben ist ir das
vermögen gnomen, das sy ein got wolt sein und selber herr, und die macht... noch vermeint zu
haben, selig oder verdampt zu werden von und aus eigner craft und nit von got, dem alles
vermögen alein zuhört.«

97 Ibid., no. 7, 44ᵛ: »Wer nit wirt durch den glouben und tauff innverzeichung der sundt
widergeborn inn die einfalt und unwissenheit zu der gehorsame des gloubenns wie ein kind, der
ist verdambt.« Cf. the Frankfurter's advice that one should abandon the vernunft and go out of
oneself »yn eym unwissen yn die eynunge des, das da ist uber all wessen und bekentnus.« *TD*,
8/18.19-21. Marpeck, therefore, links the state of the »unknowing« child with this mystical state
of »unwissenheit.«

98 *KB*, no. 7, 29ᵛ. Marpeck uses John 8:32 to relate, here, truth to freedom. See also ibid., no.
7, 28ʳ. Cf. *TD*, 50/95.9-13.

99 *KB*, no. 5, ll ᵛ: »Und solche einigkheit des h[eilige]n geists hat Christus den vatern betenn
fur die seinigen, ains zu sein in im, wie er im vatern und der vaterr in im und er inn uns eins ist,
so wir anderst die einigkheit in im undereinander halten im h[eilige]n geist. So mögen wir ouch
ein opferr vor got vaterr fur ainander sein wie Christus fur uns.« Marpeck quotes or refers to this
prayer of Jesus several times (*KB*, no. 7, 59ᵛ, no. 8, 63ʳ; and *Vermahnung*, 189.43f.

100 *KB*, no. 7, 35ʳ: »Dann Christus spricht: 'bey den fruchten (und spricht nit:bey dem pluee
oder loub) werth ir sy erkennen.'«

the fruit and not run before Jesus and obstruct the work of the unconstraining Spirit. But he made clear that Christians must also not run behind Jesus. If a believer does not judge with Christ, that is, testify to justice (*gerechtigkeit*) when evil fruit is revealed, that one is also a murderer and thief.[101] For the sake of justness and justice, a Christian must confront the fellow believer with any unwillingness or incapacity to fulfill the law, hoping for his or her correction.

»The Untransfigured Body of Christ«

While he clarified his understanding of the unity of the Anabaptist movement in conversation with the Swiss Brethren and Hutterites, Marpeck struggled against the anti–institutional tendencies of the Spiritualists (especially Schwenckfeld) for a definition of its identity. The controversy with Schwenckfeld included questions concerning the nature of the reality of Christ, before and after his transfiguration; the role of his cross; and the nature of his realm and the believer's relationship to it.

In Strassburg Marpeck had said that the Lord Christ became a human being so that the human being might be »translated through the natural into the supernatural and heavenly being [*wesen*].« Christ initiated a new order in which »the natural and supernatural« exist together. He called the new possibility of integration of the earthly and heavenly the *neues wesen* (new being) and affirmed that the Spirit, poured out in the cross of Christ, made this integration available to all of humanity. His controversy with Schwenckfeld forced Marpeck to clarify his concept and terminology for the new being (*neues wesen*) and its meaning for the gathered community. This clarification will be examined by attending to the stages of the Marpeck/Schwenckfeld debate.[102]

1538 – 39: Schwenckfeld's Christological Shift and Marpeck's *Bekenntnis an Jan von Pernstain*

As has been noted, Christ's cross was decisive in Schwenckfeld's distinction between the New and Old Covenants. Through death and resurrection, Christ became equal to God in power and majesty. Schwenckfeld did not, however, conclude with Luther that Christ's humanity thereby became ubiquitous. Rather he asserted that creatureliness itself was abolished in the transfigured or glorified Christ.[103] Christ's flesh was transformed into that heavenly flesh, which

101 Ibid., no. 7, 36[v].

102 Blough, *Christologie Anabaptiste*, 145ff., has a perceptive account of the development of the debate and the implications of Marpeck's notion of *wesen* for his Christology. I rehearse that debate in some detail because his work was published in French and he does not treat the *Bekenntnis*.

103 See McLaughlin, *Caspar Schwenckfeld*, 208-9; and Emanuel Hirsch, *Zum Verständnis Schwenckfelds*, 165.

Valentine Crautwald had called »the enduring bread which is ever Christ himself.«[104] Indeed, after Christ's transfiguration (*Verklärung*), »all externals are obsolete and do not belong to the substance [*substanz*], nature [*natur*] or essence [*wesen*] of the New Testament or the realm of Christ.« Although he referred to the glorified Christ (*glorificierte*) after the resurrection, Schwenckfeld tended to use the word transfigured (*verklärt*) to describe this state. In his controversy with Schwenckfeld, Marpeck appears to have taken over this terminology and most often wrote of Christ's transfigured body. Even in this early formulation (c. 1531), the presuppositions for Schwenckfeld's later position are evident. Using *Substanz, Natur*, and *Wesen* as equivalent terms, in accord with scholastic usage since the Fourth Lateran Council, Schwenckfeld insisted on the separation of uncreated reality from created reality: »Everything that is is either a divine or creaturely *Wesen*.«[105]

By the 1535 Tübingen Colloquy, Schwenckfeld argued that, after his elevation, Christ had no creaturely existence at all. In a 1538 letter to Fabian Eckel in Glatz, Silesia, Schwenckfeld writes:

Christ had... in the days of his temporal flesh, place and accidents, even as other human beings, yet without needing to sin.... But when he, through the cross and suffering, was led out and became an entirely new heavenly human being, he needed as little time, place and accidents... as the heavenly Father.... Christ was placed in the heavenly *wesen* [essence, substance, nature].[106]

Sometime in 1538/39 Schwenckfeld realized the logical extension of his position and projected Christ's uncreaturely existence back before the transfiguration into the earthly life of Christ.[107] He asserted two natures in Christ, but the human nature was from conception uncreated and »scarcely distinguishable from the divine nature.« Schwenckfeld applied the Nicene formula, »begotten and not made,« to the whole Christ, not just to his divine nature or eternal Logos, and could thereby also posit a preexistent Christ, whose heavenly flesh nourished even the Patriarchs.[108]

Evidently Marpeck in his *Bekenntnis* and in his *Vermahnung* was unaware of this development in Schwenckfeld's theology.[109] In any case, since each work

---

[104] Williams, *The Radical Reformation*, 111-13, describes the illuminating experience of Crautwald concerning the meaning of the Supper and its foundational character for Schwenckfeld's theology.

[105] *CS*, 6:85.21-22.

[106] Ibid., 6:81.1f. Marpeck and his collaborators knew and quoted this letter extensively. See *Antwort*, 284, 472, 475-76, 484, 494, 498-99, 503-4, 511-12, 552, 557.

[107] *CS*, 7:453. Hirsch, »Zum verstandis Schwenckfelds,« 166, observed that this projection was »logisch fast unvermeidlich.« Schwenckfeld himself, *CS*, 6:570.26f., reflects that opinion when he says that it is illogical that Christ's humanity should pray to his divinity, which would have been appropriate were his humanity creaturely.

[108] Williams, *The Radical Reformation*, 326, 332, 334.

[109] Bergsten, *Pilgram Marbeck*, 70, concurs with this conclusion.

represents a stage of Marpeck's thought concerning his own view of the *neues wesen*, they will be treated separately.

In the *Bekenntnis*, Marpeck appears to develop his trinitarian formulations in opposition to those who deny the equality of the Word to the Father and, thus, deny the divine nature of Christ.[110] Therefore, he stresses that »the eternal, sufficient, incomprehensible Word has come out of (but not out and apart from) the Father [*außgangen aber nit abgangen*],« so that the Word is »one with the Father in *natur, wesen* [substance] and *krafft*.« The Holy Spirit is also of the same *wesen* (substance).[111] Here Marpeck, as Schwenckfeld, uses *wesen* and *natur* to refer to the unified uncreated nature of God. In fact, the godhead is so unified, that, although »distinguishable by names,« the divine *wesen* (substance) is a »unified, indivisible, inseparable God without persons.«[112] Marpeck's tendency toward modalistic monarchianism is also evident in the *Vermahnung* and would be criticized by Schwenckfeld.

Having addressed one threat to the soteriological significance of the person of Christ (that is, the denial of the divine nature), Marpeck turns to two positions which seem to deny the human nature of Christ. Against those who say the Word assumed neither the seed of Abraham nor human flesh, he argues, »If this heavenly body received no accidents, then Christ did not restore the fall of Adam.«[113] Therefore, Marpeck insists on the completeness of Christ's humanity:

[He was] a true natural human being, who began in time, lived in time and fulfilled his time through suffering and death under Pontius Pilate... the true seed of Abraham... fruit of the body of Mary, therefore he can truly be called our brother... with all our weaknesses except sin.... [H]e cried, suffered, hungered,

110 He may have had Sebastian Franck, then living in Ulm, in mind here. See Franck's positive evaluation of Servetus, KR, 1:159. There is evidence for anti–Trinitarian tendencies at this time also in Moravia. A leader of the Minor Party at Letovice, under the jurisdiction of Pernstain, criticized the Austerlitz brethren for holding the erroneous beliefs of Athanasius. See Zeman, *Czech Brethren*, 246 n. 22.

111 *Bekenntnis*, 161ᵛ: »das das ewig, selfstandig, unbegreifflich wort vom vater aussgangen (aber nit abgangen) sey«; and 163ʳ: »das das ewig wort des vatters, welches ym anfang bey gott war, ja gott selbs, durch welches der vater alle ding weisslich gemacht hat, tregt und erhellt, ains mit dem vater sey in natur, wesen und krafft.« Because *Wesen* becomes later a technical term for Marpeck, I leave *Wesen* untranslated in the text and indicate its meaning in the particular context with parentheses or square brackets.

112 *Bekenntnis*, 163ʳ: »ym namen unntterschidlich, aber ym wesen ein ewige, volkumene, bestandige ainigkait, welche (von weiten, sovil sich gezimbt und die warhait zuelast) gleichait wir ynn der sunnen begreiffen kunnen«; and 161ᵛ: »wie wir glauben, ein allmechtiges, ewiges, ainiges, unzertayliches, unenndliches, unwanndlpares, götliches wesen gottes vaters, suns und heiligen geists, welches wir ain ainigen, unzertailten, ununderschidlichen, unpersonlichen gott nennen und bekennen.«

113 Ibid., 162ᵛ: »dieweil ynn die himlische corper solche accidentia oder zuefal warhafftigklich nit kummen etc. Het auch Christus nit den val des fleisches Adae wider zu recht pracht.« Among those committing the first error, Marpeck probably includes Bünderlin and perhaps Franck, while Hofmann represents those committing the second error.

thirsted, was coerced, trembled, feared death, was anxious, suffered, and died... but could not fall.[114]

Of the relationship between this human nature and the divine nature, Marpeck asserts: »In Christ these two distinguishable natures [naturen] have united with one another, but not mixed.«[115] Further, the human nature is first perfected through suffering and is thereby »transfigured into the heavenly *wesen* [being].«[116] Marpeck's terminology is very close to that of Schwenckfeld before the change in 1538-39. In fact, he distinguishes two bodies of Christ – an earthly and a heavenly: »The first we all share in common and Christ became part of it with us. The second, Christ inherited and we shall in his time inherit it with him in likeness (Philippians 3:21).«[117] Marpeck does not describe the heavenly body of Christ after the resurrection and ascension, but he probably did not detect major differences between himself and Schwenckfeld until the latter's response to the *Vermahnung*.[118] However, the publication of the *Vermahnung* precipitated the clarification and development of nascent differences between the two men.

1542: Marpeck's Vermahnung and Schwenckfeld's Juditium

As noted, Marpeck wrote the *Vermahnung* to unify the Anabaptists and to oppose the apparent indifference among certain *Geister* to physical reality and therefore social responsibility. Marpeck objected to what he perceived as a separation of the spirit and body reflected in their Christologies, whereby Christ's humanity excluded materiality. He further opposed the consequent rejection of physical acts such as baptism and the Supper by which the gathered community was constituted. In the *Vermahnung*, Marpeck began to develop a

---

114 Ibid., 162^r: »bekennen wir in ein waren naturlichen menschen, der mit der zeit angefangen und in der zeit seines lebens zuegenomen und sein zeit unntter Pontio Pilato gevollendet hat, durch leiden und sterben... das diser mensch Jesus Christus nach disem tail der warlich naturlich sam des weibs sey,... ja, der ware samen Abrahae,... die gebenedeit frucht des laibs Mariae darumben er warlich unser brueder genent wirt und wir sein fleisch und bain,... mit aller schwachait umgeben wie wir, die ainig sunndt aussgenomen... er wainet, leidt hunnger, durst, wirt betriebt, er zittert, furcht den tod, wirt geanstiget, leidt und stirbt... nit fallen kunnen.« In *KB*, no. 7, 34^r, Marpeck says that Jesus asked the Father to take the cup from him but the Spirit held this desire of the flesh in obedience so that he asked »your will not mine be done.« Expressions like this may have prompted Schwenckfeld's accusation that according to Marpeck, Christ could have sinned. But Marpeck, here, explicitly rejects that position.

115 *Bekenntnis*, 163^r: »Dise baide unnderschidlichen naturen haben sich in Christo miteinander verainigt, aber nit vermischt.«

116 Ibid., 162^r: »verklärt nach dem fleisch ynnss himlisch wesen.«

117 Ibid., 162^v : »so doch der geist gottes unns mit guetem unnterschaid alain zwaierlay corper bezeuget (1 Cor. 15:40) nemblich ainen irdischen und himlischen; den ersten, so wir yetz all gemain tragen und Christus mit unns tailhafftig worden ist, den anndern, so Christus ereerbt und wir in ime zu seiner zet gleichformig mit ym ereerben werden (Phil. 3:21).« Cf. Blough, *Christologie Anabaptiste*, 133.

118 In his 1543 letter to him, Marpeck (*Antwort*, 57) registered surprise concerning Schwenck-feld's polemical Juditium.

notion of *wesen* as first, a new being understood as an hypostasis, or entity, in which both created and uncreated realities exist together; and second, the integration of the internal (spiritual) and external (material) aspects of the human being through the Spirit.

Marpeck employed this new concept in service of his desire to maintain the complete humanity and divinity of Christ in one *wesen*, or hypostasis. According to the divine will, the Word instituted an »order of creatures,« in which the creature has »time, *wesen* [substance], place and person.« Further, without mediation, no creature may come to the fulfillment of the will of God. So, »it was also ordained with Christ, the Son of Man and seed of Abraham, that he must be according to time, *wesen* [substance] and person a creature of God. Otherwise there would have been no distinction between the creation and the Creator and all would have been a charade.«[119] Here, Marpeck stresses the created, human *wesen* (substance or nature) in Christ. He implies, but does not state, that this creaturely *wesen* (substance) is integrated with the divine *wesen* (substance) in the new *wesen* (hypostasis) of Christ. He approaches this formulation by referring later to a »newes *wesen* in Christo.«[120] Therefore, Marpeck suggests a meaning for the word *wesen* different than substance. The new *wesen* is an hypostasis, being, or person, in which the human and divine natures exist together, although they are not mixed or changed into one another.[121] The Holy Spirit seems to be the required mediator between the two *wesen* (substances or natures) of Christ, for this new wesen was an impossibility for other human beings before Christ was transfigured or »went away« and the Comforter came.[122]

Marpeck again focuses attention on the cross, under which the treasure of Christ (that is, the Holy Spirit) is hidden.[123] Through the cross, of which the resurrection and ascension are indivisible parts, Christ is transfigured (*verklärt*). At this point Marpeck appears to ascribe two aspects to this transfiguration. First, Christ receives a new kind of body. Second, the Holy Spirit, the mediator of the new participation between the divine and created realities, is made available to others. In faith, one receives the divine Spirit through acts of others and offers that Spirit to still others through one's own activity.

Here Marpeck builds on a distinction Rothmann made between *zeychen* and *wesen* to describe this process, which includes physical reality, of receiving and

---

119 *Vermahnung*, 233.26-30. Blough, *Christologie Anabaptiste*, 130-34, rejects Kiwiet's contention (Kiwiet, *Pilgram Marbeck*, 84) that Marpeck's notion of the »Ordnung Gottes« was derived from Denck's covenant theology and suggests Schwenckfeld's Strassburg writings as a possible source. It is now clear that Marpeck's use of order owes much also to the notion of *Gerechtigkeit* derived from the mystical tradition through Schiemer and Schlaffer.

120 *Vermahnung*, 227.29: »eines newen wesens in Christo.«

121 I render this use of *Wesen* by Marpeck with the English, hypostasis understood in its theological sense derived from the Greek, meaning one person, or entity, composed of two unified but unmixed natures. Grimm, *Deutsches Wörterbuch*, 14:559, notes this usage of *Wesen* in German as early as the fifteenth century: »eyn selfstendik wesyn« (*persona*).

122 *Vermahnung*, 227.36-40.

123 Ibid., 224.10-11.

giving the Spirit. Rothmann wrote, »Whoever gives or receives a sign (*zeychen*) of one unified thing and does not heed the *wesen* (substance), is he not a traitor?«[124] Marpeck changes *wesen*, from meaning substance, to expressing a unity between the internal (spiritual) and external (material) aspects of baptism:

But whoever has the truth in the heart (which one offers and manifests with the external sign [*zeychen*]) to him it is no sign but one *wesen* [hypostasis] with the internal reality.... [W]here one rightly receives the external sign, so must he of necessity bring the internal and external *wesen* [essences] with him. Wherever and whenever that happens, the sign is no longer a sign but one *wesen* [hypostasis] in Christ.[125]

By having the truth in the heart, Marpeck means that one, through faith, has experienced the »birth of the Spirit« or has received the Spirit.[126] When that person turns to another, he or she offers the Spirit to a second person through a concrete act such as baptism. If the second rightly receives that act (that is, with faith), he or she also receives the Spirit. Therefore, the external act is not simply a sign, standing for spiritual reality, but participates in and bears the divine Spirit – it is one hypostasis in Christ.

Marpeck grounds this unity in the unity of the Godhead. Again, using the Johannine theme of coinherence, he writes, »For what the Father does, the Son of Man does at the same time – the Father as Spirit internally, the Son as a human being externally... therefore, the external baptism and Supper in Christ is no sign but the external work and *wesen* [hypostasis] of the Son.«[127] Here, Marpeck develops a more comprehensive framework for his notion that baptism, the Supper, and even ordinary works of mercy of the gathered community are a prolongation of the incarnation. Christ was two natures (divine and created) in one hypostasis. According to Marpeck, this hypostatic union continues through the activity of the divine Spirit, poured out through Christ's cross (that is, his death, resurrection, and ascension). The external *wesen* of the Son is comprised of those concrete, material acts performed by believers (baptism and the Supper). The internal *wesen* is the Spirit from the Father. Since the Father and Son are one, the material acts of believers are one participative reality with the divine Spirit.[128]

124 Ibid., 206.42-43.
125 Ibid., 207.19f. Bergsten, *Pilgram Marbeck*, 54; and Fast, *Bemerkungen zur Taufanschauung der Täufer*, 140-44, note this appropriation of the term *Wesen* from Rothmann. Bergsten identified it as the key to Marpeck's teaching on the inner and outer human being. The *Theologia Deutsch* may have inspired Marpeck's peculiar use of the term. Cf. *TD*, 1/7.3-7, 9/18-10.1, 45/89.14-17.
126 *Vermahnung*, 207.35.
127 Ibid., 207.29f. Blough, *Christologie Anabaptiste*, 113, notes Marpeck's use of the contemporaneous adverb »zugleich,« while the translations of Luther and Zwingli rendered the adverb in John 5:19 as »gleich.«
128 Rollin Armour, *Anabaptist Baptism*, 120, 134, judged Marpeck's theology of baptism the most profound in his study and called this synthesis of the inner and outer aspects of baptism his most interesting contribution to the doctrine.

Again, a modalistic strain is perceptible in Marpeck's trinitarian and christological thought at this point. He asserts that the Father works through the Spirit.[129] Further, in the prolongation of the hypostatic union, Marpeck speaks of the union of the divine Spirit with external wesen of Christ, or the physical acts of believers. He tends to substitute the Spirit for the Word as the divine nature of Christ.[130] It should also be noted that Marpeck's strange use of the word *wesen*, as substance sometimes, and other times as an hypostasis of the divine Spirit and the human person whose spiritual (internal) and material (external) aspects were thereby integrated, led to confusion in his exchange with Schwenckfeld.

It appears, however, that his intention in developing the latter sense of *wesen* was to overcome the division between the spiritual and the material, perceptible among the *Geister*, in order that the material might also be included in the restoration of Christ. Because Helena Streicher maintained that external elements or acts could not be »spirit and life« because of their earthly nature, Marpeck felt that she did not understand the integrative activity of the Holy Spirit (the *mitwürkung des geistes*), through whom created and uncreated realities might participate intimately, as a spiritual reality (*geistlicher wurcklicheit*) without the loss of their own *wesen* (substance).[131]

Therefore, she denied the participation of the human nature of Christ in »spirit and life« and could not understand the pivotal role of the cross in making Spirit available to others.[132] For her part, Helena accused Marpeck of making the cross an idol and Christ merely a creature.

In the *Juditium*, Schwenckfeld calls Marpeck's affirmation that »whoever has the *wesen* [substance] or the truth in the heart,... to him is it no longer a sign [*zeichenn*] but one *wesen* [substance],« a disorderly mixture (*unordenlich gemenge*). In his view, Marpeck mixed the spiritual in the bodily and the bodily in the spiritual and put God and the creature in one *wesen* (substance).[133] He compares Marpeck's doctrine to the transubstantiation of the scholastic theologians and demands that Marpeck define what he means by external *wesen* and clarify what kind of *wesen* (substance) it is – divine or created.[134]

It is clear that, by *wesen*, Schwenckfeld means substance or essence and, by order, he means the categorical separation of the created and uncreated substances. He accuses Marpeck, therefore, of having only a created Christ whose flesh was capable of sin and of teaching a Sabellian or patripassionist doctrine of the Godhead.[135] On the same grounds, Schwenckfeld criticizes Marpeck's assertion of the unity of the internal and external aspects of the Supper and baptism. According to the Latin definition, a sacrament is a sign of a holy thing.

---

129 Ibid., 125 nn. 67, 68, Armour notes this Sabellian tendency of Marpeck.

130 Blough, *Christologie Anabaptiste*, 184, observes Marpeck's occasional identification of the Spirit with the divine nature of Christ.

131 *Antwort*, 182.18f.

132 Ibid., 181.17f.

133 *CS*, 8:182.39, 186.29f.

134 Ibid., 8:184.35f., 183.26f.

135 Ibid., 8:184.23ff., 183.38f., 284.28-30.

Therefore, there are two different things present, not one as Marpeck claims. The elemental sign does not and cannot participate in the uncreated thing itself.

1543: *Verantwurtung*

In answer to Schwenckfeld's charge that he mixes the *wesen* (substances) of the created and uncreated realities, Marpeck replies that he never said that he regarded the »elemental substance« (*substanz*) of the water as the inner *wesen* (substance of the Spirit).[136] He explicitly draws attention to and defends his double usage of the word *wesen*: »Consider well the word (*wesen*), whether one ought not distinguish or whether it might not be helpful to understand it [*wesen*] not just as the invisible godhead itself, but to distinguish between *wesen* (substance) with *wesen* (hypostasis).«[137] In support of this distinction, Marpeck refers to the reality of the untransfigured Christ on earth which was »one bodily, visible *wesen* [hypostasis] in and with the invisibility of the Word as the third person of the Godhead.«[138] Therefore, Marpeck states explicitly what had been implied in the *Vermahnung* – that *wesen* in one sense is the unified, concrete hypostasis or person combining the two distinct but not separate natures of Christ. With this notion of *wesen*, Marpeck fills out the content of his Strassburg statement, »the natural and supernatural may exist together.«

He objects that Schwenckfeld teaches only the »inner and transfigured, majestic, impassive Christ in heaven and not the suffering Christ on earth, the Word in its glory and majesty and not in its cross and affliction.«[139] Marpeck, for possibly the first time, responds to the 1538-39 shift in Schwenckfeld's Christology. By stressing the heavenly nature of the transfigured Christ, Schwenckfeld, according to Marpeck, excludes both now (since Christ's transfiguration) and then (during his earthly existence) the creaturely component.

Since Marpeck's primary commitment was to the inclusion and therefore salvation of created humanity, he responded by questioning the nature of that transfigured Christ, which allowed Schwenckfeld to exclude all natural, created realities. Marpeck, therefore, asserts, »Christ is not yet fully glorified; he lacks his untransfigured body [*unverklerten leib*]« which is »his community.«[140] In response

---

136 *Antwort*, 165.12f. See also ibid., 124.30f.: »bleibt wasser wasser, wein, wein, brot, brot.«

137 Ibid., 136.49-137.2: »Gedenk man dem wort (wesen) wol nach, obs nit zu unterschaiden sey, obs auch auf nichte gang, raicht oder verstanden mög werden, dann allein auf die unsichtbare gottheit selbs und nit zwischen wesen mit wesen underschaid sey.«

138 Ibid., 137.2f.: »Betracht man, wie Christu als das unverklärt haubt auf erden in und mit der unsichtbarkeit des worts als dritter person der gottheit ein leiblich wessen was.« It is unclear what Marpeck means by this odd expression. It is possible that dritter is mistaken reading of zweiter by Loserth, because Marpeck speaks elsewhere (*Bekenntnis*, 161ʳ) of the »götliches wesen gottes vaters, suns und heiligen geists.« If it is not a false transcription, it is possible that, since the Spirit mediated the union of Christ's divinity (Word) and humanity (*leiblich wesen*), Marpeck conceived of the bodily hypostasis as a manifestation of the Spirit, or third person of the Trinity.

139 *Antwort*, 160.33f.

140 Ibid., 154.25f.

to Schwenckfeld's projection of the heavenly nature of Christ back into his earthly existence, Marpeck projected, as it were, in the opposite direction – the earthly nature of Christ, which included created, physical reality, into the heavenly nature of Christ. After Christ's death, resurrection, and ascension, his earthly nature (untransfigured body) was henceforth to be constituted by those believers who received his Spirit. Marpeck refines his statements concerning the contemporary reality of Christ in the *Bekenntnis* and the *Vermahnung*. Rather than two different bodies, a pre– and a post–transfigured body of Christ, Marpeck posits a twofold body of Christ – the transfigured body of Christ (which is not yet perfect) at the right hand of the Father and the untransfigured body of Christ (composed of earthly members gathered by his Spirit). Marpeck writes, »Therefore we speak of the right inner and outer aspects of the believer, that is an actual *wesen* [hypostasis] according to the inner and outer aspects even into the eternal majesty of the heavenly [*wesen*].«[141] Here Marpeck appears to go a step farther to say that the outer aspects (created, physical reality) will be, eternally, a constitutive part of the heavenly nature.

Marpeck goes on to use *wesen* as hypostasis to develop a conceptual framework by which he identifies the gathered community as the untransfigured body of Christ in its internal (spiritual) and external (physical) and thereby in its individual and social aspects. To describe the relationship of the believer to the Spirit of Christ and to the community, he employs two formulations – *wesen des glaubens* and *wesen im herzen*.

As we have seen, faith is that receptivity through which the Spirit »reaches into and secures [the believer's] spirit.« The divine Spirit and human spirit thereby become one *wesen* (hypostasis) of faith.[142] The external aspect of the human being is, in turn, ordered by the internal human spirit and the two become one *wesen* (integrated being) in the heart:

that the *wesen* [integrated being] in the heart of believers reports everything which is attested to through faith. It manifests one truth, the external with the internal, and the internal with the external. Just as there are two parts or two human beings which attests one whole human being as internal and external in two obediences.... The inner obedience with our spirit (which is first born to purity, Matt. 23) belongs to the Spirit of Christ, who secures our spirit (Romans 8). The external obedience of the external human being (understand the absorbed body of the believers) belongs to the spirit of that human being vitalized by God.[143]

---

141 Ibid., 126.21f. See Blough, *Christologie Anabaptiste*, 200, for his comments on the »deux corps.«

142 *Antwort*, 112.20-23.

143 Ibid., 123.26f. Cf. *TD*, 37/71.3-8. In the union the »ausser mensch von dem ynnen wol geordnet und gelert das man da keiner ausser gebot oder lere darff.« But Marpeck goes beyond the Frankfurter to imply that the right and left eyes, in the Frankfurter's words, are harmonized in the new human being. Cf. also *TD*, 8/18.3f.

Marpeck describes two movements through which the whole human being participates in the divine. The human spirit receives (through faith) the vitalizing Spirit of Christ and then acts (from the heart or love) to order the body. The new human being is one integrated entity (*wesen im herzen*), which enjoys participation in, or is one hypostasis (*wesen des glaubens*) with, the divine Spirit.

Because of the dependence of the body on physical reality, this integration or harmony of body and spirit necessarily involves one with others: »With this external obedience, the whole believing human being, according to one's internality and externality, as with spirit, soul and body, becomes, in the obedience of the body of Christ, that is his holy community, a member of that body... where one member serves the other for the improvement of the body of Christ.«[144] Therefore, whatever is done in the community – baptism, the Supper, foot – washing, or other acts of brotherly love – is all »one work in and through the Spirit.« The community as the »untransfigured body of Christ« is constituted by the Spirit through the concrete acts of believers.

In contrast to the old human being (*alte mensch*), characterized by a self – enclosed mode of existence (*aigen annemen*), the new human being (*neuer mensch* or *neues wesen*) is characterized by a participative or relational mode of existence. Participation in the divine through the Spirit necessarily involves the human being in relationships of receiving and giving with other human beings. One cannot receive the Spirit except through concrete acts of others. So, the many believers are bound together in one interdependent body through the Holy Spirit.

As to Schwenckfeld's question about what he means by an »external *wesen*« and whether it is of a created or a divine status, Marpeck says that it is »[t]hat work, which takes place externally from faith, an external testimony of love, such as a gift and help for the poor from unselfish love, an inner working of the Spirit. Is that not one thing or deed? So that the external enacts what the internal attests and it is true of the internal what the external indicates.«[145] The ontological status of the gift remains unchanged, but it bears the reordering Spirit, through which the human being receives participation in the divine reality and thereby a harmony in the whole person. For Marpeck, it is not an either/or issue. The gift remains a natural, created reality but it participates in and therefore bears the uncreated.

Marpeck manifests here a pervasive sacramental theology. Through an act of a believer, who has received the reordering Spirit of Christ, grace, or that Spirit, is conveyed to a willing recipient. As Marpeck said in the *Vermahnung*, »whoever has the truth [that is, the Holy Spirit] in the heart (which one offers and manifests with the external sign), to him it is no sign but one *wesen* [hypostasis] with the internal reality.« For example, because the body and external acts of the believing elder are one hypostasis with the Spirit, the water (which remains water substantially), with which he baptizes another believer, bears that Spirit. If

---

[144] *Antwort*, 123.38f.
[145] Ibid., 125.31f.

received by the recipient in faith, the elder and the baptizand are bound through the Spirit in one participative reality (the untransfigured body of Christ). The water is not only a zeugnis, or testimony, of the willingness of the baptizand, but also may be seen as a *zeug*, or means, by which the Holy Spirit is conveyed by the elder.[146] His understanding is unusual in at least two ways. First, there is a twofold rejection of an *ex opere operato* character of a ceremony.[147] For grace to be conferred, the recipient must be willing or manifest the receptivity of faith, and the ceremony must be administrated by a person of faith, that is, someone who has received the reordering Spirit. Second, Marpeck extends those external acts which convey the grace of the Spirit to virtually any act of love or gift given to another, such as a gift to the poor.

Schwenckfeld had used wesen to denote substance and he defined order as the division of created from uncreated substances. For Marpeck, order described that participation of created realities in the uncreated which was embodied in the new *wesen* (hypostasis). Far from excluding it, the new *wesen* of the believer and even the »heavenly *wesen* of Christ« necessarily includes created, material reality:

And it cannot be said that the external *wesen* [hypostasis] exists, is or is effectuated without the physical creature, for the members of the body of Christ... do not work without physical creatureliness. It may not be said that the human being may be blessed outside the flesh of his body and that must happen in the flesh of his body through the grace of Jesus Christ.[148]

Further, Marpeck asserts that Christ in his new heavenly *wesen* may not otherwise be known than through the physical existence of other believers, for they through faith in Jesus Christ do outwardly what they see the Father doing inwardly.[149] Therefore, Marpeck not only defines the identity of the gathered community as the untransfigured body of Christ, but also insists that a person can neither know nor be saved by the transfigured Christ apart from the concrete life of that community.

---

146 See chapter 4 where Marpeck's use of the word zeug suggests that this notion of the element as a means might stand behind his understanding of zeugnis.

147 Blough, *Christologie Anabaptiste*, 160, points out Marpeck's rejection of an *ex opere operato* character of ceremonies, noting that it is necessary for the believer to accept the divine reality offered. It should be added that Marpeck manifests a Donatist tendency in that it is also necessary for the one administering the ceremony to be operating from the new *Wesen*.

148 *Antwort*, 126.25-30.

149 Ibid., 126.31-35.

Chapter 6

AUGSBURG: CONFESSIONAL PLURALISM AND POLITICAL CONFLICT

During Marpeck's residence (1544-56) in the imperial city, Augsburg was embroiled in the struggle between Charles V and the Schmalkaldic League. Since the Augsburgers held conflicting political and ecclesiastical loyalties, the events on the battlefield had wrenching consequences in the city. Therefore, the final phase of Marpeck's work and thought is considered in the context of the social, political, and ecclesiastical dynamics which led to the 1555 Peace of Augsburg.

AUGSBURG'S SOCIAL AND POLITICAL STRUCTURE

Augsburg experienced its guild revolution even earlier than did Strassburg. In 1368 the weavers led a popular uprising against the patriciate in which the city books, seal, and keys to the gates were seized. The ensuing negotiations produced the first *Zunftbrief*, which prohibited any »imperial, royal or ecclesiastical law« from interfering with the city's own social contract. The second *Zunftbrief* made guild membership a requirement for all merchants and created eighteen large guilds. The thirty – four guild masters (some guilds had two) and fifteen patricians (picked by the guild masters) comprised the Smaller Council *(Kleiner Rat)*. This council, along with the Bürgermeister, was the city's most important deliberative body. The Larger Council *(Großer Rat)* combined the Smaller Council and twelve representatives from each guild.[1]

The next century saw a decrease in the number and power of the patrician families, while a new commercial class gained economic and political power. The Fugger family is a notable example of these increasingly influential merchants. In the late fifteenth and early sixteenth centuries the Fuggers invested in Hungarian copper mines, manufactured weapons in Augsburg, opened trade connections to Lübeck, Danzig, and Antwerp, and participated in the Indian spice trade. Their 500,000 guilder loan to Charles for his imperial election was repaid with a contract for copper, silver, and salt, as well as with a monopoly in the East

---

[1] Martha White Paas, *Population Change, Labor Supply, and Agriculture in Augsburg 1480-1618*, 10-11.

Prussian amber trade and in the Spanish tin and mercury trade.[2] By 1545 the
house of Fugger held assets of 6.25 million guilders and sizable debts from
Charles V (2 million guilders), Ferdinand I (593,108 guilders), and even Henry
VIII.[3] This powerful group of merchants encouraged more local control by the
city government over against the episcopal administration.[4] However, during the
Reformation period, they joined the patricians in maintaining loyalty to the Old
Church. In fact, since the number of patrician families had dwindled to seven
(including Rehlinger, Welser, Langenmantel, Herwart, and Ilsing), thirty – eight
families were raised to the patriciate in 1538 (including Fugger, Baumgartner, and
von Stetten).[5]

Below this upper class of patricians and rich merchants, a broader group of
large craftsmen and city officials exercised significant political influence. At the
top of the guilds' political structure, they dominated the city's councils, as well as
the office of Bürgermeister. Even some of the smaller craftsmen enjoyed a degree
of political participation in decisions concerning their own craft.[6] The evangelical
movement took firm root and found its strongest advocates in this group.

Wage earners and those outside the guild structure (that is, domestic servants
and beggars) comprised a lower class in Augsburg. Having little upward mobility
or political power, this group, nevertheless, bore a disproportionate burden of
the city's military responsibilities.[7]

In 1544, when Marpeck arrived in this imperial city of some 30,000 residents,
the middle – class guildsmen, mostly sympathetic to the Lutheran cause, were at
the height of their political power. Although Charles V had supported the Old
Church at the Diet of Augsburg and suspended evangelical services in June 1530,
popular pressure for the reform had slowly produced change. In December 1531
the council called for new Protestant preachers (Zwinglian).[8] By 1534 only seven
churches kept the mass and the Carmelites, Dominicans, and Franciscans left the
city. Two years later Augsburg joined the Schmalkaldic League and secured its
protection by endorsing the Wittenberg Concord (May 1536). On January 17,
1537, the Larger Council abolished the mass, dissolved the cloisters and required
all clerics to buy citizenship.[9] In 1545 Jakob Herbrot, the Bürgermeister and
master of the furrier guild, headed this powerful Protestant faction. In opposition
to the patricians and great merchants, he raised property taxes, fortified the city,
and prepared for war with Charles V.

    2 Ibid., 22-24. See chapter 1 where the Fuggers invested in the Rattenberg mines during the
time of Marpeck's activity there.

    3 Wolfgang Zorn, *Augsburg: Geschichte einer deutschen Stadt*, 183-86.

    4 Rolf Kießling, *Bürgerliche Gesellschaft und Kirche in Augsburg im Spätmittelalter*, 355. By the
sixteenth century the city controlled its own currency and finances and the bishop had moved his
residence to Dillingen.

    5 Zorn, *Augsburg*, 183.

    6 Claus – Peter Clasen, *Die Augsburger Weber*, 74.

    7 Paas, *Population Change*, 15.

    8 Hugo Steiger, *Geschichte der Stadt Augsburg*, 118-19.

    9 Zorn, *Augsburg*, 180f.

Although weakened, the loyalists to the Old Church could, for several reasons, never be totally suppressed in Augsburg. First, they benefited from the external influence of Cardinal Otto Truchseß and Charles V and had the considerable internal, financial support of the Fuggers, Welsers, and Baumgartners. Further, the unity of the Protestant movement suffered from disputes among the evangelical preachers concerning the nature of the presence of Christ in the Supper.[10]

We turn now to a brief survey of the eventful period of Marpeck's residence, giving attention to Augsburg's internal and external political affairs and their impact on the city's ecclesiastical situation.

ECCLESIASTICAL CONTEXT

The Political and Church Struggle, 1546–55

Strengthened by a 110,000 guilder loan from the Fuggers, Welsers, and Baumgartners, Charles V marched against the Schmalkaldic League in the early summer of 1546.[11] Four days before the council decided to enter the fray, the evangelical preacher Michael Keller, in a sermon at St. Moritz on Luke 12:1-12, compared the activity of the pope to »the whoredom of the Pharisees« and exhorted: »O dear councilmen, you are in the hands of Christ and no one can snatch you from them... strengthen and increase the faith and let us not abandon the cross.... Act, so that we do not now shame ourselves.«[12] Schertlin von Butenbach, the Stadthauptmann, gathered a force of 4,000 in June and left about 1,500 men to guard Augsburg while he took to the field on July 9.[13] By July 23, Dillingen, the abandoned residence of Cardinal Truchseß, had fallen. This represented the first step in the plan of the city fathers to establish a territorial sovereignty outside the city walls, free from episcopal domination.[14]

With the support of another sizable loan from the Fuggers and 180 horsemen contributed by the cardinal, Charles V won the upper hand in September. By

---

10 Friedrich Roth, *Augsburg Reformationsgeschichte*, 1:201ff. In the late 1520s Urbanus Rhegius and Stephan Agricola (Castenbaur) had argued for the Lutheran position against Michael Keller and Johann Seifrid. Bürgermeister Rehlinger had supported this view. But under Herbrot a Zwinglian tendency increased, particularly with the advent of the preachers Johann Haller (Zurich) and Bernardino Ochino (Geneva) in 1542.

11 Paas, *Population Change*, 22. This money was lent to Charles V without the knowledge that he intended to use it in the war against Augsburg. When the council learned of this, it forced the Fuggers, Welsers, and Herwarts to lend an equal amount to the city's war effort. Hans Baumgartner refused.

12 Steiger, *Geschichte der Stadt Augsburg*, 125.

13 See below concerning the Anabaptists from Marpeck's circle who were arrested July 8 for rejecting military service.

14 Jürgen Kraus, *Das Militärswesen der Reichstadt Augsburg 1548-1806*, 19.

October Truchseß was back in Dillingen and the Augsburg council capitulated on January 24, 1547. After capturing John Frederick, the elector of Saxony, and Philip of Hesse in the spring of 1547, Charles returned to Augsburg in July with an occupation force of about 3,500 soldiers. There he called a diet, lasting from September 1547 until January 1548, to bring the empire's political and religious factions to order. The result was the transfer of political power to the patricians and the reestablishment of the Old Church.

As with twenty–five other cities in Southern Germany and Austria, Charles dissolved Augsburg's Protestant–dominated guild government and reinstituted the political dominance of the patriciate. Two Stadtpfleger (one Protestant, one Catholic) replaced the Bürgermeister and, with five patricians, comprised the Privy Council (Geheimer Rat), which ran the city's business, finance, and appointments to office. Of the forty–one members of the Smaller Council, thirty–one were patricians. The Larger Council was reduced to a forum for the artisans, who were in the minority, and merely confirmed decisions from above.[15] In the summer of 1549 the Privy Council dissolved the powerful guilds, sold or took over their halls, and appointed deputies to oversee the particular crafts.[16]

As the basis for unity in church affairs, the Augsburg Interim was proclaimed as imperial law on May 17, 1548. While reinstituting the daily mass, confession, vestments, and the observance of holy days, the Interim allowed a modified version of the doctrine of justification by faith, the marriage of priests, and the Supper in both kinds. After the emperor's departure in September, the council appointed a commission to oversee the order of the six churches left to the Protestants. In these churches the worship service proceeded as before until after the sermon, when one of the four specially appointed priests stepped in to celebrate the mass.[17]

It was a disheartening time for Augsburg's Protestants. At the 1548 celebration of the Feast of Corpus Christi, all must have seemed lost. Cardinal Truchseß headed the procession carrying the monstrance under a canopy held by six princes, including the Lutherans, John Frederick and Philip of Hesse. Behind them, Charles V and his brother, Ferdinand I, bore candles followed by a host of German nobles, princes, and other dignitaries.[18] Then in August the evangelical preachers were required to swear an oath to observe the Interim. However, the evangelicals, led by Johann Held, resisted the reinstitution of confession and baptism according to the old rite. In the meantime, the cathedral chapter had returned and Cardinal Truchseß had called Michael Helding to preach in the city. Helding's sermons on 1 John, stressing the sacrifice of the mass, faith and works, and the sacrament of penance, were published and widely circulated in the city.

15 Ibid., 34-35; and Zorn, *Augsburg*, 190-91.
16 Clasen, *Die Augsburger Weber*, 74.
17 Roth, *Augsburg Reformationsgeschichte*, 4:249-50.
18 Ibid., 4:130.

However, the Catholic population of the city had effectively diminished to about 10 percent and attendance at the mass was very small.

The long occupation (July 1547-September 1548) of Augsburg by Charles and his Spanish troops evoked antipathy among the city's lower classes. In order to quarter the 3,500 foreigners, the working craftsmen had to sacrifice food and in some cases their beds, and many sent their wives and daughters out of the city for protection. Because of the chronic shortage of firewood, the Spaniards at times burned the citizens' furniture and flooring. Further, the February 1548 public execution of Sebastian Vogelsberger, apparently innocent of the charge of collaborating with the enemy, aroused strong opposition from these working craftsmen. The result was a deeper resentment toward the Old Church in whose name Charles acted.[19]

In the years 1549 and 1550 Protestant life flourished again in the city, in spite of the restrictions imposed by the Interim.[20] However, Charles's return to the city in 1550 for another imperial diet ended this period of relative calm. When Spanish troops disturbed a Protestant service a street fight broke out at St. Ulrich's. Then in July Charles examined and dismissed all but four of the Protestant preachers and fourteen teachers in the city's schools. From August until December 1551 there were no Protestant services in Augsburg. It appears that most people stayed away from the churches. As few as ten persons attended mass in any one parish; and few brought their children for baptism. Some went to Strassburg to be married and fathers served as emergency pastors in the homes.[21] Because of popular unrest, the council recalled Caspar Huber in December to minister to the Protestants at St. Anna's parish, but under its strict supervision. Wolfgang Musculus, who had left the city for Bern in 1549 after eighteen years as an evangelical pastor, wrote a book (April 1552) of comfort and instruction to the city's oppressed Protestants. Drawing a distinction between suffering under unjust coercion and doing injustice, Musculus said that a Christian is obligated to either suffer or flee coercion but should not resort to retaliation (*gegengewalt*).[22]

The fortunes of Augsburg's Protestants took another turn as King Henry II of France along with Elector Maurice of Saxony, Landgrave William of Hesse, and Margrave Albrecht Alcibiades initiated the so–called War of Liberation against Charles in the spring of 1552. Seizing the opportunity afforded by the advance of Maurice's troops, Augsburg, led by the merchant Georg Österreicher, returned to the pre–1548 guild government. On April 5, 1552, Jakob Herbrot was elected Bürgermeister and the Smaller Council consisted of forty guildsmen and only fifteen patricians.[23] Having Charles on the defensive, Maurice negotiated with Ferdinand the Passau Treaty which allowed Lutheran worship in the empire

19 Ibid., 4:57.
20 Ibid., 4:341.
21 Ibid., 4:391, 399.
22 Ibid., 4:396-98.
23 Zorn, *Augsburg*, 193.

until the next diet. In August the emperor's troops entered Augsburg once again and Charles dissolved the guild government. However, he gave the Protestants permission to observe services prescribed by the 1530 Augsburg Confession.

On September 24, 1552, the council asked Melanchthon to suggest pastors to fill the depleted ranks. By the end of the year five Lutheran pastors, including Georg Melhorn, Jakob Rülich, and Stephan Agricola (son of Castenbaur), had joined the older, mostly Zwinglian, pastors in Augsburg. Led by Melhorn, the new pastors denounced Zwingli and Oecolampadius from the pulpit and criticized the divergence of the older pastors from the definition of the real presence in the Wittenburg Concord. Georg Meckart and Leonhard Bächlin defended Zwingli and Oecolampadius and led the opposition to the Lutheran emphasis on the real presence. The Augsburgers seem to have supported the Zwinglian view as Melhorn's congregation dropped from seven hundred to about thirty. After a heated literary exchange with Bächlin, Melhorn was relieved of his pastoral responsibilities by the council in May 1555.[24]

From February to September 1555 a diet met in Augsburg to establish peace in the empire. Convened by Ferdinand I, the diet lacked strong papal representation and support from Charles V, the German electors, and many of the princes. The Catholic and Protestant princes, concerned for their own territorial prerogatives, were forced to accept disagreement on the religious issue. The Augsburg Peace, issued on September 25, provided that each estate could choose between Lutheranism and Catholicism.[25] Since those in Augsburg's ruling regime had mixed allegiances, this principle, *cuius regio eius religio*, meant that both churches, despite Cardinal Truchseß's objections, could exist without restriction from the other.

Anabaptist Activity to 1544

From 1524 to 1527 Augsburg was the center of South German Anabaptism. Many of the movement's leading figures visited the city: Ludwig Hätzer (twice), Hans Hut (thrice), Hans Denck (twice), Balthasar Hubmaier, Hans Bünderlin, and Jakob Groß. In August 1527 the so–called »Martyr's Synod« convened to discuss differences concerning the relation of the Christian to civil authority and eschatology. The sources reflect three groupings among the participants: first, sympathizers of the increasing Spiritualism of Denck and Jacob Kautz; second, a group of Swiss Brethren led by Groß, Hans Beckenknecht, and Gregor Maler; and third, the followers of Hut.[26] Hut's testimony reveals a disagreement between the last two groups on the oath and the carrying of weapons.[27] The

---

[24] Roth, *Augsburg Reformationsgeschichte*, 4:275f.
[25] Ibid., 4:194.
[26] Werthan Gerhard, *Zur Geschichte der Augsburger Täufer im 16. Jahrhundert*, 63.
[27] C. Meyer, *Die Anfänge des Wiedertäufertums in Augsburg*, 227-28.

Swiss forbade both to the Christian.[28] However, Hut maintained that God had forbidden neither the swearing of oaths nor the carrying of weapons.[29] Others such as Jakob Dachser and Hans Schlaffer agreed with Hut on these issues but resisted his speculative eschatology.[30] The city fathers, alarmed by the large number of Anabaptists in the city, passed ordinances in October 1527 and May 1528 forbidding rebaptism and the housing of Anabaptists.[31] We have already seen the impact this exodus of Anabaptists had on Strassburg in the spring of 1528.

By 1533 a small group of Anabaptists had reemerged in the city. Concerned about the violent tendencies exhibited in Münster, the council had several suspects arrested. One was Jörg Probst Rothenfelder, or Jörg Maler. Maler had been baptized in 1532 by Sebolt Feuchtner, the leader of a small group which included Sabina Hieber. Most of those arrested recanted and were expelled from the city.[32] After trips to Moravia and Switzerland, Maler returned to Augsburg for his wife, Anna, and was arrested again in 1535. His testimony reveals two groups with whom he then had contact. One group centered in the house of Helena von Freyberg in Rosenau, just outside the city gate to the east. The members included Pauls Weckerlin (weaver), Philip Schloßer, and Bernhart Schmidt (wool carder). The other group, including Sixte Bartholome, Jörg Weckerlin (brother of Pauls), and Matheus Ott (weaver), gathered in the valley between the city and the Wertach River to the west.[33] This latter gathering evinced a Swiss influence perhaps mediated by Maler, for one of their number, Matheus Ott, rejected the oath.[34] Helena von Freyberg, Maler, and Schmidt were banned from the city on April 15, 1535, while Jörg Weckerlin and many of the others recanted.[35] A 1536 letter to the Barons of Hesse reveals the attitude of the council toward the Anabaptists. Anabaptists were expelled, not because of their faith but because of their »frechait, ungehorsame und widersessigkeit,« and tendency to withdraw and therefore destroy the »gemainen burgerschaft.«[36]

There was also a small Schwenckfeld following in Augsburg. After his departure from Strassburg, Schwenckfeld resided in Augsburg (1534-35) and won

---

28 For Groß see chapter 3.

29 Some have doubted the reliability of this source because of Hut's earlier rejection of the sword against Hubmaier at Nicolsburg. However, Werner Packull, *Mysticism and the Early South German–Austrian Anabaptist Movement, 1525-1531*, 103-4, has shown that the *Hutterite Chronicle* confused the Hubmaier–Hut conflict with the later controversy between Jacob Wiedemann and Johann Spittelmaier. Therefore, this testimony very likely reflects Hut's genuine position.

30 For Schlaffer see chapter 2.

31 Friedwart Uhland, *Täufertum und Obrigkeit in Augsburg im 16. Jahrhundert*, Disser-tation, 159, 176-77.

32 St–A.A, Strafbuch 1533-39, 12^V.

33 St–A.A, Urgichten, April 5, 7. Heinold Fast provided transcripts of these hearings.

34 St–A.A, Strafbuch 1533-39, 50^V. Ott testified that he had received in 1534 a letter from Ma-ler, who was then in Switzerland. As we shall see, Maler later testified that he also rejected the oath at this time.

35 St–A.A, Strafbuch 1533-1539, 50^V, 52^r.

36 Uhland, *Täufertum und Obrigkeit*, 258.

the sympathies of the Bürgermeister, Ulrich Rehlinger, and several members of the city's most influential families, including a Welser, a von Stetten, and Regina Regel.[37] In view of their later correspondence, he may also have become acquainted with Helena von Freyberg.

Maler returned to Switzerland, first to St. Gallen and then to Appenzell, where he was the Vorsteher of the community criticized by Marpeck in 1542-43 for its strictness.[38] Because of the intercession of her two sons, Helena was allowed back into Augsburg in 1539 and lived there until her death in 1545.[39] Although never cited to appear before the council, she continued her Anabaptist activity. Hans Jakob Schneider, an important leader in the later group around Marpeck, testified in 1562 that, as Helena's tailor in 1542, he had been instructed by her in the fundamentals of the Anabaptist faith.[40] At about the same time she received the *Vermahnung* from Marpeck and forwarded it to Schwenckfeld and relayed Schwenckfeld's letter to Marpeck.[41] It is likely that Marpeck visited her in Augsburg during this time and she probably played a role in his settling there in the beginning of 1544.

MARPECK IN AUGSBURG, 1544–56

Professional Activity

From the first year of his residence in the city, Marpeck took a leading role in two of the city's most important public works – the wood supply and the water system.

In the first notices of Marpeck's presence in Augsburg, he is referred to as »Herren Paumgartners diener« and was paid on February 16 and May 10, 1544, for his work in »meiner Herren wälder.«[42] Since Hans Baumgartner was lord of Hohenschwangau in the southern, upper Lech River region and the city bought firewood from a mining work in the same region, it is possible that Marpeck worked first for Baumgartner and thereby became involved in delivering wood to the city.[43]

---

[37] Steiger, *Geschichte der Stadt Augsburg*, 112.

[38] See chapter 5.

[39] Gerhard, *Zur Geschichte der Augsburger*, 113.

[40] St – A.A, Urgichten, 1562, August 5.

[41] See chapter 5.

[42] St – A.A, Baumeisterbuch (BMB), 1544, »Gemeines Ausgeben,« 68ʳ-68ᵛ. Marpeck's acquaintance with Hans Baumgartner may stem from Baumgartner's investment in the Rattenberg mining works 1518-25. Bayerisches Hauptstaatsarchiv, Gerichtsliterialien: Hohenschwangau 2: Codex diplomaticus, 361ᵛ.

[43] Baumgartner was a strong Catholic supporter and was raised to the patriciate in 1538. He married Anton Fugger's niece, Regina. In 1548 Charles V named him an imperial Freiherr and

We have already noted the adverse effects of Augsburg's chronic wood shortage on its citizens during the emperor's occupation of 1547-48. According to one contemporary observer, the forests were depleted for several miles around the city and Cardinal Truchseß, his rentmaster, and other lords and nobles who controlled the outlying areas, sold wood to Augsburgers at ever–increasing prices.[44] In April 1545 the council appointed a commission of four, including the guild master Joachim Langenmantel, to consider the problem and bring a recommendation for its solution.[45] As in Strassburg, Marpeck suggested to the commission that the city buy its own forests in the upper Lech region, oversee the timbering, and float the wood into Augsburg on the river. On May 12 the council ordered the city *Baumeister* to hire Marpeck and on June 27 signed a twenty–eight–year lease on a forest belonging to a convent in the area of Hoheneck.[46] The following month Marpeck was paid sixty–five guilders for his »*muehe und arbait*« on behalf of the city and engaged as a full–time employee to supervise the work in the city forests.[47]

The Schmalkaldic War, the imperial diet, and the change in the city government delayed the project until 1548, when the city Baumeister was replaced by the three patricians, Melchior Ilsing, Anthony Welser, and Heinrich Rechlinger. With the permission of Wilhelm of Bavaria and Ilsing's enthusiastic support, Marpeck had a large amount of timber cut in the forest near Füssen and bound together in rafts for the trip to Augsburg. The results were just short of disastrous. The Lech's turbulence and frequent twists and turns wreaked havoc on the rafts. After three unsuccessful attempts, several flotillas finally reached Augsburg. Because of the wastage, a toll by Wilhelm, and the extra wages paid for the dangerous work done in the winter, a cord of wood cost three times the normal price.[48] In spite of this early setback, it appears that Marpeck continued

appointed him as one of the five patricians, who with the Stadpfleger comprised the powerful Privy Council.

[44] Paul Hektor Mair, *Grundliche und ordenliche Beschreibung der notwendigsten und fürnembsten Handlungen... in des löblichen Reichs Stadt Augsburg... 1548–1565*, 69.

[45] St–A.A, Ratsprotokolle (RP), 1545, I, 58[r].

[46] Ibid., I, 84[r]; and BMB, 1548, 48[v]. The council paid 2,400 guilders. Hoheneck may refer to Hochegg, which lay between the vogtei belonging to the bishop of Augsburg and the Pflegamt at Füssen and is near present–day Roßhaupten.

[47] July 18, 1545. BMB, 1545, »Amtsleute Sold,« 63[r]. In 1546 Bürgermeister Herbrot bought two more forests, BMB, 1546, »Gemeins Ausbegen,« 50[v], 52[v]. Marpeck's responsibilities also included a new waterwork.

[48] Mair, *Gründliche und ordenliche*, 70-73. See also Paul von Stetten, *Geschichte des Heiligen Römischen Reichs Freyen Stadt Augsburg*, 451-52. Marpeck estimated that about 100 cords were delivered on this first attempt. It is possible that up to 50 men worked for Marpeck in this project, for he bought 45 pairs of wading boots in December 1548. BMB, 1549, »Gemeins Ausgeben,« 41[r].

to supervise the city's timbering in the upper Lech forests.[49] In 1549 he was provided with a horse and an expense account for his work outside the city.[50]

During this time the city tax records show that Marpeck lived in a house owned by Constantius Müller, the city *Baumeister* until the change of government in 1548.[51] Just north of the St. Moritz Church, the house was located on the same block as the prominent guildhalls of the weavers, the merchants, and the patricians.[52] The records also show that Marpeck was never taxed. Because of a housing shortage and a recent increase of foreigners in the city, the council decided in 1544 not to accept any new applications for citizenship.[53] As an *Einwohner*, or registered resident, and city employee, Marpeck was exempt from city taxes and military service.[54] Sometime between October 1552 and October 1553 Marpeck moved to the water tower beside the Haustetter gate at the southern end of the city.[55] He lived there until his death in 1556.

At the same time that he was supervising the wood supply, Marpeck undertook a major project in Augsburg's water system. Between October 18, 1544, and February 28, 1545, the city paid him forty-three guilders to draw plans for a new project.[56] In May, when the council ordered the Baumeister to hire Marpeck, Bürgermeister Hoser paid a city cabinetmaker twenty – eight guilders to produce a model of the project.[57] When he entered the city's employ in the summer of 1545, Marpeck directed the construction of the »new waterwork« (*newen   prunnenwerckh*).[58] Usually   referred   to   simply   as   »Pilgrins Pronnenwerckh« in the records, it appears that this project corresponds to the new work, which the records indicate was »at the bleacher outside Jakob's gate.«[59] So Marpeck may have duplicated the work he had done earlier in St. Gallen by providing water conduits to a bleacher to aid the city's important weaving industry. By 1550 the Augsburg Baumeisterbuch lists »Pilgrins

[49] BMB, 1551, »Pilgrins Prunnenwerkh,« 38[r]. On September 27 he was reimbursed for supplies he provided for the »Holzknecht im Oberland.«

[50] BMB, 1550, »Gemeins Ausgeben,« 62[v]. J. C. Wenger, »The Life and Work of Pilgram Marpeck,« 157, reports that Marpeck may have been in Allgäu near Bregenz in 1549, which is quite believable. Bregenz is just southwest of the city forest in Füssen.

[51] St – A.A, Steuerbücher, 1544, 61[b]. The Steuerbücher for the years 1545-52 show Marpeck at the same address.

[52] The Steuerbücher refer to this tax district as »Vom Weberhaus.« I am grateful for Claus – Peter Clasen's personal assistance in deciphering these books.

[53] Von Stetten, *Geschichte des Heiligen Römischen*, 378. In 1546 this decision was extended for three more years. See ibid., 390.

[54] Claus – Peter Clasen, *Die Augsburger Steuerbücher um 1600*, 49, observed that the »nit – nemen,« which was often written by Marpeck's name, referred to the Einwohner, who paid no tax. Kraus, *Das Militärswesen*, 99.

[55] St – A.A, Steuerbücher, 1553, 16.

[56] St – A.A, BMB, 1545, »Gemeins Ausgeben,« 42[r], 43[v].

[57] Ibid., 46[v].

[58] Ibid., 1547, »Gemeins Ausgeben,« 53[v]: Pilgrins pronnenwerckh; 63[r]: newen prunnenwerckh.

[59] Ibid., 1554, 238[v].

Pronnenwerckh« as a special rubric, rather than including payments authorized by Marpeck in the general expenditures (*Gemeins Ausgeben*).[60]

The payments to craftsmen, itemized by Marpeck from 1550 to 1556, indicate the other projects he supervised. A significant amount of money and time went to renovate the old water tower near the Haustetter gate. There were two towers at this location. The first and oldest tower provided water for the city. Built in 1416, this tower contained a pumping mechanism driven by the current of the spring entering the city at this southern gate, forcing water through wooden pipes to the public fountains throughout the southern part of the city. Marpeck probably lived in or around this tower. The second one–story tower was built in 1470 to feed more water into the system. Marpeck added two stories to this tower.[61] Further, it appears that he helped expand the network of pipes in order to furnish water to more outlets.[62] In addition, Marpeck supervised the beginning of Conrad Wiedenmann's construction of a dike on the Reichstraße and may have been involved in building a dam on the Lech to direct more water to the city.[63]

Because of his varied responsibilities, the title of Marpeck's position is difficult to determine. When employed by the city in 1546, he received a yearly salary of 150 guilders (paid quarterly) and was listed under »Werckleute.«[64] His contract and the oath he took upon entering office are unfortunately no longer extant. But, as was customary, he probably laid two fingers or his hand on the contract and swore to uphold the interests of the city in performing his responsibilities. From 1547 to 1550 he is listed second, behind Hans Tirol, the city *Bauvogt*. Thereafter, Marpeck's name is the first among the »Werckleute.« Thus, Stadt–*Werkmeister*, or public works director, seems to be the most accurate title.[65]

Georg Loscher was Augsburg's *Brunnenmeister* and directed the important pumping station providing water for the northern end of the city.[66] However, Marpeck seems to have had responsibility for as much or more of the water system as Loscher.[67] In addition to the numerous craftsmen he commissioned to

60 Ibid., 1551, 38^r-39^v.

61 Wilhelm Ruckdeschel, *Das Untere Brunnenwerk zu Augsburg durch vier Jahrhunderte*, 86-88. Wilhelm Ruckdeschel, *Die Brunnenwerke am Roten Tor zu Augsburg zur Zeit des Stadtsbrunnenmeisters Caspar Walter (um 1750)*, 64, says that the small tower was raised between 1556 and 1559. However, the data shows that the work began before Marpeck's death in 1556.

62 Von Stetten, *Geschichte des Heiligen Römischen*, 389, dates this work around 1546.

63 In 1551 Wiedenmann took responsibility for this job (St–A.A, BMB, 1552, »Conrat Wideman,« 48^v). In 1554 the Augsburg council got permission from Albrecht of Bavaria to build this dam. See von Stetten, *Geschichte des Heiligen Römischen*, 476, 506.

64 St–A.A, BMB, 1546, »Amtleute Sold,« 89^r. Marpeck's salary was comparable to those of other city officials: Stadtschreiber: 400 gld.; Ratschreiber: 248 gld.; Steuerschreiber: 150 gld.; and Stadtartzt: 120 gld.

65 Von Stetten, *Geschichte des Heiligen Römischen*, 451.

66 This »Machina Augustana« fascinated the Italian physician, Hieronymous Cardanus, who included a description and drawing of it in his *De Subtilitate* (1553).

67 Loscher's (40 gld.) salary was considerably lower than Marpeck's. His expenditures were also less. For example, in 1556 Marpeck signed for over 2,214 gld., while Loscher spent close to 127 gld.

produce parts and materials for the various projects, Marpeck employed a number of wage earners across the city.[68] Anthony Hildebrand, who also lived in the water tower, worked closely with Marpeck and took over the city's southern waterworks after Marpeck's death.[69]

In conjunction with the work of Loscher and Wiedenmann, Marpeck's extension of the old tower, expansion of the piping network, and damming of the Lech had a significant impact on the city.[70] Between 1558 and 1560 citizens of Augsburg, for the first time, could connect to the pipelines and have running water in their houses for the yearly rate of ten guilders.[71]

Anabaptist Activity

From his entry into Augsburg in 1544 until his death in 1556, Marpeck was the leader of a persistently strong Anabaptist group.[72] Information about the group's life comes from the letters of Marpeck and Jörg Maler, preserved in *Das Kunstbuch*,[73] as well as from the protocols of hearings of group members in 1545, 1546, 1550, and 1562.[74] These sources reveal: 1. something of the group's strength, composition, and meeting places; 2. its internal order and literary production; 3. its relation to civil government; and 4. its relation to Augsburg's evangelical and Catholic churches.

Members and Meeting Places

The nature of the sources makes it difficult to determine the precise strength of the group. Even under physical torture, members were reluctant to identify associates and letters carried only occasional special greetings from or to particular persons. However, between 1544 and 1562, forty–five people are identified by name or profession or both. Among the men there were two city employees (Marpeck and Hildebrand); twenty craftsmen (five tailors, three

---

[68] Called »Pilgrams volck,« the average weekly wage was about 12 gld.

[69] St – A.A, BMB, 1557, 141ʳ.

[70] Marpeck may have advised other cities concerning waterworks, or, perhaps, timbering. See Johann Walch's report in KR 1:186, and chapter 3 n. 49.

[71] Jürgen Zimmer, *Die Veränderungen im Augsburger Stadtbild zwischen 1530 und 1630*, 28.

[72] Hans Jakob Schneider (St – A.A, Urgichten, 1562, July 22, August 5) testified: »Der Bilgram selig sei ir vorgeer und lerer gewesen hab.... Seins glaubens genossen seien alle vom B[ilgram] seligen herkommen.«

[73] *KB*, nos. 2, 3, 13, 14, 15, 16, 17, 18, 19, 27, 28, 33, 34, 35, 36, 37, 38, 40.

[74] St – A.A, Urgichten, 1545, 1546, 1550, 1562. The hearings of 1545-46 were occasioned by the refusal of some in the group to participate in the Schmalkaldic War. In 1550 Maler and Jörg Seifrid (not a member of Marpeck's group) were arrested because both had been previously expelled from the city. Several of the group were arrested because Hans Herzog, a new arrival in Augsburg who associated briefly with the group, published a tract under Johann Flinner's name. Flinner was a former evangelical pastor who had moved to Strassburg.

shoemakers, two weavers, two cutters, one tinsmith, one mason, one watchmaker, and one furrier); and eight domestic servants. In addition, there were ten women, who worked in their own homes. Further, some of the laborers involved in Marpeck's public works projects may have been participants.[75] Therefore, the bulk of the known members came from the working craftsmen and servants.[76] The meetings took place in the homes of leading members: Marpeck's apartment near the weavers' hall and the water tower, where he, Anna, their maid (Barbara Nagensenfftig), and Anthony Hildebrand lived; Jörg Maler's apartment after his return to the city in 1548; the apartment of Hans Jakob Schneider and his wife, Kunigunda; and Hans and Anna Schmidt's house after 1550.

Order and Writings

Although there is no church order from the hand of Marpeck, there is an undated one by Marpeck's associate, Leupold Scharnschlager, preserved in *Das Kunstbuch*.[77] While quite similar to the 1527 Rattenberg order, Scharnschlager's articles reflect some adjustments made during the 1530s and 1540s. For example, Article 1 states that a person should not forsake the assembly but, during times of persecution, the group should gather with discretion. Also, Articles 3 and 5 stress that the sharing of goods should be strictly voluntary and the elder responsible for the distribution should examine the lives, circumstances, and motivations of the recipients. This was probably directed against perceived excesses among the Hutterites. Article 6 emphasizes, against the Swiss congregation, that the *Gewalt Christi* exercised in mutual discipline should not ruin or tyrannize but improve the fellow believer. A confession, written by Helena von Freyberg, indicates that both private and public confession of sin were practiced in the group, followed by a word of promise and reconciliation through the blood of Christ, spoken by the Vorsteher or an elder.[78]

Aside from letters, Marpeck and members of the group produced two major theological works during this period: the *Testamenterleütterung* and the *Verantwurtung II*. The *Testamenterleütterung* is a large concordance of biblical verses arranged in 118 topics relating the Old Testament (*Gestern*) to the New Testament (*Heute*). Its purpose was to refute those who, by projecting the merits of Christ back to the Old Testament believers, denigrated the suffering and

75 St–A.A, Wiedertäufer– und Religionsakten, Facs. III, 1562, August 12. Hildebrand testified that he »hab gleichwol meinen herrn werckhleut vil bei sich gehabt.«

76 This distribution corresponds to the analysis of Gerhard, *Zur Geschichte der Augsburger*, 115, as to the social composition of all Augsburg Anabaptists in hearings 1526-73. Of 323 Anabaptists, 2.5 percent came from the upper–class nobles, patricians, and rich merchants, 78 percent from the middle–class working craftsmen and city employees, and 14 percent from wage earners and domestics.

77 *KB*, no. 19.

78 Ibid., no. 28.

resurrection of Christ and denied the article of the Apostles' Creed concerning the necessity of the descent of Christ to proclaim redemption to the patriarchs. By confusing the covenants, the opponents also perverted the rightful use of earthly power and allowed it to be used against God's purposes.[79] This concordance seems to have been compiled by Scharnschlager in Ilanz.[80] However, according to the 1550 testimony of Jörg Seifrid, Marpeck's »brotherhood« published it in Augsburg with their own printing press.[81] Published before 1550, and perhaps before May 1, 1547, the *Testamenterleütterung* was used extensively in the *Verantwurtung II*.[82]

This latter book was the promised second part of Marpeck's answer to Schwenckfeld's *Juditium*. It appears that Marpeck wrote the first part of the *Verantwurtung II* – concerning original sin, the children of God, the Word of God, civil government, the churches, the disciples of Christ, and the faith of the patriarchs – between 1547 and his death in 1556.[83] Then Scharnschlager probably finished the work, possibly by 1558, adding the last section containing contradictions in Schwenckfeld's writings.[84]

Relation to Civil Authority

As we have seen, the attitude of the Augsburg council was relatively mild toward Anabaptists in the 1530s. Concerning his 1533 expulsion from the city, Jörg Maler later reported a private conversation at the time with Wolfart

[79] CC, 52.

[80] The writer of the first part of the *Verantwurtung II*, whom I judge to be Marpeck (see following) cites the *Testamenterleütterung* (hereinafter listed as *TE*), and writes: »Mit welches buechs inhalt in disen und andern sachen wir dann wol zufriden seind« (*Antwort*, 343). It is possible then, that Marpeck did not compose the *TE*. Gerhard Hein, *Leupold Scharnschlager: Ein Mitarbeiter Pilgram Marpecks*, 6-12, concludes that Scharnschlager composed the *TE*. Klassen in *CC*, 52, also thinks that the evidence points in Scharnschlager's direction.

[81] St–A.A, Urgichten, 1550, May 5. It is possible, then, that an Augsburg printer was associated with Marpeck's group or at least sympathetic with it.

[82] Schwenckfeld (*CS*, 11:21) wrote that the Anabaptists had published a big book against him dealing with the faith of the patriarchs.

[83] Jan J. Kiwiet, *Pilgram Marbeck*, 64, 76, correctly detected two different writing styles. The first section (to p. 408 in Loserth's edition) reflects Marpeck's style and argumentation. Although Walpurga von Marschalk includes among the authors the elders Sigmund Bosch, Martin Blaickhner, Valtin Werner, Anthoni Müller (Hildebrand?) and Hans Jakob (Schneider), the latter three do not appear to have had the literary capacity to actually have written the work, and the first two probably represent two of the »alten brüder und glaubigen in allen landen« who received, judged, and passed the manuscript on.

[84] Valtin Werner wrote to Scharnschlager August 26, 1559, reporting that he had learned through a Veit Schneider about »die fertigung des buechs« through Scharnschlager's »vil feltigen müe und arbait.« See *Zwingliana* 4 (1926): 332-37, for the text of the letter. Perhaps Scharnschlager took over the work after Marpeck's death because no one in Augsburg was capable of finishing it. It is possible that Marpeck made and carried with him a manuscript copy of a tract written by Schwenckfeld against Bucer and cited it in the *Verantwurtung II*. See Blough, *Christologie Anabaptiste*, 79.

Bonifatius, the evangelical preacher at St. Anna's. Bonifatius confided that the council did not want to force Maler from his faith or expel him. He would be allowed to meet with four or five people for discussions and works of mercy if he would swear the oath read to him. Maler replied that he could not agree with certain things in the oath. Then the preacher assured him that the oath was only important as a sign of willing obedience because the »councilmen, themselves, were divided – some favoring the Old Church and others the Lutheran.«[85]

However, because of the increased strength of the Protestant party under Herbrot and the impending Schmalkaldic War, the council began to take sterner measures against the city's Anabaptists. In the summer of 1545 the councilmen passed ordinances providing stricter controls of midwifery and printing.[86] Further, when he was hired on July 16, 1545, Marpeck was reprimanded concerning »seiner sect.«[87] The following month the city's street patrols were instructed to watch for gatherings of the »gartenbrüdern« (a term used in Augsburg for Anabaptists). In September the council appointed a commission of three councilmen and the evangelical pastors Musculus and Johann Held to handle Anabaptist cases.[88]

On October 29, 1545, Jörg Weckerlin, Hans Jakob Schneider, Jörg Seifrid, and Hans Schleiffer were given one month to agree not to baptize anyone and to bring their children to their parish churches for baptism. Apparently the last three men agreed, for only Weckerlin was expelled.[89] The following summer on July 8, the day before Schertlin von Butenbach entered the field against Charles V, five Anabaptists – Schneider, Seifrid, Georg Kraft (furrier), Hans Eberlin (weaver), and Ulrich Knoll (mason) – refused to take their turn at the watch on the city walls. Schneider seems to have been the spokesman for those associated with Marpeck (Kraft and Knoll).[90] Asked if he had sworn the yearly oath, Schneider replied that he had. When queried as to why he now refused to do what he had sworn to do with his oath, he responded that he had, up until then, and wanted to continue to carry out all of his civil responsibilities so far as that was possible. However, he could not find it »in his conscience« to keep the watch and especially to assail the enemy. He confessed that he would rather die than do so. All five Anabaptists were banned from the city on July 29.[91]

In April 1550 Jörg Maler was arrested and questioned concerning his Anabaptist activities. Maler testified that he was expelled from Appenzell because

---

85 St – A.A, Urgichten, 1550, April 28.

86 Von Stetten, *Geschichte des Heiligen Römischen*, 386-87.

87 Roth, *Augsburg Reformationsgeschichte*, 3:279 n. 80.

88 Ibid., 3:247.

89 St – A.A, RP, 1545, II, 42^V, 43^V.

90 St – A.A, Urgichten, 1546, July 16. Schneider named Knoll, Kraft, and Marpeck as brothers. Seifrid does not appear to have belonged to Marpeck's group.

91 Ibid., Strafbuch, 1543-53, 82^r. A note on the margin says that Schneider was allowed back in the city in 1561, but he must have returned before then because a 1555 letter from Hans Bichel (*KB*, no. 36) reports on the status of Pilgram and Hans Jakob in Augsburg. Seifrid recanted on December 18 and was allowed to live in the city.

he refused to fight against the emperor, and came to Augsburg at the time of Vogelsberg's execution (February 1548). When asked about his position on civil authority, he expressed his disagreement with the prohibitions of the Swiss against all oath – taking, the carrying of weapons, and the recognition of civil courts.[92] Maler maintained that a Christian may and should swear oaths because they furthered the need of the brother, maintained love, and promoted justice (gerechtigkhait).[93] Further, carrying a sword was no sin, but misusing it was. Unfortunately there is no source to determine Maler's criteria for judging what constituted a misuse of the sword. As for civil courts, Maler said that since the Obrigkeit was established by God and had power over adultery and other matters, it was appropriate to go before a public court to confess to or accuse another of public misconduct.[94] Under torture, Maler asserted that he kept his opinions to himself unless he was asked and then he was dutybound to reply. Asked whether they would create a regime as in Münster if the Anabaptists grew in numbers, Maler replied that they would do nothing except comport themselves as Christians so as not to offend anyone. Further, he had »absolutely nothing to do with the Münster insurrection« and did not consider the Münsterites Christians.[95] Refusing to recant, Maler was expelled April 26, 1552, after a long imprisonment.[96]

Schneider and Maler, two of Marpeck's closest associates, agreed that the Christian could and should swear the oath and wanted to fulfill their civil responsibilities. However, Schneider categorically rejected any use of deadly force, while Maler approved of it when it was justified and not misused. Apparently, Maler's refusal to fight against the emperor in Appenzell reflected his judgment that that constituted a misuse of the sword. Marpeck's own position on civil government will be developed in chapter seven. Here we note that, although Schneider (1546) and Maler (1550) both mention his name and Jörg Seifrid testified that he had printed the Testamenterleütterung in the city, there is no record of an interrogation of Marpeck. As in 1545, he was warned two more times, 1553 and 1554, but apparently no action was taken.[97] His value to the city as public works director probably outweighed the embarrassment of the gatherings in the water tower.

---

92 See chapter 5.

93 In another statement on the oath (KB, 157ʳ), Maler states that he formerly agreed with the Swiss on the basis of the dominical command (Matt. 5:34). But, on the basis of Jesus's implicit acceptance of oaths (Matt. 23:12-22), Paul's appeal to God to testify to his soul (Rom. 1:9), and Paul's acceptance of those who swear by one greater than they (Hebr. 6:16), he concluded by saying that Christ never forbad oaths and that love of neighbor should be the criterion for every act, including oaths.

94 St – A.A, Urgichten, 1550, April 23.

95 Ibid., Urgichten, 1550, May 3.

96 Ibid., RP, 26, I, 50a.

97 Ibid., RP, 1553, II, 17ʳ: September 26, 1553; and RP, 1554, II, 18ᵛ: September 20, 1554.

Relation to the Religious Establishment

The only records of discussions between members of Marpeck's group and Augsburg's established clergy are those of Maler's discussion with Bonifatius (1533) and his exchange, in 1550, with the Lutheran preachers Johann Held (St. Anna), Johann Flinner (Helige Kreuz), and Johann Meckart (St. Georg), as well as with Johann Faber, the Catholic Domprediger.[98] From Maler's account, the brief arguments dealt strictly with infant baptism and achieved no common agreement.[99]

Relations to Other Groups

Inside Augsburg

In 1545 there was a small group of about fourteen Anabaptists who were influenced by the Moravian Hutterites. Gathered around Magdalena Rayserin, this group received Leonhard Sailer and Hans Klöpfer from Schakwitz and decided to resettle in Moravia. They paid an Augsburg raftsman, Hans Penntz, to take them down the Lech to the Danube and then headed east. However, they were apprehended at Grafenwerdt in lower Austria and taken to Vienna for hearings.[100] Whether Marpeck had contact with this group is uncertain, but in his letters he did maintain his criticism of the Hutterites' strict insistence on the community of goods.[101]

From Jörg Seifrid's 1550 testimony, we learn of another group of Anabaptists, which gathered in Sabina Hieber's house in the Khappenzipfel district.[102] According to Seifrid, who had recanted and returned to Augsburg in 1546, the group included five women (Hieber, a Margareth, Regina Weißhauptin, an Elß, and an Appel) and met together four times per year or whenever a meeting was needed. Shortly before his hearing, he had left the group because he felt that Sabina Hieber had not properly cared for the older Appel when she was sick and he disagreed with some foreign brothers who taught in one of the meetings.[103] Contact between this group and the Marpeck group is uncertain, although Seifrid had expressed interest in buying a copy of the *Testamenterleütterung*.

98 *KB*, 164ʳ. Roth, *Augsburg Reformationsgeschichte*, 3:248-49, states that the preachers also had discussions with Marpeck, but gives no source.

99 As a result of his discussion with Maler, Faber wrote two tracts in 1550 against the Anabaptists: *Christliche undterweisung an die Widertauffer and Von dem Aydschwören*. See Roth, *Augsburg Reformationsgeschichte*, 4:399-400 n. 20.

100 See Uhland, *Täufertum und Obrigkeit*, 261-62; and Gerhard, *Zur Geschichte der Augsburger*, 85, 134. See Karl Schornbaum, ed., *Bayern II: Abteilung*, 141-54, for the protocols of the hearings.

101 See chapter 7.

102 As we have seen, Hieber was arrested in 1532. Apparently she recanted and remained in Augsburg in 1533 and discreetly sponsored this small group.

103 St–A.A, Urgichten, 1550, May 5.

The 1553 investigation of the Schwenckfelders, Bernhard Unsinn, Balthasar Marquart, and Leonhard Hieber, reveal that the Silesian had a significant following in Augsburg during these years. In addition to these craftsmen, members of some of the city's most distinguished families (Ulrich Rehlinger, Ulrich Welser, Simprecht Hoser, Anna Regel, and Hans Jakob Fugger) manifested interest in Schwenckfeld's spiritualistic piety.[104] The sympathy of his fellow townsmen to Schwenckfeld's position no doubt impressed upon Marpeck the importance of refuting Schwenckfeld and setting forth his own more structured ecclesiology in the copious *Verantwurtung II*.

Marpeck's Influence Outside Augsburg

As he had done in the years before settling in Augsburg, Marpeck continued to work for the identity and unity of the Anabaptist movement. One means to that end was the circulation of general letters in Switzerland, Alsace, Southern Germany, and Moravia on particular theological themes. Preserved in *Das Kunstbuch*, these letters represent Marpeck's attempt to shape a theological identity for the Anabaptists. They deal with: three kinds of human beings (no. 38), the dead in sin (no. 2), repentance (no. 18), the love of God and cross of Christ (no. 4), the humanity of Christ (no. 5), Christian service and servants (no. 16), and the church (no. 33). Unfortunately two other letters on Gelassenheit and the Lord's Supper have been lost.[105] Further, Marpeck travelled or wrote letters to congregations in Switzerland, Moravia, Southern Germany, and Strassburg, addressing specific issues and attempting to forge a basis for unity among the groups.

We have noted Marpeck's ongoing relationship to Leupold Scharnschlager in the production of the *Testamenterleütterung* and *Verantwurtung II*. In 1545 he wrote a letter to him as the Vorsteher of the Ilanz congregation and relayed one of Scharnschlager's letters to the Austerlitz community.[106] The previous year he had travelled to Chur, where members of the congregation had suffered persecution.[107] During the Schmalkaldic War, he wrote letters of consolation to Graubünden, Appenzell, and St. Gallen on Christ's cross and the depths of Christ's suffering.[108] His disagreement with the strictness of the Appenzell – St. Gallen congregation reemerged in 1551, when he refused to take sides in a dispute and urged the members to bear with one another.[109] Later, Marpeck's group

---

[104] Roth, *Augsburg Reformationsgeschichte*, 3:245-46.
[105] *KB*, no. 16, 167^r. These were sent along with the *Vermahnung* to Eibenschitz in 1552.
[106] *KB*, no. 27, 37.
[107] Ibid., no. 33.
[108] Ibid., no. 35, 4.
[109] Ibid., no. 34.

provided leadership to this congregation in the persons of Jörg Maler and Jörg Weckerlin.[110]

Moravia commanded considerable attention during this Augsburg period. Concerned that Cornelius Veh and his coworker, Paul, might take his rejection of Hutterite legalism to the extreme, Marpeck wrote in 1544 warning them against a »fleshly freedom.«[111] He may have also visited several congregations around 1550.[112] Three years later, Maler carried three of Marpeck's letters and twenty copies of the *Vermahnung* to Moravia.[113] Elders of congregations in Eibenshitz, Poppitz and »umb den Stein,« Jamnitz and »am Wald,« Znaim, and Vienna responded to Marpeck's letters, saying that they had been read in all the gatherings and thanking him for his special ministry to them.[114] In 1558 the leaders from the Eibenschitz and Znaim congregations initiated a dialogue with the Czech Brethren.[115] Apparently, some of these »Pilgramite« congregations in Moravia survived into the seventeenth century.[116]

Marpeck also had contact with a group of Anabaptists in Langenau, near Ulm. Having lived or visited there earlier, Marpeck responded quite personally in a 1555 letter concerning several members who had visited him after their expulsion from Langenau.[117] He advised the *Vorsteher*, Abraham Brendlin, to encourage an »old sister and brother« to return to Langenau and act more discreetly.[118] He also sent along a description of a remedy for the wife of a Lorenntz in Lebertal who suffered from rheumatism.[119] In the same letter he briefly developed his notion of the humanity of Christ.

This latter theme may have reflected recent developments in Strassburg. In early 1554, 600 Anabaptists met there for the first so–called Strassburg Conference. Although it is unclear from the sources, one modern scholar believes

---

110 Maler travelled to St. Gallen after his 1552 expulsion from Augsburg. See his letter, dated October 15, 1552, from St. Gallen, to Ulrich Agemann in Constance (*KB*, no. 14). Weckerlin wrote a letter (1555) as »diener der Schweizer Brüder« to Hans Jakob Schneider. Gerhard, »Zur Geschichte der Augsburger,« 82.

111 *KB*, no. 3.

112 Josef Beck, *Die Geschichts–Bücher der Wiedertäufer in Österreich–Ungarn (1526 bis 1785)*, 188 n. 1, reports that at the 1550 Landtag in Brunn, Ferdinand I discovered that »die Brüder im landt herumzogen, wie Pilgram« and ordered a strict persecution of the Anabaptists. Further, the Moravian congregations thanked Marpeck (1553) for »die Mühe and Arbeit« which he had exercised for some time on their behalf. (*KB*, no. 17).

113 *KB*, no. 16. Evidently, Maler had returned from St. Gallen by January or February 1553 and served as the carrier for this letter as well as the response (ibid., no. 17).

114 Ibid., no. 17.

115 Jarold Knox Zeman, *The Anabaptists and the Czech Brethren in Moravia, 1526-1628*, 250-52.

116 Ibid., 255.

117 *KB*, no. 15.

118 This old woman appears to have been expelled from Langenau on January 18, 1555, with her three daughters. Heinold Fast provided me with his transcripts of the Ulm Ratsprotokolle dealing with these members of the Langenau group.

119 The Vienna Royal Library, Medical Codex (no. 11, 182), no. 36, preserves Marpeck's cure for syncoma made from blackthorn juice.

Marpeck attended and was a principal motivating force behind these colloquies between the High and Low German Anabaptists.[120]

The second conference took place in August 1555 and dealt solely with the incarnation. With the Swiss Brethren, Hutterites, and Pilgramites insisting on the Adamic flesh of Christ, and the Mennonites, or Hofmannites, maintaining that Christ's flesh was celestial, the participants decided to limit their formulations to the New Testament expressions, which allowed both interpretations.[121] In his letter of January 22, 1555, Marpeck insisted that Christ's flesh »is of the creaturely kind.«[122] As the letter was also sent on to the members of the congregation in Lebertal, perhaps they had asked for Marpeck's opinion in preparation for the conference and were the »Pilgramites« who participated in the August gathering. It is doubtful that Marpeck would have been satisfied with the compromise with Hofmann's Christology, but his unifying work among the Swiss Brethren and Hutterites seems to have come to fruition in their cooperation in 1555 and again in 1557.[123]

Sometime during the week between October 31 and November 7, 1556, Pilgram Marpeck died a sudden death at about sixty – one years of age.[124] Anna probably received his last salary payment on December 16 and moved out of the water tower soon thereafter.[125]

---

[120] Kiwiet, *Pilgram Marbeck*, 66. He conjectures Marpeck's presence without documentation.

[121] George H. Williams, *The Radical Reformation*, 496-97.

[122] *KB*, no. 15, 159ʳ.

[123] The Third Strassburg Conference (1557) was less successful in unifying the High and Low German Anabaptists. The Netherlands refused to go and the High Germans refused to accept Menno's recommendation of the »hard« ban. Later that year the Netherlanders banned the High Germans. See Williams, *The Radical Reformation*, 497.

[124] On October 31 Marpeck signed for a payment having to do with the waterworks. The next entry, November 7, reads: »11 gld. 59 K[reuzer] zalt Anthoni [Hildebrand] so Bilgerumb selig verwishen.« St – A.A, BMB, 1557, »Pilgerumbs Pronnenwerck,« 45ᵛ.

[125] She may have moved in with Hans Jakob and Kunigunda Schneider, for Kunigunda testifies in 1562 that Anna had been with her during childbirth. St – A.A, Wiedertäufer – und Religionsakten, Facs. III, 1562, August 10. Roth, *Augsburg Reformationsgeschichte*, 4:249, reports: »Mancher eifrige 'Junger' mag ihm betrübt ins grab nachgeblickt haben.« A check of his sources – Buff, Christell, and Gasser – produced no reference to this.

Chapter 7

GERECHTIGKEIT AND MARPECK'S SOCIAL THEOLOGY

In the last phase of his life, Marpeck experienced some of the sixteenth century's most important events in the religious and political life of the empire. His professional responsibilities and religious activities brought him into sustained personal contact with Augsburgers from every social class, including patricians, craftsmen, laborers, servants, housewives, midwives, and wet nurses. From the vantage point of an apartment in the middle of the city and the water tower on its edge, Marpeck observed the political struggle for control of the city and the empire – a struggle often justified in the name of the true faith and the church, but fought by many who had little influence in that church or in political life.

During the final phase of his theological development, Marpeck employed the formula »a spiritual, real justice« (*geistlicher wesentlicher gerechtigkeit*) to express the individual and social transformation wrought by acceptance of the cross of Christ.[1] In this chapter we will examine Marpeck's final reflections on the new being and explore the implications of his notion of justice for his social theology.

FURTHER DEFINITION OF THE NEW BEING

In the second part of the *Verantwurtung* to Caspar Schwenckfeld and in his correspondence, Marpeck further clarified the individual and social aspects of the new being and their mutual relation. This discussion is focused on the further nuances of Marpeck's understanding of sin, the unique role of Christ's cross, and the rebirth of the human.

Sin

Schwenckfeld's charge that he denied original sin and thus perpetuated the »heresy of Pelagius« forced Marpeck to clarify his understanding of the corporate and individual character of sin and to employ a more precise terminology. In the

---

[1] *Antwort*, 261.18.

Vermahnung, Marpeck had said that original sin (*erbsünd*) was present in children before the age of *wissenheit*, but that it was not actual sin, nor reckoned as sin before God. Therefore, he also called this original sin the root of sin. In the *Verantwurtung II*, Marpeck explicitly rejected the traditional notion that original sin is transmitted in marital intercourse or inheres in physical flesh and blood.[2] He then abandoned the term inherited sin altogether, replacing it with inherited weakness (*erbbresten*): »[T]hat which comes over and in them [unknowing children], from and through Adam's fall, also because of the above mentioned inherited weakness [*erbbresten*] of children, cannot be called nor be thought of as sin or original sin [*erbsünd*].«[3] This distinction between *erbbresten* and *erbsünd* reflects Marpeck's concern to hold a dynamic tension between the individual and the community. For him, sin cannot be defined strictly in terms of the influence of the community by means of a mechanical transmission. It must also involve personal choice, which presupposes a process of individuation or personal transcendence. Marpeck further, developed both the social and individual aspects of sin.

Concerning the impact of social interaction on the child, Marpeck states more explicitly what he had implied earlier.[4] He describes the inherited weakness as a »general, worldly, natural, self–enclosed knowledge, recognition, or understanding of good and evil.«[5] It is an inherited »evil mode« which »comes over all human beings... which flows into children and is manifest in them.«[6] As has been noted, the self–absorbed mode of a child's parents and peers inevitably produces a weakness or tendency toward that mode in the child. However, this proclivity is not reckoned as sin before God. Marpeck gives two arguments for this. First, he recognizes an original grace: »For just as original sin, inherited weakness and impurity came over and in the children in Adam's loins through his fall, so also have they received the original grace [*erbgnad*] as described above through the promise in Adam's loins.«[7] After the fall, Adam and Eve received the promise of God that Eve's seed would destroy the snake (Genesis 3:15). Since all children lay then in Adam's loins, the promise and work of Christ covers them in their state of unknowing (*unwissenheit*).[8] Second, Marpeck insists that sin does not occur unless one »takes and eats from the forbidden fruit for himself in the recognition of good and evil apart from the guilt, recompense, or responsibility of Adam and Eve's sin and guilt.«[9] Therefore, sin also has a necessarily personal component.

2 Ibid., 190, 191.

3 Ibid., 213.33-36. Marpeck probably borrowed the word *erbbresten* from Zwingli.

4 See chapter 5.

5 *Antwort*, 197.12f.

6 Ibid., 205.41; 198.9.

7 Ibid., 206.46.

8 See ibid., 198.21f.; 203.40f. I concur with the opinions of Torsten Bergsten, *Pilgram Marbeck und seine Auseinandersetzung mit Caspar Schwenckfeld*, 80; and Horst Quiring, *Die Anthropologie Pilgram Marbecks*, 2:15, who identify this promise with Marpeck's *erbgnad* and disagree with Neal Blough, *Christologie Anabaptiste*, 174-76,; and Jan J. Kiwiet, *Pilgram Marbeck*, 92, who interpret erbgnad as a natural tendency toward the good.

9 *Antwort*, 199.16-17.

According to Marpeck, the child exists in a state of »created simplicity« or »unknowing« in which there is no understanding and therefore no sin.[10] In childhood two countervailing forces lie dormant. The first is that »general, worldly, natural, self – enclosed knowledge« experienced from parents and others in proximity. The second is a »good or natural light which is given by God in creation,« but which is not yet awakened.[11] In adolescence, both of these forces grow into actuality and an individuating process takes place by which the child becomes an adolescent (*jugent*), »the reason begins and the created simplicity dies and comes to an end.«[12] Inevitably, the adolescent »abandons the good and chooses or does evil which he knows and (Psalm 52) loves more than the good.«[13] There is, then, a personal volitional choice. Here, Marpeck quotes the *Theologia Deutsch* twelve times to emphasize the character of sin as knowing disobedience.[14]

But even here Marpeck mentions »the impulse and work of the snake« offering the forbidden fruit which it promises will make the adolescent as a god.[15] That promise of self – sufficiency is a tempting one for the adolescent who, surrounded by self – obsessed persons, perceives that no one else will provide for him or her. Marpeck describes the steps by which one »grows out of created simplicity« into the »general, human, natural knowledge of good and evil.« First, there is an opening of the eye or consciousness to an evil for the sake of the self. Second, a person experiences, meditates on, and remembers oneself and one's needs. Third, the acts of abandoning the Creator, of preferring creation and one's own life, and worrying about one's own care issue into all manner of »fleshly, sinful lust, desire, selfishness, evil thoughts, murder, etc.«[16] Therefore, every aspect of the human – the spirit, soul, and body – is involved in the sin.[17] Although he agrees with the Frankfurter that Adam would have sinned (that is, his spirit and soul had already fallen through his grasping, lust, and desire) had he never bitten the apple, Marpeck says that the act and injury was not complete until Adam did so. He thus stresses the concrete, material act. In this conscious movement, the human being turns from the Creator to secure his or her own life. Marpeck calls this the human being's »own distorted life« (*aigen verkert leben*) and attributes to that person an »unjust or distorted mind« (*ungerechten oder verkerten synn*).[18]

It is important to note that Marpeck insists that a process of individuation or personal transcendence must exist before sin has any meaning. It appears that this

---

10 Ibid., 194.1, 6-7.

11 Ibid., 206.4-5. With respect to the origin of individual souls, Marpeck here appears to tend toward a creationist rather than a traducianist position.

12 Ibid., 194.11-12.

13 Ibid., 208.15-17: »daraus er das guet... verlasst und erwölt oder thuet das bös, das er kennt und Psalm. 52 mer liebt dann guets.«

14 Ibid., 213.38-39; 214.3-6, 32-35; 215.2-7, 13-15, 25-31, 38-40; 259.21-26; 266.31-32, 41-42; 267.23-24; 269.43-45.

15 Ibid., 258.24-25.

16 Ibid., 208.18ff.

17 Ibid., 251.32-33.

18 Ibid., 221.26; 216.12.

same concern stands behind his insistence on the preservation of the sovereignty of the individual conscience, if faith and love are also to have meaning.

Christ

While disorder or injustice (*ungerechtigkeit*) was introduced in Adam and spread by the contagion of disordered relationships throughout all of humanity, Marpeck claims: »Before the ascent of Christ and his going to the Father, no one was justified in the justice [*gerechtigkeit*] of grace.«[19] To appreciate Marpeck's final position on the role of Christ and his cross in the restoration of social justice and individual justness in humanity, we shall examine the person, the work, and the justice of Christ.

The Person of Christ

In his 1555 letter »On the Humanity of Christ,« Marpeck continued his polemic against the *Geister* and the celestial flesh Christology of the Melchiorites by insisting on the full humanity and Adamic flesh of Christ: »the Son of Man, who was born from the virgin of the race of Judah and the seed of David.«[20] Further, the human being, Jesus, »was taken into God the Father and God the Father into the son who from eternity is one substance [*wesen*], spirit and God.« In the incarnation the human nature of Christ was drawn by the Word into intimate participation in the community of the divine life: »the incarnate word is taken in according to the measure of time – one in and with God two natures, one human being; two natures, one God, divine and human in one.«[21] As we have seen previously, this renewal of human participation in the divine life in Christ was made available to other human beings: »In him [Christ] alone all the fullness of the Godhead dwells bodily. From the fullness of the Son of God, all the true believers are filled with the Holy Spirit,« and »The transfer [*ubergab*] of the Spirit happened in the humanity of Christ.«[22] Therefore, the interruption of human participation in the divine life, introduced by Adam and spread throughout all of humanity through social interaction, was restored in the human person of Jesus.

---

[19] *KB*, no. 35, 294[r]: »Vor diser auffart Christi und zuganng zum vater ist kein mensch gerechtfertigt worden inn grechtigkheit der gnaden?«

[20] Ibid., no. 15, 158[r]-58[v]: »der sun des menschens, der im geborn ist von der jungfrouen vom geschlecht Juda und vom somen David.«

[21] Ibid., no. 13, 129[v]: »das vermenscht wort ist eingenomen nach mass der zeit ains inn und mit got. Zwu natur, ein mensch, zwu natur, ain got, götlichs und menschlichs in eins.«

[22] Ibid., no. 15, 158[v]-159[r]: »In im alein woneth die fölle der gotheit leiplich. Aus der fölle des suns gotes werden erfült alle wargloubigen mit dem h[eilige]n geist,... Die ubergab, die geschechen ist, die ist der menscheit Christi beschechen.«

The Work of Christ: the Cross, Resurrection, and Ascension

According to Marpeck, Christ voluntarily offered the Holy Spirit and, therewith, participation in his humanity and in the divine life to other human beings through his cross: »[Christ] conquered evil in the highest patience with love and truth; paid and redeemed with all good, love, fidelity, truth and mercy; gave his human and blessed life on the cross in unfeigned patience; and became a still, silent sacrificial lamb for the sins of humanity to effect their release.«[23] By stressing the love, fidelity, mercy, and patience of Christ's submission to death, Marpeck underlines the voluntary character of the act and thus the maintenance of Christ's transcendent human self within the intimate communion with the divine.

Marpeck also offers a new image for the offer and outpouring of the Holy Spirit in the death of Christ:

That is the same lord, king and true God, who gave himself with all his treasures and gifts as an acceptable new year [Luke 4:19]. That treasure was hidden or enclosed in the trunk or chest of the new covenant (that is his body), until this chest of the covenant was smashed and opened on the cross. There the consummation (*consumatum*) [John 19:30] was accomplished.[24]

Again Marpeck draws on the Johannine passion narrative in his elaboration that the consummation of Christ's work was the giving up of the treasure or the Spirit in his death. As a part of Christ's cross, Marpeck includes the descent into hell where his soul preached the gospel to the dead.[25] In Christ's death and descent into hell, »life broke out because of the power of life [*des lebens macht*], which the Lord had in him against all the power of hell.«[26] Marpeck again echoes a Christus victor motif. In his conception, the Spirit's power to restore the relationship of the human Jesus to the divine and thus to life was greater than the power of death and evil to obstruct and end it. Therefore, Christ »took life to

---

23 Ibid., no. 13, 142^V: »der inn höchster gedult mit lieb und warheit uberwunden das böss mit aller guet, lieb, treu, warheit und barmhertzigkeit, bezalt und vergolten had mit herzlichen furbit fur seine feind, sein menschlichs und seligs leben an creutz beschlossen, inn aller unfermailigterr gedult ein stilhaltend, stum und stilschweigennt opferlamb worden fur di sundt der menschen, zu irer erlösung.«

24 Ibid., no. 35, 279^V: »Das ist derselb herr, kunig und warer got, hat sich selbs mit alle seine schätzen und gaben zu einem angenemen neuen jar geschennckt, wölcherr schatz inn der truhen oder lad des punnds (das ist sein leib) verborgen und verschlossen send gwesen, bis dise lad des bunds am creutz zerschlagen und aufgespert ist worden. Do ist das consumatum gmacht worden.«

25 *Antwort*, 280. Marpeck uses Jesus's cry, »Why have you forsaken me?« (Matt. 27:46) and the Apostles' Creed to establish the descent. See *CC*, 183ff., for a discussion of Marpeck's sources and use of the descent. Bergsten, *Pilgram Marbeck*, 52, notes Marpeck's rejection of the triumphant character of the descent in Schwenckfeld. We shall return to Marpeck's implicit belief in the soul's survival of death and his expectation of a bodily resurrection.

26 *KB*, no. 35, 281^r: »do brach das lebenn aus des lebens macht (das der herr in im het, wider allen gewalt der hellen).«

himself again and ascended out of death into the heights with all who had hoped for their release in the Lord.«[27] Christ offered, through the »outpouring of the promised Holy Spirit« participation in the divine life to the living and the dead.[28]

The »*Gerechtigkeit Christi*«

Marpeck calls the restoration of human participation in the divine, justice: »[T]he Lord Christ should restore Adam's fall, sin and injury to all peoples and heathen (Acts 3, Gal.3)... and restore justice [*gerechtigkeit*] to the earth (Isaiah 28, 42) and, indeed, bring everything to order (Mark 9).«[29] Concerning the social aspect of that justice, Marpeck draws on the Old Testament prophetic tradition. Citing Isaiah 42:1-4, and Jeremiah 33:15, he affirms that the human being, Jesus Christ, »restored to and reconstituted for the earth its justice... from all of our injustice.«[30] With Christ, then, there was an establishment of right order among peoples. In addition, order was restored in the individual »in order that the human being might return to him who created him (Isaiah 17[:7]) and be converted from the devil's noose by which the devil imprisoned the human being according to the devil's will (II Timothy 2[:19]).«[31] As we have seen before, both of these aspects of Christ's justice must be held together in order to understand the process and nature of rebirth or individual and social transformation.

Rebirth

Just as sin involves social influence and personal decision, so also does its correction. Individual rebirth is impossible without social transformation and social transformation is impossible without individual rebirth. One requires and contributes to the other: »It is also pure fabrication and deceit, that some claim that the Holy Spirit inspires without the apostolic service of the churches.«[32] But, »[T]hey deceive themselves who believe that wherever they serve, teach, and baptize it must follow that therefore the Holy Spirit also inspires and teaches because of them.«[33] As has been observed, the effectuation of the new being or

27 Ibid., no. 35, 281[r]: »darfür aus der hörrligkheit, gwalt und macht des lebens, das leben wider an sich ze nemen mitten aus dem tod sambt allen, so auf den herren seiner erlösung gehoft heten.«

28 *Antwort*, 204.7.

29 Ibid., 198.30-35.

30 Ibid., 290.3-6.

31 Ibid., 290.11-13. The order brought to the individual is, apparently, that order into which the person would have grown had the adolescent not abandoned the good and chosen evil.

32 *KB*, no. 35, 295[v]: »Es ist ein lauters dicht und betrug, das etlich furgeben, als solt der h[eili]g geist geisten on die appostolisch dienstbarkhiet der kirchen.«

33 Ibid., no. 35, 296[r]: »Herwider betruegen sich die all selbs, die do maynen, wo sy dienen, lernen und touffen, do muess volgen, das darum ouch der h[eili]g geist geiste und lerne umb desswillen.« Emphasis added.

participation in the humanity and justice of Christ presupposes a strongly individuating experience of suffering and the mediation of the reordering Spirit by the community. In the Augsburg period Marpeck further elaborates these two aspects of the process toward the new being.

Personal Repentance: The »*Schuldkreuz*«

According to Marpeck, the »self–obsessed, distorted life« chosen by the adolescent results in considerable pain and suffering. The »good and natural light« given by God in creation is obscured by that distorted life but not extinguished. Marpeck also calls that light an »infused breath or spirit,« which is »of the divine mode« yet not divine itself.[34] The purpose of this light is to reveal the law of God which brings a consciousness of sin so that the human being cannot excuse him or herself from sin.[35] Therefore, the conscience is »crushed, wounded and sick.«

Marpeck calls this state the »guilt cross« (*schuldkreuz*). Citing the story of the two thieves crucified with Christ (Luke 23:33, 39-42), Marpeck distinguishes two guilt crosses. He calls the cross of the thief on the left the »guilt cross of the world,« for that thief wanted only to be released from the suffering caused by his sin (»If you are the son of God, help us and yourself down from the cross«) and not from his sin. Whereas, the thief on the right recognized that his suffering resulted from his own sin and asked to be released from the sin and not from the suffering.[36] This is the »guilt cross of the believer« and is an element of true repentance.

In the 1550 letter »On the Five Fruits of True Repentance,« Marpeck outlines the individuating process whereby a person recognizes and assumes responsibility for one's own sin. First, by means of the natural light of good, one recognizes the »justice and angry wrath of God,« realizes that »pain, anxiety, destruction, suffering and eternal death« are fruits of a sinful, self–obsessed mode of existence, acknowledges that one is guilty of eternal death without the comfort of any creature, and experiences shame in the presence of God.[37] Second, God gives a ray of hope of pardon so that the believer waits humbly for grace. Third, the true penitent wishes to be released from sin and not the suffering which is its result. Fourth, sin remains but does not rule the penitent. Although there is no comfort for the conscience, one still hopes for grace. Fifth, the true penitent »blames no creature on heaven or earth« for his or her own sin, but realizes that evil has its origins in himself or herself. So, one takes responsibility for one's

---

[34] *Antwort*, 218.51: »eingeblassnen athem oder geist«; and ibid., 223.1: »ein abgesunderter lediger geist des lebens und nit gott selbs, ob er wol göttlicher art ist.« Marpeck uses Rom. 1:20, and Matt. 8:22-23, to support the existence of this inner light. The *Theologia Deutsch* may be a source for his notion of this light.

[35] *Antwort*, 226.30; 234.13; 232.7.

[36] *KB*, no. 13, 140ᵛ.

[37] See ibid., no. 8, 173ff. See also *TD*, 11/25.1-8, for a similar affirmation concerning the abandonment by every creature.

own mode of life and does not seek to escape from the consequences of that mode, but desires that that mode be changed. Here it is important to note that this process of suffering protects the sovereignty of the individuated conscience. Through the conscious confrontation of human contingency and the deserved fruits of the self–chosen mode of dealing with that contingency, a person chooses to change.[38] Since sin involved such a choice, rebirth or healing must also include an unconstrained decision. And just as sin involved social influence, so the rebirth or change cannot be effectuated by the penitent. A person must wait patiently for grace which comes from outside the self – from God through the community of saints.

The New Community

As the human being waits, hoping for a change of his or her mode of living, the »good deeds [for example, preaching, teaching, miracles, baptism, and discipline] of the truly believing true community« serve as a necessary preparation and mediator of the Holy Spirit.[39] The believing body is the »true fountain« (rechten prunnenquellen) from which eternal life flows.[40] Through it the Holy Spirit flows into the hearts of all believers and secures them,[41] thereby releasing them from the hopeless task of securing themselves. The Holy Spirit comes from outside, grants participation in the communal and divine life and, thus, secures the human spirit in a transcendent reality. The believer participates in the first resurrection: »[T]hrough the free out–going of his [Christ's] power [craft] from above... death is no longer death, but through faith in Christ we are carried through death with the love which is stronger than death.«[42] As had been the case with the human Jesus, the Holy Spirit's power to maintain the believer in the life–giving relationship with the divine is greater than the power of death to separate the believer from that participation. Therefore, »[N]o one can overpower us again as we had done before with the deceit of our self–obsessed love of ourselves and the idolatrous love of creatures by which we, in a disorderly way, loved over and against God and our neighbor.«[43] By being secured in a reality greater than the self, the believer is freed from »the slavery of sin,« that is

---

[38] The »natural light,« given in creation, evidently enables the individual to receive the offer of the saving Spirit. Blough, Christologie Anabaptiste, 176, notes that before the advent of the Spirit, the »natural light« is capable of a natural piety – a piety which, however, does not constitute salvation.

[39] KB, no. 35, 294ᵛ, 295ʳ.

[40] Ibid., no. 35, 297ʳ.

[41] Ibid., no. 5, 297ᵛ; and Antwort, 216.18f.

[42] KB, no. 27, 238ᵛ: »durch den freyen ussganng seiner craft von oben herab.... [D]urch den glouben inn Christo send wir vom tod zum leben hindurch drunngen mit diserr lieb, die starckh ist wie der tod.«

[43] Ibid., no. 27, 239ʳ: »das uns dero keins mer begweltigen mag, wie wir vor gethon haben mit betrug eigner lieb unserr selbs sambt abgötischerr lieb zum creaturn, so wir unordennlicherweis uber got und wider got und den nechsten geliebet haben.«

from the attempt to secure the self in the world by anxious grasping. A person is freed from the compulsion to serve the self by taking from the neighbor or to serve for a reward. Rather, the believer is free to serve the neighbor »out of free grace.«[44] For Marpeck, freedom is that unconstrained receptivity and giving made possible by participation in the communal and thereby in the divine life. The Holy Spirit, poured out in the cross of Christ, grants the »participation in the love and friendship of God« and effectuates a »real, supernatural, spiritual life.«[45] Again, he employs Johannine coinherence language to describe this participation: »[W]e know that Christ Jesus is in God, the Father and God, the Father, is in Christ Jesus... and we know, acknowledge and also feel that Christ is in us and we are in Christ and remain so in eternity.«[46]

Integrated Life of the Christian

Echoing his earlier reflections concerning the *wesen des glaubens* and *wesen im herzen*, Marpeck affirms that the internal, spiritual aspect of the Christian is integrated with the external, physical aspect so that the whole human being acts in one, consistent mode. The Holy Spirit pours into the hearts of believers and »reproduces and recapitulates the perfect law of freedom of Christ« in the »lowest part of the inner human being« effecting a »purified mind« (*synn* and *gemüet*).[47] The believing spirit and soul, in turn, »maintain a rule against the undisciplined, noisome flesh.«[48] The human spirit leads the body and flesh into »a purification and turning from sin,« making them »weapons of justice.«[49] By receiving the Spirit, one's whole being is reordered and the Christian, who is part of the humanity of Christ, becomes an agent of Christ's justice in the world, through the concrete acts of his or her body.

Marpeck identifies the vocation of the Christian and the new community with that of Christ:

Therefore, also the Lord gave his messengers and servants the Holy Spirit for this office, as Isaiah wrote: The Spirit of the Lord is upon me, for the Lord has anointed and sent me to preach good news to the poor, to bind up the brokenhearted, to announce release to the captives, to open the chains of the bound, to announce the year set by the Lord and the day of God's wrath, to

---

44 Ibid., no. 27, 239[r].

45 *Antwort*, 225.40: »die werden tailhaftig der lieb und freundtschaft gottes«; and ibid., 223.40: »wesentlich ubernatürlich geistlich.«

46 *KB*, no. 7, 302[v]: »das wir wissen, das Christus Jesus inn got vaterr und got vaterr inn Christo Jesu ist und pleibt... das wir ouch wissen und erkennen und ouch empfinden, das Christus in uns und wir inn Christo send und pleiben von ewigkheit zu ewigkheit.«

47 Ibid., no. 35, 297[v], no. 13, 141[v]; and *Antwort*, 294.12.

48 *KB*, no. 13, 131[v].

49 *Antwort*, 285.32: »begebt euch selbs gott, als die aus den todten lebendig seind und eure glider gott zu waffen der gerechtigkeit.« See 2 Cor. 6:7.

comfort the sorrowful... that God may call them to justice [*gerechtigkeit*] − a plant of the Lord to which he turns.[50]

The believer's task is to serve and call others to the new order of Christ − an order in which the self−obsessed mode of individuals is broken, leading to mutuality among people. Freed from grasping and taking from the neighbor, the believer serves the neighbor, offering a share in the Spirit through concrete acts, and opposes, in word and deed, the pursuit of self−interest among others as an obstruction of the new order. The believer and the community of saints are, then, a transformed and transforming new being in the world.

It is likely that Marpeck understood much of his own activity as service to his neighbors and a calling of them to the justice of Christ. As we have seen in Strassburg and Augsburg, he sponsored a common collection to be shared with the poor. His letters to persecuted colleagues in Switzerland, as well as his exposition of the salvific potential of suffering, can be viewed as attempts to bind up the brokenhearted and to comfort the sorrowful. Further, he denounced the Schmalkaldic War as the wrath of God on those who attempted to coerce the faith of others.

Cross of the Christian

While this service and call to justice may have come as good news to some, Marpeck was convinced that these activities would inevitably elicit opposition from the unjust and thus suffering for the believer. Calling this opposition and suffering the »innocent cross of Christ« (*unschuldig creutz Christi*), he placed the activity of the believer in the cosmic context of the dramatic struggle between the snake and the seed of Eve.[51] The snake bites the heel of the incarnate Word and his bride (that is, those still present as members of the untransfigured body of the Christ). However, »the head of the serpent will be trod down, overcome and demolished by the heel, that is the weakness of the flesh and blood of Christ in his believers.«[52] Christ overcame the power of sin and death (that is, the power to separate one from the divine life through self−obsession) by submission to his unjust persecutors in the power of the reordering Holy Spirit. Having received

---

[50] *KB*, no. 35, 284[r]: »Darum auch der herr seinen gesannten und dienern zu disen ampt den h[eilige]n geist geben hat, wie Esaies [Isaiah 61:1-3] meldt: 'Der geist des herren ist bey mir, dann der herr hat mich gesalbt und gesannt, gute botschaft den armen zu verkunden, das ich die verwunnten hertzen verbind, das ich den gefanngnen erledigung verkund und den gebunndnen den kerckher aufthuee, das ich das jar verkund, das der herr angesehen hat, und den tag der rach unsers gotes, das ich tröste alle, die trauren,... das sy got der grechtigkheit genannt werden ein pflanntz des herren, deren er sich rueme.'«

[51] Ibid., no. 13, 141[r].

[52] Ibid., no. 13, 141[v]: »so wirt doch ir kopf von den versen, das ist von allerr schwech des fleischs und pluts Christi, inn seinen gloubigen durch alle gedult zerdreten, uberwunden und hingericht.«

the life–giving Spirit, the believer also overcomes the fear of death and is therefore free to offer that Spirit to the persecuting enemy. Therefore, the believer, as a member of the untransfigured body of Christ, also overcomes injustice (that is, the disordered and disordering mode of others) or restores order by the patient, noncoercive offer of the reordering Spirit poured out in the cross of Christ.[53]

As observed in chapter four, Marpeck insists that the believer makes this sacrificial offer, not in order to earn an inheritance for himself or herself, but »to offer grace and salvation and to announce through him [Christ] and in his name remission and forgiveness of sins.«[54] In the face of those who would do harm to him or her, the believer, as Christ, does not grasp and cling to his or her own life, but freely offers the Spirit to his or her enemies as the only source of their salvation.

MARPECK'S SOCIAL THEOLOGY OF THE CROSS

The task of the transformed community and the transformed individual within it is the extension of Christ's humanity and thereby Christ's justice in the world. As we have consistently observed in Marpeck, that justice involves the reordering of social relationships, as well as of the life of the individual. The reordering Holy Spirit, willingly poured out by Christ in his cross, constitutes and is mediated by the new community, which patiently offers that Spirit to others without coercion. This extended humanity of Christ, the »new being« (*neues wesen*), or »realm of Christ« (*reich Christi*) is then a social entity in which personal transcendence is maintained within social interdependence. From his notion of the realm of Christ, Marpeck drew two principles by which he developed his ecclesiology and determined the proper relation of the Christian and the Christian community to civil authority: first, the pervasive physical and spiritual interdependence of human life; and second, the sovereignty of the individual conscience.

»Reich Christi« and the Church

During the Augsburg years, Marpeck often referred to the gathered Christian community as the »community of saints« (*gmeinschaft der heiligen*).[55] Probably

---

53 Ibid., no. 13, 142ᵛ: »Das ist das aller geheiligtisch creutz Christi unnd kein schuldcreutz, darinnen... alle nachvolger Christi uberwunnden, dardurch sy den freyen einganng in got und zu got haben.«

54 Ibid., no. 27, 239ᵛ-240ʳ: »Und gar nit, das wir erst dardurch den lon oder erbschaft erlanngen. Es ist uns vor mit Christo geschennckt und verdient... sonder innen zu dienen, die gnad und heil anzebieten und verkunden durch in, undter seinem namen verzeichung unnd vergebung der sünd ussrueffen.«

55 Ibid., no. 37, 306ʳ.

taken from the Apostles' Creed, this phrase, rather than including the dead among the faithful, referred to the living, local community and expressed the dynamic tension between the individual and the community which was of primary concern to Marpeck. The church is a transformed and transforming community of individuals who have been and are being transformed. Throughout his literary career, Marpeck criticized ecclesiologies which he believed resolved the tension in either direction, thus obstructing the transformation of the individual or the community and, ultimately, both.

Critique of Radical Individualism

From Marpeck's perspective, the *Geister* resolved the tension in the direction of the individual, ignoring the physical and spiritual interdependence of human life. In chapters three and four we saw that he published his first books in opposition to the perceived denigration, by Bünderlin and Entfelder, of the material world, their lack of concern for the physical well–being of others, and their refusal to share their gifts in the concrete life of the community. He focused his refutation on the importance of the full humanity of Christ and the ordinances, such as baptism and the Supper, as a continuation of that humanity. During the Interim Years, he further developed his position in the controversy with Schwenckfeld. Stressing the created, fully human nature of Christ, including his flesh, Marpeck rejected Schwenckfeld's projection of the transfigured body of Christ back before his death and resurrection. In response, Marpeck projected Christ's earthly, untransfigured body in the opposite direction, positing a twofold body of Christ. He identified the untransfigured body of Christ as the community of saints, including all its material elements, and insisted that individual rebirth could not take place apart from mediation by and participation in that untransfigured body.

As noted, Marpeck's Augsburg activity evinces his concern for the physical well–being of others. For example, his group made a communal collection for the aid of its poorer members. He also offered medical advice to those suffering from physical maladies.[56] For Marpeck, these concrete acts were potentially sacramental in the sense that they were possible mediators of the Holy Spirit from believers to the recipients. These acts of charity and others, such as preaching, teaching, baptism, the Supper, and the ban, bound believers together in the new community to which the Spirit had been promised. Identifying that community as the spouse of Christ and the mother of the children of God, Marpeck insists that, »whoever despises the birth, care, and discipline of the mother, that one also despises the Father along with her.«[57] Because the

---

[56] See chapter 6.

[57] *KB*, no. 33, 269ᵛ: »Darum ist die gsponns Christi ein geberin, ein pflegerin und ein erziehe-rin der kinder gotes, der himlisch vater inn Christo ein versorger, ein erhalterr und ein ernörer

Spiritualists so stressed the sovereignty of the individual, Marpeck believed that they closed themselves off from the resources of the community and thus participation in the divine life.

Critique of Coercive Collectivism

While the Spiritualists overemphasized the individual, Marpeck thought that many of his contemporaries erred by resolving the tension in the direction of the community. By attempting, in the interest of the collective uniformity, to coerce faith through physical force or legalistic social control, these Christians violated the individual conscience and thereby obstructed both personal and communal transformation.

»Coerced Faith«

Marpeck's conviction that physical force was not only futile but also obstructive in matters of faith probably dates from his intercession with Archbishop Lang for Stephan Castenbauer in 1523 and his eventual refusal to obey Ferdinand I's order to extradite miners sympathetic to the Anabaptist preachers. These experiences must have inspired his warning to Bucer and Capito against relying on the civil power of Strassburg's council to reform the city's religious life. Contrasting the *gewalt* of the sword to the *kraft* of the unconstraining Spirit, Marpeck argued that only the latter could effectuate individual transformation and thus constitute a new, just community. After his exile from Strassburg, he criticized the peasants, the Swiss reformers, and the Münsterites, in addition to the Catholics and Lutherans, for the same mistake.

In Augsburg, Marpeck closely observed the often mercurial fortunes of the city's religious parties as the Protestants, led by Michael Keller and Jakob Herbrot, and Catholics, led by Cardinal Truchseß and the Fuggers, struggled for dominance. After Charles V's victory over the Schmalkaldic League and during his occupation of Augsburg in February 1547, Marpeck wrote an unpublished letter criticizing the »supposed Christians« (*vermeinten christen*) who support a »coerced, forced faith« (*gezwungner gewaltglouben*). [58] Because they replaced the unconstraining, unifying Spirit with their own power, he calls theirs a »sectarian, superficial, coerced religion.«[59]

The result is a superficial faith which cannot survive opposition and persecution, much less offer the Spirit patiently to the enemy. In a gloss on the Biblical passage, »Whoever lives by the sword will die by the sword« (Matthew

der muterr und dere kinder. Und wer der muterr geburt, pfleg und zucht veracht, der hat den vaterr sambt ir veracht.«

58 Ibid., no. 13, 136^V, no. 35, 296^V.

59 *KB*, no. 35, 296^V.

26:52), Marpeck contends: »For all humanly coerced or required faith (or whoever trusts or gives themselves to human protection and power in order to believe the word of truth) will also be destroyed again by human coercion and driven to denial, as was Peter.«[60] Echoing his Strassburg descriptions of Petrine and Iscariot Christians, Marpeck maintains that »the affliction of Christ is to them an affront and shame.« The former deny their Lord, while the latter betray him and both send »with all impatience... soldiers with shield, spear, and mace.«[61]

Of his fellow Augsburgers whom he viewed as Petrine Christians, Marpeck may have had in mind the Protestant preachers, and particularly Michael Keller. After having exhorted the city's councilmen in 1546 to take the field against Charles and Cardinal Truchseß – for the sake of the gospel – Keller was one of the Protestant pastors forced to sign the 1548 Augsburg Interim, an act which for some Protestants was tantamount to a denial of the gospel. From Marpeck's perspective, Keller's appeal to the councilmen »to strengthen and increase the faith... and not to abandon the cross« was itself a denial of the cross of Christ, which cross resulted from Christ's refusal to transgress the sovereignty of the individual conscience and to coerce faith. Among the Iscariot Christians, Marpeck numbered the »offensive and evil merchants« whom he judged worse than the pharisees who »bought the Lord from Judas out of jealousy and hatred.« In a slightly veiled reference to the Fuggers and perhaps to his former employer, Hans Baumgartner, Marpeck writes that they: »betray, sell, and buy entire lands and peoples, as well as armies through their lending, finance, and simony from greed, jealousy, and hatred in order to maintain their human glory, pride, and noble honor.«[62] He viewed their self–interested pursuit to maintain their economic and political control in the name of the true faith as the most extreme betrayal of the self–giving cross of Christ.

For Marpeck, those who exercised coercive force in matters of faith betrayed the cross of Christ in that they transgressed the sovereignty of the conscience. Therefore, they also misunderstood the nature of faith which must be a willing receptivity to the Spirit. Coercion which threatens the existence of the human being cannot secure the conscience and thus open one to resources beyond the self. It only serves to intensify the defensive activity of the self–obsessed, grasping mode. Only the patient, nonthreatening offer of the unconstraining Spirit encourages and empowers the human being to faith – to that willing receptivity. Having received that Spirit, the conscience is secured in a reality greater than the self (that is, the divine life) and is thus able freely to give to and receive from others (that is, to pursue justice). Therefore, the self–sacrificing

---

[60] Ibid., no. 33, 291^v: »Dann aller menschlischer gezwungner und genoterr gwaltgloub (oder wer sich schon, zun wort der warheit zu glouben, auf menschlich schutz und gwalt vertrost und begibt) die werden all durch menschlichen zwang wider zerstort und atriben zum verlougnen, wie Petrus.«

[61] Ibid., no. 35, 291^r.

[62] Ibid., no. 35, 292: »das jetz nit ergere und bösere kaufleuth verhannden weren,... gantze land und leuth sambt hörlegen, verraten, verkouffen und kouffen durch ir furleihen, fynanntz und wucherr aus geitz, neid und hass, irn menschlichen bracht, hofart und eytle eer zu erhalten.«

cross of Christ is a permanent protest against the transgression of the individual conscience and a witness to the futility of coercion to effect true justice in the world.

In a 1547 letter concerning the cross of Christ, Marpeck surveys those whom he believed repeated the mistake of some of the first century Jews who »expected a Messiah who would free them from all power of the heathen through physical and human arms and weapons and lead them to a promised land.« The Jews take comfort in the »Turks and sects [Protestants] carrying the name of Christ« against the emperor. The Catholics rejoice in the emperor for their protection and deliverance against the sects and Turks. The Evangelicals rejoice in everyone who opposes the emperor, whether the Turks, the French, the cities, princes, or peasants. Finally, certain sects wish to be delivered from the physical affliction and cross of Christ and take false hope and comfort in a miracle whereby God will avenge them against all their opponents with the advent of a new prophet.[63] In contrast, Marpeck maintains that followers of Christ's cross do not rejoice in these »wars, conflicts and shows of force,« but mourn for the souls of the corrupt and rejoice in the delivery of the pious.[64]

»Legalistic Coercion«

During the Interim Years, Marpeck criticized the Swiss Appenzell congregation and the Hutterites for exercising a legalistic coercion with the same results. They crushed consciences and destroyed unity by replacing the strength of the unconstraining Spirit with their own self–rationalizing power. In Augsburg, Marpeck continued his warning against judging too quickly and encouraged elders to wait for the fruit in order to judge the mode of anyone's living. He wrote the Swiss that interference in the life of another without special »prompting or a command from God« caused injury, not healing.[65] To the Hutterite leaders he advised that »whoever will be master must be the servant and slave of all and not rule over others with coercion.«[66] Again, the defensive self–obsessed mode of the individual was not lessened, but rather heightened by coercive social pressure to conform. In Marpeck's view, this rigid legalism also betrayed the free offer of the Spirit in the cross of Christ and the necessary experience of the cross of the Christian which prepared one for willing receptivity to that Spirit. For him, the »community of saints« is characterized by the members' attention to their physical and spiritual interdependence and by their respect for the sovereignty of each other's consciences. There is no healthy individual who does not realize his or her dependence on others. Therefore, Marpeck encouraged a communal penitential discipline which held each member

---

63 Ibid., no. 13, 138^r.
64 Ibid., no. 13, 138^v.
65 Ibid., no. 34, 273^v.
66 See chapters 5 and 6.

accountable for the pursuit of justice and the fulfillment of social responsibilities.[67] There is no healthy community which did not respect the sovereignty of the individual conscience. Therefore, Marpeck insisted that participation in the life of the new community must be voluntary.

»Reich Christi« and Civil Authority

To appreciate Marpeck's position concerning civil authority, one must recall that, during his formative years in Rattenberg, he was the son of a prominent councilman and Bürgermeister; he served as a city councilman, Bürgermeister, and as a representative to the *Landtag*; and filled the office of mining magistrate, exercising full civil jurisdiction over the mining community with powers to arrest, try, judge, sentence, and punish. We have observed his concern for social responsibility and his willingness to fulfill various civil duties. He then experienced a crisis of conscience when Ferdinand I demanded that he use his civil power to aid in the coercion of the recantation of those miners responding to the Anabaptist preachers' call to repentance and personal justness. Through that crisis and in his later reflection, Marpeck apparently came to the conviction that true social justice and therefore civil order was impossible without respect for the sovereignty of the individual conscience. Hence, his critical participation in civil life was also governed by his commitment to social responsibility and respect for the sovereignty of the individual conscience. The nature of that critical participation will be examined by treating his views concerning the proper role of civil authority and the Christian's responsibilities to it.

Role of Civil Authority

Marpeck's writings and activities reveal a consistent appreciation of both the negative and positive roles of civil authority, which he recognized as a good ordinance of God.

Concerning its negative aspect, we have noted Marpeck's Strassburg affirmation of the protection of the just from the civilly unjust by civil power. In the *Bekenntnis an Jan von Pernstain*, Marpeck called civil authority a »servant of God for vengeance« to maintain the pious in peace and punish the evil. During the Augsburg years, Marpeck expressed his opinion more clearly in response to an accusation by Schwenckfeld. In the *Juditium*, Schwenckfeld criticized Marpeck for stating in the *Vermahnung* that »no true Christian should assume, protect or direct with force any city, country or people (as earthly lords).«[68] In the *Verantwortung II*, Marpeck responded by saying that Schwenckfeld had left out the key words that such force does not belong to true Christians »in the guise or

---

[67] See chapter 6.
[68] *Antwort*, 303.1f.

in the name of faith in Christ« as the »papists and so–called evangelicals« exercise.[69] He then clarified the meaning of his words in the *Vermahnung* by saying: »[N]o true Christian should use coercion (as the worldly power and sword in and over the realm of this world must) in and under any name or the guise of Christ or of the gospel or faith in Christ.«[70] His objection was not that physical force should not be used, or even used by a Christian as a civil servant, but that the Christian should not use force in the name of Christ to coerce faith. He protested that Schwenckfeld wronged him by accusing him of finding fault with »God's good order.« In fact, he affirmed that even its misuse and the chaos caused by unjust rulers did not lead him to reject the exercise of force by civil authority in the »worldly rank and realm,« for it »is ordained and has power from God to do so.« Indeed, he asserted that he not only did not find fault with that order, but he prayed and gave praise, honor, and thanks for it.[71] In a letter Marpeck revealed his belief that the civil authority would continue to be a mediator between »piety and evil, the just and the unjust« until the »last human being was made blessed who should be.«[72] After that all authority would be suspended and house would fall upon house. Therefore, he construed one purpose of the civil authority to be a divinely ordained maintenance of order so that the justice of Christ might be extended. However, while civil power could secure an environment in which that justice might be extended, it could not assure its extension, that is, it could not produce faith or receptivity to the reordering Spirit.

In addition to this negative role, Marpeck implicitly affirmed the positive contribution civil authority made to social welfare. Most of his professional career was spent serving city councils in public works projects. He began that career working in Rattenberg's city hospital. As its *Holzmeister*, Marpeck provided Strassburg with wood and supported the city's office for poor relief. The St. Gallen council commissioned him to build water flumes for that city's weaving industry and domestic needs. In Augsburg, Marpeck served as the city engineer, administering projects providing the city with wood and water.

It is not surprising, therefore, that Marpeck counselled obedience to civil authority. For example, in his 1555 letter concerning the Anabaptists expelled from Langenau, he wrote that the city council's order did not seem to him so strict that it could not be obeyed. Further, he observed that civil authorities often preferred not to persecute Anabaptists but did so only because they feared punishment for themselves.[73] Hence, he advised their *Vorsteher*, Abraham

---

69 Ibid., 303.34-35.

70 Ibid., 303.40-44.

71 Ibid., 304.9-12: »Welche ordnung und verordnung gottes wir dann ungetadlet lassen und gott vil mer darfür bitten, auch lob, ehr und dank sagen.«

72 *KB*, no. 13, 135ᵛ: »Dann alle obrigkeit als hir inn diser zeit göterr und mitler sein zwischen frumkheit und possheit, zwischen rechten und unrechten... bis das gricht, gut und böss zu scheiden, besetzt wirt, des dann geschechen wirt, wann der letst mensch, der selig soll werden, volenndt wirt.«

73 Ibid., no. 15, 162ᵛ.

Brendlin, to act more discreetly and avoid unnecessary provocation lest the opportunity for witness in the city be lost. However, he also insisted that, if the civil authority required that they deny the honor due God or God's truth, they should refuse and endure persecution unto death. So Marpeck proposed a discriminating obedience to civil authority. We turn now to the various civil responsibilities required of a sixteenth–century burgher to determine which expectations Marpeck thought were legitimate and which illegitimate for the Christian citizen.

Civil Oath

We have observed in several contexts Marpeck's willingness to swear oaths in the interest of the public order. He took Rattenberg's civil oath and, as a councilman, prosecuted a case of its violation. He doubtless required oaths in his courtroom as mining magistrate. Marpeck also swore Strassburg's civil oath, as well as many lesser oaths when he was hired by the council and in the course of daily business transactions. He did, however, reject an oath requiring him and other Anabaptists to desist from their meetings. During the Interim Years, he disagreed with the Appenzellers' strict prohibition of swearing the civil oath, maintaining that the matter should be left to the individual conscience.

As we have seen, the groups of Anabaptists in Augsburg had a history of divided opinions on the oath. During his Augsburg residence, we have no explicit statement by Marpeck concerning the oath and, as a registered resident (*Einwohner*), he was not required to swear it. However, indirect evidence indicates that his position had not changed and that he probably would have sworn the civil oath had Augsburg allowed applications for citizenship when he arrived in 1544. First, the oath of obedience to Augsburg's council would have been fully consistent with his view in the *Verantwurtung II* that that civil body and its power were a good ordinance of God. Second, two members of Marpeck's circle, Hans Jakob Schneider and Jörg Maler, had both sworn the civil oath. Maler even defended it as furthering the need of the brother, maintaining love, and promoting justice.[74] Third, Marpeck himself swore a similar oath upon entering the employ of the city in 1546. Therefore, it is likely that Marpeck viewed the civil oath as legitimate civil responsibility to be performed by the Christian. Besides a general obedience to the city's council, the oath entailed two major responsibilities – the payment of taxes and military service.

[74] See chapter 6.

Taxes

Because he was employed by the city, Marpeck was not required to pay Augsburg's yearly property tax. However, earlier statements and his professional activity in Augsburg establish that he viewed the payment of taxes to be consistent with the social responsibility of the Christian. In his Strassburg Confession, and the *Bekenntnis an Jan von Pernstain*, Marpeck affirmed the right of civil authority to »all taxes, tolls and tribute.« Indeed, for most of his life, he not only disbursed large amounts of public funds for the public good, but he also received his salary from them.

Military Service

Marpeck's final position on the use of coercive force by the Christian is more difficult to determine. We have noted that the two prominent members of the Marpeck circle, Schneider and Maler, appear to have disagreed on the issue. When arrested for his refusal to participate in the Schmalkaldic War, Schneider seems to have categorically rejected the use of any force, saying that his conscience would allow him neither to help keep watch nor assail the enemy. However, Maler's was a selective rejection of the war against the emperor. He claimed that the misuse, and not simply the use, of the sword was a sin.

Some evidence indicates that Marpeck approached Maler's position. We have noted that in his *Bekenntnis an Jan von Pernstain*, Marpeck expressed his willingness »to protect your (Pernstain's) subjects according to your command.« Also, he not only did not find fault with the »worldly power and sword« in the *Verantwurtung II*, but prayed for it and gave it praise, honor, and thanks. It seems, then, that Marpeck also endorsed a critical participation in the use of coercive force. However, we have little data concerning his criteria for evaluating the extent of that participation.

Since Marpeck was exempt from the obligation of military service, he was not forced to declare himself publicly concerning participation in the Schmalkaldic War. It is clear, however, that he categorically rejected the use of force by the Christian in matters of faith. We have already developed in detail his reasons for viewing such use of coercive force as not only futile, but also as obstructive to true justice. Claiming that the Evangelicals and Catholics who put »false hope in war and fighting« were »imprisoned in their own vengeance,« Marpeck probably judged the Schmalkaldic War to be a misuse of the sword because the combatants fought »in the name of Christ and the true faith.«[75] Further, he also criticized the self–aggrandizing motives of those financing the war. It appears, therefore, that he doubted that the civil sword was being used by either side to protect the just

---

75 *KB*, no. 13, 138[V]: »Und wer einer andern erlösung verhoft, der bauth uff diss zergenncklich leben als uff ein sand und ist inn gmeinschaft allerr obanzeigterr valscherr hoffnung mit krieg und kriegsgschrey in eigner rach erst recht gefanngen.«

from the unjust. It is possible that these are at least two criteria by which Marpeck judged the proper use of deadly force: first, does it leave the individual conscience inviolate in matters of faith? and second, does it serve social justice by protecting the just from the unjust? Because the Schmalkaldic War, in Marpeck's opinion, failed to meet both criteria, it is conceivable that he might have counselled Schneider not to participate on those grounds.

However, there are other indications that Marpeck may have shared Schneider's unqualified rejection of deadly force. In his 1531 *Clare Verantwortung*, Marpeck wrote that since, after the incarnation, the »Spirit is more powerful to overcome through patience... Christ forbade such revenge and resistance« and commanded Christians to overcome through patience.[76] We have seen that he returned to this theme when treating the cross of the Christian in his Augsburg writings. Just as Christ overcame sin and death by submission to his unjust persecutors, so also the Christian overcomes injustice, not by armed resistance, but by the patient, noncoercive offer of the reordering Spirit.

The relationship between these two strands in Marpeck's thought is unclear. It is possible that he, viewing civil power as a good and necessary order of God, simply left that office to nonbelievers, prohibiting any participation of the Christian in it. However, this solution seems unlikely for two reasons. First, Marpeck did not oppose the Christian's payment of taxes which supported the city's police and military forces. Second, as we shall see, he did not rule out, on principle, the Christian's service as a civil magistrate who had ultimate responsibility for those forces. A second possibility is that Marpeck endorsed the use by the Christian of coercive restraints in order to maintain a degree of social justice. However, it appears that, for him, that restraint stopped short of the use of deadly force. Perhaps Marpeck's concern for the sovereignty of the individual conscience lay behind this refusal to kill. By taking the life of even the unjust, one not only restrains but obliterates the sovereign human person and eliminates any future contribution that person may make to the interdependent human community. Hence, the use of deadly force cannot be justified either with respect to the good of the individual or of the community. The Christian, therefore, refuses deadly force for the sake of both the individual and the community and patiently offers to the unjust the reordering Spirit, preferring to be killed rather than to kill.[77]

---

[76] See chapter 4.

[77] We have noted (chapter 4 n. 126) that the *Theologia Deutsch* may have informed this refusal by Marpeck: »[the Christian] should resist nothing or anything with force or war in the will or in deed« (*TD*, 44/88.22-25). For the Frankfurter, the motivation for the rejection of deadly force lies in one's love for God. »All things are in One and the One is in all things, therefore one has love for all things« (*TD*, 44/ 88.26-28). Since life comes through participation in other created things, »it would never come into the will, desire or mind [of the believer] to cause suffering or disturbance« or death and, thus, to separate another from the possibility of that participation (*TD*, 3/63.10-13). Even if the *vergottet mensch* were killed a hundred times and would live again, that one must have love for the one who killed him (*TD*, 31/61.26-62.1).

Christian Magistrate

The question as to whether the Christian may serve as a magistrate is an interesting test case for Marpeck's critical participation in civil authority. Marpeck had been, by his own account, a pious councilman and mining magistrate in Rattenberg. In Strassburg he wrote that a Christian could be a magistrate but insisted that such a person should not use civil power in matters of faith or church reform. Although he said, in the *Vermahnung*, that Christians do not need civil authority for themselves, he did not rule out the possibility that a Christian might serve in the civil magistracy for the sake of those beyond the conventicle. During the Augsburg years, Marpeck affirmed the possibility of a Christian magistrate but was dubious about the duration of his term: »[I]f a Christian received such an office and ruled and ordered every matter of the realm of this world according to the just, human order of God without abuse, how long would he remain a civil authority?«[78] His own surmise was that the Christian would soon either endure abuse and disorder to his own conscience and therefore resign or »abandon the Lord Jesus Christ, Christian patience and the knightship of Christ.« His assessment probably reflected his own experience when, in early 1528, he resigned his office in order to avoid participating in the use of deadly force to coerce the religious faith of his miners.

Marpeck proposed, then, a critical participation in civil authority. He participated because the civil order provided protection for the civilly just from the unjust and facilitated the fair exchange of goods and services required by the physical interdependence of human life. Marpeck, therefore, endorsed the payment of taxes, the development of public works, the civil and lesser oaths, and perhaps even police and military service, short of taking the life of another. There were, however, limits to that participation. When the civil authority transgressed or required the Christian to violate his or her own conscience or that of another, Marpeck believed the Christian should not do so. Therefore, he refused to desist from Anabaptist meetings or coerce others to do so. He insisted on speaking the truth as it was given to him by the Holy Spirit and believed the Christian should not use deadly force.

---

[78] *Antwort*, 304.13-26.

CONCLUSION

Pilgram Marpeck's social theology shares a number of commonalities with the »lay theology« described recently by Paul Russell.[1] Concerning eight »commoners« from Southwest Germany, who wrote pamphlets containing the »first expressions of Protestant piety,« Russell draws several conclusions. In developing their theologies, these literate laypersons drew eclectically from their immediate environment. Luther, as well as other major, magisterial reformers, constituted only one among many influences, which usually also included the local pastor. They seemed »to have no difficulty in combining biblical conservatism, an important hallmark of Reformation theology, with a mystical anthropology and a vision of the city as sacred community that were very medieval.« Critical of the abuse of Christian freedom among Luther's adherents, they »manifested a vocation to redeem the world,« and therefore concerned themselves more with sanctification than justification. Insisting on a »active life in the secular world,« they rejected monastic withdrawal from society. Consequently they believed that obedience in things pertaining to property and external order was due the state, but rejected »state interference in the affairs of the church, especially imprisoning evangelical preachers and calling crusades against the Turks and Jews.« They were neither chiliastic, nor revolutionary; the fruition of their egalitarian society awaited the nearing end of their age, before which they might well experience martyrdom.

Marpeck also drew eclectically from a number of sources available to him in the various contexts in which he found himself. These included magisterial reformers (Luther and Zwingli), medieval mysticism (*Theologia Deutsch*), spiritualizing reformers (Schwenckfeld and Franck), apocalyptic restitutionists (Rothmann), local reform–minded pastors (Castenbaur and Kern), and itinerant Anabaptist preachers (Schiemer and Schlaffer). His appropriation of ideas from these diverse traditions was a critical one which had as one of its central organizing principles his own sense of vocation to »redeem the world,« or in his own words, »to be diligent in all things unto the fulfillment of all justice, not only internally before God, but also externally before humanity.« This study has focused on his appropriation of a notion of justice (*Gerechtigkeit*) from the medieval mystical tradition, mediated by the Theologia Deutsch, Leonhart Schiemer, and Hans Schlaffer, which integrated his dual concern for personal

---

[1] Paul Russell, *Lay Theology in the Reformation*. This summary is drawn from his conclusions, 212-27.

repentance and social responsibility. The »justice of Christ« was established by
the reordering Holy Spirit in the »humanity of Christ«; spread abroad by the
pouring out of the Spirit through Christ's cross; received through faith issuing
from the »guilt cross« of the Christian; and extended through the
nonconstraining offer by Christians resulting in their own »innocent cross.« For
Marpeck, the realm of Christ, constituted by that justice, encompassed both
individual and social transformation – one was impossible apart from the other.

James Preus has observed: »The fastidious depoliticization of the doctrine of
justification, via the two–kingdoms doctrine, has served the church's interests
well – politically. But has it served the world?«[2] Marpeck, with the other lay
theologians of Russell's study, would have answered Preus's question negatively
and developed a sixteenth–century alternative both to this depoliticization and
to the theocratic tendencies of their time. Because of Marpeck's sense of the
spiritual and physical interdependence of human life, the individual and
communal transformations within the new community had political implications
beyond the conventicle.

Marpeck conceived of a transformed community of transformed persons,
transforming the larger human community. In the resolution to be diligent to
fulfill justice *coram hominibus*, as well as *coram deo*, the believer served not only
the body of Christ but also the whole world. The extension of that justice took
place through the individual and communal acts of believers which bear to others
the reordering Spirit. Therefore, Marpeck exhibited a strong sense of responsibility for the physical and spiritual welfare of those beyond the conventicle. We
have noted his participation in the provision of wood, water, and poor relief for
his fellow townsmen in Strassburg, St. Gallen, and Augsburg. Further,
recognizing the social character of knowledge and one's mode of living (for
example, his concept of *erbbresten*), Marpeck felt dutybound (*schuldig*) to witness
to the justice of God wherever there was an opportunity.[3] He did so, however,
without coercion, leaving the individual conscience »*frei und allein*« to the work
of the unconstraining Spirit.

This sense of responsibility committed Marpeck to a stricter political metaphor
than those of many of his contemporaries. Like those lay theologians and in
contrast to many of his Anabaptist colleagues (for example, the Swiss Brethren
and Hutterites), Marpeck endorsed political participation as an appropriate
expression of the Christian's social responsibility. He even developed a
sacramental notion of that participation in that any act of charity by a believer
(for example, the provision of drinking water) could bear the Spirit if received in
faith. That participation had, however, a more critical edge than that of many of
the magisterial reformers or Catholic clergy. For him »diligence in the fulfillment
of God's justice« meant a criticism and alleviation of economic injustice (for
example, his participation in Strassburg's poor relief and his criticism of the
Fuggers' financing of the Schmalkaldic War), as well as a refusal to coerce the

2 James S. Preus, *The Political Function of Luther's Doctrina*, 598.
3 *KB*, no. 15, 161[v].

consciences of others (for example, his 1528 resignation and, perhaps, his refusal to use deadly force).

His thought might be described, then, as a social, or even a political, theology of the cross.[4] It is a social theology of the cross, because he believed that the cross of Christ both freed him, by the outpouring of the Holy Spirit, for this participation and provided the criterion (that is, the refusal to violate the individual conscience) by which that participation was to be judged. The believer is free to act for the neighbor in order to establish a new social order characterized by liberal mutuality instead of the pursuit of self–interest. However, this new order is only possible in conjunction with the unconstrained transformations of individuals.[5] In contrast to the Peace of Augsburg's acceptance of confessional pluralism, precipitated by a military standoff, Marpeck advocated the separation of church and state for the sake of both individual and social transformation.

In Marpeck's view, the realm of Christ might spread to include all of Strassburg, Augsburg, or the empire but, if so, it would grow from the bottom up, by the work of the unconstraining Spirit, and not be imposed from the top down through coercive power. Consequently he, along with the lay theologians, not only opposed the exercise of civil power in matters of faith, but also a violent imposition of a new order, whether that imposition took the form of armed revolution or the apocalyptic expectations of some of his Anabaptist colleagues (for example, Hofmann).[6] Instead, Marpeck expected that the realm of Christ would be extended on earth through the activity of believers until all were blessed who »should be blessed.« Until that time or until his or her own death, after which the conscious soul awaited the resurrection of the body, the believer patiently offered »grace and salvation« to others.[7]

Marpeck, unlike the lay theologians, was not a commoner, but came from a family of considerable means and influence. Although he forfeited his estate when he left Rattenberg and chided Schwenckfeld for looking for the gospel among the »elite, nobles, and in the castles« and not among »poor Anabaptists,« Marpeck was, because of his technical skills, never »poor« and continued to count among his associates persons from the middle and upper strata of sixteenth–

---

4 The term »political theology« here does not carry the more technical sense of Dorothee Soelle, *Political Theology*, 59, but the more general sense of a »deprivatizing of theology« wherein theology cannot be isolated from its social, political, and economic spheres. See the early work of Johannes Baptist Metz, *Theology of the World*, 110.

5 John H. Yoder, *'Anabaptists and the Sword' Revisited*, 138-39, presents a brief characterization of Marpeck's position which is accurate. James Stayer, *Anabaptists and the Sword*, 181, correctly points out that Marpeck's position is not to be identified with the unqualified rejection of the civil magistracy and that he objected to that identification by Schwenckfeld.

6 See chapter 3; Torsten Bergsten, *Pilgram Marbeck und seine Auseinandersetzung mit Caspar Schwenckfeld*, 63; J. C. Wenger, *The Theology of Pilgram Marpeck*, 253: and Heinold Fast, *Pilgram Marbeck und das oberdeutsche Täufertum*, 236, note Marpeck's aversion to apocalyptic speculation.

7 See chapter 7 for Marpeck's implicit acceptance of the soul's survival of death, and *Antwort*, 287.25, for his affirmation of the bodily resurrection.

century German society.[8] He also, however, associated with, worked among, and counted as fellow members of the »untransfigured body of Christ« many who were on the economic and political margins of that society, including craftsmen, gardeners, journeymen, laborers, maids, housewives, and wetnurses.

Marpeck's social theology of the cross served them in two significant ways. First, it gave them a meaningful theological context in which to understand their own suffering. Through that suffering they were prepared to receive voluntarily the Holy Spirit poured out in the suffering and death of Christ. That Spirit brought healing and order to their lives, constituted the new community, and enabled them to communicate it further through an offer to others. Therefore, Marpeck opposed those whom he thought violated the sovereignty of the individual conscience. By coercing faith through physical force (Zwingli, the Peasants, the Münsterites, Michael Keller, and Cardinal Truchseß) or legalistic social control (the Hutterites and Swiss Brethren), these abandoned the cross of Christ and had no appreciation of the salvific potential of human suffering. They threatened the unity of the body of Christ by obstructing individual receptivity to the unifying Spirit.

Second, Marpeck's theology provided those in his sphere of influence with a new sense of identity, worth, and dignity. As members of the »untransfigured body of Christ,« these »poor Anabaptists« bore the Spirit through the performance of the conventicle's ordinances, through their daily work, and through concrete acts of mercy. The activity of their everyday lives carried sacramental significance. They were Christ to one another and for others.

The vision they shared of a lay apostolate connected them with »Franciscans, Beguines, and Hussites of earlier centuries.«[9] And the vocation they pursued toward a redeemed world connects them with movements like the base Christian communities of succeeding centuries.

---

[8] *Antwort*, 247.15f. In a contemporaneous letter (*KB*, no. 38, 312ʳ), Marpeck calls only those born of the Holy Spirit nobles. Russell, *Lay Theology in the Reformation*, 214, notes that the term »poor« as used by some of his lay theologians does not mean that they were, in fact, »have–nots.« The use of the term, therefore, was not very significant when employed as a self–description in the sixteenth century because »in general in the Middle Ages, it was always more advantageous to call oneself poor, rather than rich.«

[9] Russell, *Lay Theology in the Reformation*, 227.

BIBLIOGRAPHY

PRIMARY SOURCES

Marpeck's Works

Books and Confessions

1. *Clare verantwurtung ettlicher Artickel / so jetz durch jrrige geyster schrifflich vnnd mündtlich außschweben / von wegen der ceremönien deß newen Testaments / als Predigen Tauffen Abendtmal / Schrifft. etc. zu trost vnd sterck warhaffter Christen / newlich außgangen. Auch betreffent Christi befelch / sein jüngern gethan. Und die außgiessung deß heyligen Geystes. Gegründt in heyliger schrifft.*
8° [Strasbourg: Jakob Cammerlander, 1531] A-Cvi
Württembergische Landesbibliothek, Stuttgart
Signature: R16 ver. 2, formerly Theol. oct. 18515.
This booklet is bound together with 4a in a small leather cover.
Translation: *WPM*, 43-68.

2. *Ain klarer / vast nützlicher unterricht / wider ettliche Trück / vnd schleichendt Geyster / so jetzt in verborgener weiss außgeen / dadurch viel frommer hertzen verirrt vnd verfürt werden / kürtzlich / getrewer warnungweiß herfür gebracht.*
8° [Strasbourg: Jakob Cammerlander, 1531] A-Dvii
British Museum, Signature: no. 3906.a.77.
Universitätsbibliothek, Jena
Translation: *WPM*, 69-106.

3. *Confession of Faith.* January 1-10, 1532, in Manfred Krebs and Hans Georg Rott, *Quellen zur Geschichte der Täufer, Elsaß, I. Teil*, Gütersloh: Gerd Mohn, 1959, 416-518. See also the text edited by J. C. Wenger, »Pilgram Marpeck's Confession of Faith Composed at Strassburg, December 1531-January 1532.« MQR 12 (1938): 167-202.
Translation: *WPM*, 107-58.

4. *Aufdeckung der Babylonischen hürn / und Antichrists alten unnd newen geheymnuß unnd grewel / Auch vom sieg / fried und herschung warhaffter Christen / unnd wie sie der Obergkait gehorsamen das creutz on auffrür und gegenwär / mit Christo*

*in gedult und lieb tragen / zum preiß Gottes / und Gotsuchenden zu dienst / sterck
unnd besserung / an tag gebracht.*
a. 8° [Strasbourg: Jakob Cammerlander, c. 1532?] A-Cvi
Württembergische Landesbibliothek, Stuttgart,
Signature: R16 ver. 2, formerly Theol. oct. 18515
b. 4° [n.p: n.p., n.d.] A-Dii
Bayerische Staatsbibliothek, München, Sign.: 4° Polem. 3342 (21)
Augsburg, Stadtbibliothek, Signature: 4° ThH 190.
This edition incorporates corrections listed on the last page of the above edition.
See photostatic reproduction of the Augsburg copy in Hans Hillerbrand, »An
Early Anabaptist Treatise on the Christian and the State,« *MQR* 32 (1958): 29-47.

5. *Bekenntnis an Jan von Pernstain.* c. 1535-39.
Regensburg, Stadtarchiv, Signatur Eccl. I, 52, 74.
Published by Hans Hillerbrand, »Ein Täufer Bekenntnis aus dem 16. Jahrhundert.« *ARG* 50 (1959): 40-50. Dr. Heinold Fast will publish this with his critical
edition of *Das Kunstbuch.*

6. *Vermahnung / auch gantz klarer / gründlicher vnd vnwidersprechlicher bericht /
zu warer Christilicher / ewigbestendiger pundtßvereynigung / allen waren glaubigen
frummen / vnd gutthertzigen menschen zu hilff vnd trost / mit grund heyliger schrift
/ durch bewerung warer Tauff vnd Abentmals Christi / sampt mitlauffung vnd
erklärung jrer gegensachen vnd Argumenten / wider alle vermeynte Christliche
Pünndtnus / so sich bißher vnd noch / vnder dem nammen Christi zutragend.*
a. British Museum (Department of Printed Books),
Signature: 3908.a.1, as »Christian Confederate Union«
b. Württembergische Landesbibliothek, Stuttgart.
Christian Hege, *Gedenkschrift zum 400–jährigen Jubiläum der Mennoniten oder
Taufgesinnten 1525-1925.* Ludwigshafen, 1925, 185-281, published this text.
c. There is a manuscript copy of this book in a codex dated 1574 in the Universi-
tätsbibliothek, Budapest, Hungary,
Signature: Codex Ab 10.
Translation: *WPM,* 159-302.

7. *Verantwurtung über Casparn Schwenckfelds Judicium.* 1542
a. Bayerische Staatsbibliothek, München, Signature: Cod. germ. 925.
b. Statui Védecká Knihovna, Olomouc, CSSR: Codex III, 19.
c. Zürich, Stadtbibliothek, Signature: MSS B 72.
Published by Johann Loserth, *Quellen und Forschungen zur Geschichte der oberdeutschen Taufgesinnten im 16. Jahrhundert, Pilgram Marbecks Antwort auf Kaspar
Schwenckfelds Beurteilung des Buches der Bundesbezeugung von 1542.* Wien/Leipzig,
1929, 61-578.

Correspondence

1. »To the Strassburg Council,« c. January 12, 1532, in KR, 1:529-30. Translation: *WPM*, 306-8.

2. »Von der Liebe,« undated, in *KB*, no. 4, 8^v-10^v. Translation: *WPM*, 516-20.

3. »An die Auserwählten um Straßburg, im Elsaß, im Kinzig–und Lebertal: Von der Einigkeit und der Braut Christi,« Graubünden, December 21, 1540, in *KB*, no. 5, 11^r-14^v. Translation: *WPM*, 521-27.

4. »An die Schweizer Brüder: Von jähen Gerichten und Urteilen,« c. 1542, in *KB*, no. 7, 27^r-62^v. Translation: *WPM*, 309-61.

5. »An Helena Streicher.« Summer 1542, in *Antwort*, 179-88. Found in each of the codices containing the *Verantwurtung*. Translation: *WPM*, 376-89.

6. »An Caspar Schwenckfeld.« December 31, 1543, in *Antwort*, 55-59. Found in each of the codices containing the *Verantwurtung*. Translation: *WPM*, 369-75.

7. »An die Schweizer Brüder in Appenzell: Über die Ursachen des Zwiespalts,« 1543 in *KB*, no. 8, 63^r-66^v. Translation: *WPM*, 362-68.

8. »An die auserwählten Wahr gläubigen in Württemberg und anderswo: Von der Christlichen und der Hagar'schen Kirche,« August 15, 1544, in *KB*, no. 33, 264^r-271^v. Translation: *WPM*, 390-401.

9. »An Cornelius Veh und Brüder Paul in Austerlitz: Von den Fleischfreien.« 1544, in *KB*, no. 3, 6^r-8^r. Translation: *WPM*, 402-6.

10. »An Magdalena von Pappenheim und andere: Von den Verstorbenen in Sünden,« 1545, in *KB*, no. 2, 3^v-5^v. Translation: *WPM*, 407-11.

11. »An Leupolt Scharnschlager: Von der Erbschaft, dem Dienst und dem Blutfluß der Sünde.« 1545, in *KB*, no. 27, 238^r-240^v. Translation: *WPM*, 412-17.

12. »An die in Austerlitz: Von der innerlichen Kirche,« c. 1544, in *KB*, no. 37, 302^r-306^v. See also Torsten Bergsten, »Two Letters by Pilgram Marpeck,« *MQR* 32 (1958): 201-15. Translation: Bergsten, 192-95; *WPM*, 418-26.

13. »Von der Liebe Gottes und vom Kreuz Christi,« c. 1547, in *KB*, no. 13, 129^r-143^v. Translation: *WPM*, 528-48.

14. »An die Gemeinden in Graubünden, Appenzell, St. Gallen und im Elsaß: Von der Tiefe Christi,« February 1, 1547, in *KB*, no. 35, 278^r-301^v. Translation: *WPM*, 427-63.

15. »An alle Auserwählten Gottes, besonders an Magdalena von Pappenheim: Von dreierlei Menschen im Gericht und Reich Christi; vom bäurischen Adel,« December 9, 1547, in *KB*, no. 38, 307^r-317^v. Translation: *WPM*, 464-83.

16. »Von fünferlei Früchten wahrer Buße,« August 24, 1550, in *KB*, no. 18, 171^r-179^r. Translation: Heinold Fast, ed., *Der Linke Flügel der Reformation*, 103-17; *WPM*, 484-97.

17. »An die Gemeinde in St. Gallen und Appenzell: Warnung vor dem verborgenen Feuer des Feindes in den Herzen,« August 9, 1551, in *KB*, no. 34, 272^r-277^v. Translation: *WPM*, 498-506.

18. »An die Gemeinden in Mähren: Vom Dienst und von den Dienern der Kirche.« 1552-53, in *KB*, no. 16, 164^r-170^r. Translation: *WPM*, 549-54.

19. »Von der Menschheit Christi,« January 22, 1555, in *KB*, no. 15, 158^r-163^v. See also Torsten Bergsten, »Two Letters by Pilgram Marpeck,« *MQR* 32 (1958): 205-10. Translation: Bergsten, 196-200; *WPM*, 507-15.

Medical Prescription

Medical prescription for female hemorrhaging, 1555

Österreichische Nationalbibliothek, Wien: Codex no. 11.182/36, Sammelband, Bl. 294.

Anonymous Work Attributed to Marpeck

Testamenterleütterung. Erleütterung durch außzug / aus Heiliger Biblischer schrifft Heiliger Biblischer schrifft, tail und / gegentail sampt ains tails angehangen beireden / zu dienst und fürderung ains klaren urtails / von wegen underschaid Alts und News Testaments / vnd irer beder sündtvergebung / Opfer / Erlösung / Gerechtigkait / Gnad / Glauben / Gaist / Folck und anderem / so grundtlich / lauter und nutzlich zue ersehen / genant Testamentserleüterung.
417 folios
Zürich, Zentralbibliothek, Signature: MFA 139.
Berlin, Deutsche Staatsbibliothek, Signature: Bf 8370.

Archival Material/Manuscripts

Bayerisches Hauptstaatsarchiv, München
    Gerichtsliteralien: Hohenschwangau 2: Codex diplomaticus

Rattenberg, Pfarrarchiv (RPA)
    Urkunde nos. 23, 603, 605

Rattenberg, Stadtarchiv (SAR)
    Baumeister Rechnungen, Schuber 269
    Brückenamts Rechnungen, Schuber 279
    Ratsprotokolle, vols. 167 (1 and 2), 168
    Schuber nos. 250, 251, Stadtkammer Rechnungen (SR), 1516-42
    Schuber no. 279, Brückenamts Rechnungen
    Stadtkammer Rechnungen, 1514-28
    Urkunde no. 168

Stadtarchiv Augsburg (St – A.A.)
    Baumeisterbücher (BMB), 1544-62
    Ratsprotokolle (RP), 1545, 1553, 1554
    Stadtpläne, B, 34
    Steuerbücher, 1544-62
    Strafbücher, 1533-39, 1543-53
    Urgichten, 1545; 1546, July 16; 1550, April 23, 28, May 3, 5; 1562, August 5
    Wiedertäufer – und Religionsakten, Facs. III, 1562, August 10, 12

Strasbourg, Stadtarchiv (S.St – A)
    Bürgerbuch 1:635
    Handschriften, III 120/1; V 145/16.5; 850
    Das große Ratsbuch der Stadt Straßburg, no. 863
    Spital – Archiv, 1477
    Stadtordnungen, vol. 4

Tiroler Landesregierungsarchiv in Innsbruck (LRAT)
    Bekennen, 1525
    Causa Domini, 2, 1527-29
    Dekanalarchiv, Reith in Alpbachtal, Urkunde no. 110
    Embiet und Bevelch, 1525, 1526, 1528
    An und von den fürstlichen Durchlaucht
    Gemeinen Missiven, 1528, 1529
    Handschrift, no. 663
    Hofreg., Reihe A, Abt. XII, pos. 1, 11
    An den Königlichen Majestät, 1521-22, 1527-29
    Von den Königlichen Majestät, 1527-29
    Schatzarchiv, I:7344; I:729

Maler, Jörg. *Das Kunstbuch*. 1561. Bürgerbibliothek, Bern, MSS Codex 464.

Published Sources

Beck, Josef. *Die Geschichts–Bücher der Wiedertäufer in Österreich–Ungarn (1526 bis 1785)*. Nieuwkoop B. de Graaf, 1967.

Bossert, Gustav. *Herzogtum Württemberg. Quellen zur Geschichte der Wiedertäufer.* Vol. 1. Leipzig: M. Heinsius Nachfolger Eger u. Sievers, 1930.

Bucer, Martin. *Martin Bucers Deutsche Schriften*. Ed. Robert Stupperich. Gütersloh–Paris: Gerd Mohn–Presses Universtaires de France, 1969.

Bünderlin, Johannes. *Ausz was ursach sich Gott in die nydergelassen und in Christo vermenschet ist / Durch welchen / und wie erdes menschens fall / in jm selbs durch den gesandten Messiah versunet / und wid(er) bracht hat*. Straßburg, 1529.

– *Erklerung durch vergleichung der Biblischen geschrifft / das des wassertauff sampt andern eüsserlichen gebreüchen / in der Apostolischen kirchen geubet. On Gottes befelch und zeügniß der gschrifft / von etlichen diser zeit / wider efert wird. Seiten mal der Antichrist die selben all zehand nach d'Apostel abgang verwustet hat. Welche verwustung dann biß an das end bleibt. Dan. XI*. 1530.

Castenbaur, Stephan. *Ain trostlicher / qutter / notwendiger Sermon / von Sterben / wie sich der mensch darzu schicken / soll mit etlichen Schlüßreden vom / leyden Christi / Ausgangen von / Doctor Steffan Castenbaur / Augustiner ordens in seiner / gefancknuß umb gottes / wort willenn / zu / Mühldorff*. 1523.

– *Artickel wider den / Doctor Steffan Castenpaur / Eingelegt. auch was / er darauff geannt / wort hat, auß / seiner gefen / cknuß, ne / welich / von im außgangen*. n.p., 1523.

– *Ein bedencken des agricola / Boius wie der warhafftig Gottes dienst / von Gott selbs geboten und aufge / setzt / möcht mit besserung ge / meyner Christenheyt wi / derumb auffgericht werden*. n.p., n.d.

Denck, Hans. *Hans Denck. Schriften*. Vol. 2. *Religiöse Shriften*. Ed. Walter Fellmann. *Quellen und Forschungen zur Reformationsgeschichte*. Vol.24. Gütersloh: Gerd Mohn, 1956.

Entfelder, Christian. *Von den manigfaltigen im glauben zerspaltungen / dise jar erstanden. Inn sonderhait von der Tauff spaltung und iren urtail / Ain bedacht*. Straßburg, 1530 (MZ).

– *Von Gottes unnd Christi Jesu unsers herren erkandtnuß / ain bedacht / Allen schulern des hailigen gaists weiter zebendencken auffgezaichnet / mit freyem urthail*. Strasßburg, 1533.

– *Von warer Gotseligkayt / wie der mensch allhie in diser zeyt darzu kommen mag / ain kurze (aber gar nutzliche) betrachtunng*. Straßburg, 1530.

Fast, Heinold. *Der linke Flügel der Reformation*. Bremen: Carl Schunmann, 1962.

Fast, Heinold, ed. *Ostschweiz*. Vol. 2. *Quellen zur Geschichte der Täufer in der Schweiz*. Zürich: Theologischer, 1973.

Franck, Sebastian. *Chronica, zeytbuch und geschychtbibel von anbegyn biss inn diss qegenwertig....* Straßburg, 1531.

– *Paradoxa duccenta octoginta das ist / CCLXXX Wunderred und gleichsam Räterschafft / aus der heiligen schrift.* n.p., n.d.

Hoffman, Bengt, trans. *The Theologia Germanica of Martin Luther*. New York: Paulist, 1980.

Hubmaier, Balthasar. *Balthasar Hubmaier: Schriften*. Ed. T. Bergsten and G. Westin. *Quellen zur Geschichte der Täufer*. Vol. 9. Gütersloh: Gerd Mohn, 1962.

Kessler, Johannes. *Sabbata. Mit kleineren Schriften und Briefen*. Ed. Emil Egli and Rudolf Schoch. St. Gallen: Historischer Verein des Kantons St. Gallen, 1902.

Klassen, William. »Leupold Scharnschlager's Farewell to the Strasbourg Council.« *MQR* 42 (1968): 211-18.

Klassen, William, and Walter Klaassen. *The Writings of Pilgram Marpeck*. Scottdale, Penn.: Herald, 1978.

Krebs, Manfred, ed. *Quellen zur Geschichte der Täufer*. Vol. 4, *Baden und Pfalz*. Gütersloh: Gerd Mohn, 1951.

Krebs, Manfred, and Hans Georg Rott, eds. *Quellen zur Geschichte der Täufer*. Vol. 7, *Elsaß, I Teil: Stadt Straßburg, 1522-1532*. Gütersloh: Gerd Mohn, 1959.

– *Quellen zur Geschichte der Täufer*. Vol. 27, *Elsaß, II Teil: Stadt Straßburg, 1533-1535*. Gütersloh: Gerd Mohn, 1960.

Luther, Martin. *D. Martin Luthers Werke*. Weimar Ausgabe (WA). Vol. 1. Leipzig: Hermann Böhlau, 1883.

Mair, Paul Hektor. *Gründliche und ordenliche Beschreibung der notwendigsten und fürnembsten Handlungen, Geschichten... 1548 in des löblichen Reichs Stadt Augsburg... 1548-1565. Die Chroniken der schwäbischen Städte, Augsburg*. Vol. 17. Ed. historische Commission bei der Königlichen Akademie der Wissenschaften. Leipzig: von 5. Hirzel, 1917.

Mandel, Hermann, ed. *Theologia Deutsch*. Leipzig: A. Deichert'sche Verlagsbuchh. Nachf., 1908.

Mecenseffy, Grete, ed. *Österreich*, part 1. *Quellen zur Geschichte der Täufer*. Gütersloh: Gütersloher Verlagshaus, Gerd Mohn, 1964.

– *Österreich*, part 2. *Quellen zur Geschichte der Täufer*. Vol. 13. *Quellen und Forschungen zur Reformationsgeschichte*. Vol. 41. Gütersloh: Gütersloher Verlagshaus, 1972.

Müller, Lydia, ed. *Glaubenszeugnisse oberdeutscher Taufgesinnter*. Vol. 1. *Quellen und Forschungen zur Reformationsgeschichte*. Vol. 20. Leipzig: M. Heinius Nachfolger, 1938.

Reublin, William. »Letter to Pilgram Marpeck.« *Geschichte des Münsterischen Aufruhrs.* Vol. 2. Ed. C. A. Cornelius. Leipzig, 1860, 253-59. See translation by J. C. Wenger. *MQR* 23 (1949): 67-75.

Röhrich, T. W. »Zur Geschichte der Straßburgischen Wiedertäufer in den Jahren 1527-1543.« *Zeitschrift für die historische Theologie* 30 (1860): 3-122.

Rothmann, Bernhard. *Die Schriften Bernhard Rothmanns.* Ed. Robert Stupperich. Münster: Aschendorffsche Verlagsbuchhandlung, 1970.

– *Zwei Schriften des Münsterischen Wiedertäufers Bernhard Rothmann.* Ed. H. Detmar and R. Krumbholtz. Dortmund: n.p., 1904.

Schiess, Traugott, ed. *Briefwechsel der Brüder Ambrosius und Thomas Blaurer, 1506-1548.* Vols. 1-3. Freiburg, 1908-12.

Schornbaum, Karl, ed. *Markgraftum Brandenburg: Bayern I Abteilung. Quellen zur Geschichte der Täufer.* Vol 2. Leipzig: M. Heinsius Nachfolger, 1934.

– *Markgraftum Brandenburg: Bayern II: Abteilung. Quellen zur Geschichte der Täufer.* Vol. 5. Gütersloh: Bertelsmann, 1951.

Schwenckfeld von Ossig, Caspar. *Corpus Schwenckfeldianorum.* 15 vols. Ed. C. D. Hartranft and J. E. Schultz. Leipzig: 1907-39.

Schweyger, Franz. *Franz Schweygers Chronik der Stadt Hall, 1303-1572.* Ed. David Schönherr. *Tirolische Geschichtsquellen I.* Innsbruck, 1869, 81-82.

Waldner, F. »Dr. Jakob Strauß in Hall und seine Predigt vom grünen Donnerstag... 17 April, 1522.« *Zeitschrift des Ferdinandeums für Tirol und Vorarlberg.* Series 3, vol. 26, Innsbruck, 3-39.

Williams, George H., and Angel Mergal, trans. and eds. *Spiritual and Anabaptist Writers. Documents Illustrative of the Radical Reformation.* Philadelphia: Fortress, 1957.

Zieglschmid, A. J. F., ed. *Die Älteste Chronik der Hutterischen Brüder.* Ithaca, N.Y.: Cayuga, 1943.

SECONDARY SOURCES

Books

Adam, J. *Evangelische Kirchengeschichte der Stadt Straßburg.* Strasbourg, 1922.

Armour, Rollin. *Anabaptist Baptism.* Scottdale, Penn.: Herald, 1966.

Barge, Hermann. *Jakob Strauß. Ein Kämpfer für das Evangelium in Tirol, Thüringen, und Süddeutschland. Schriften des Vereins für Reformationsgeschichte.* Vol. 162. Leipzig, 1937.

Baring, Georg. *Bibliographie der Ausgaben der Theologia Deutsch (1516-1961): Ein Beitrag zur Lutherbibliographie. Bibliotheca Bibliographica Aureliana.* Baden – Baden: Hertz, 1963.

Barth, Ludwig. *Die Geschichte der Flößerei im Flußgebiet der oberen Kinzig.* Karlsruhe, 1895.

Baum, Adolf. *Magistrat und Reformation in Straßburg bis 1529.* Strasbourg, 1887.

Baumen, Clarence. *Gewaltlosigkeit im Täufertum.* Leiden: E. J. Brill, 1968.

Beechy, Alvin. *The Concept of Grace in the Radical Reformation.* Nieuwkoop: de Graaf, 1977.

Bellardi, Werner. *Die Geschichte der »christlichen gemeinschaft« in Straßburg (1546-1550).* Leipzig: M. Heinsius Nachfolger, 1934.

Blough, Neal. *Christologie Anabaptiste: Pilgram Marpeck et l'humanité de Christ.* Genève: Labor et Fides, 1984.

Brady, Thomas A. *Ruling Class, Regime and Reformation at Strasbourg.* Leiden, E. J. Brill, 1978.

Bücking, Jürgen. *Michael Gaismair, Reformer – Sozialrebell – Revolutionär. Seine Rolle im Tiroler »Bauernkrieg« (1525-32).* Stuttgart: Klett – Cotta, 1978.

Chrisman, Miriam U. *Strasbourg and the Reform.* New Haven, Conn.: Yale University Press, 1967.

Clasen, Claus – Peter. *Anabaptism: A Social History, 1525-1618.* Ithaca, N.Y.: Cornell University Press, 1972.

– *The Anabaptists in South and Central Germany, Switzerland, and Austria.* Ann Arbor, Mich.: Univ. Microfilms Int. 1978.

– *Die Augsburger Steuerbücher um 1600.* Augsburg: Hieronymus Mühlberger, 1976.

– *Die Augsburger Weber.* Augsburg: Hieronymus Mühlberger, 1981.

Conrad, Franziska. *Reformation in der Bäuerlichen Gesellschaft. Zur Rezeption Reformatorischer Theologie im Elsaß.* Stuttgart: Steiner – Verlag – Wiesbaden, 1984.

Cornelius, C. A. *Geschichte des Münsterischen Aufruhrs.* Vol. 2. Leipzig, 1855.

Crämer, Ulrich. *Die Verfassung und Verwaltung Straßburgs von der Reformationszeit bis zum Fall der Reichsstadt (1521-1681). Schriften des Wissenschaftlichen Instituts der Elsaß – Lothringer im Reich, N.S.* 3. Frankfurt/M., 1931.

Davis, Kenneth. *Anabaptism and Asceticism: A Study in Intellectual Origins.* Scottdale, Penn.: Herald, 1974.

Deppermann, Klaus. *Melchior Hoffman: Soziale Unruhen und apokalyptische Visionen im Zeitalter der Reformation.* Göttingen: Vandenhoeck and Ruprecht, 1979.

Eells, H. *Martin Bucer.* New Haven, Conn.: Yale University Press, 1931.

Elgi, E. *Die St. Gallen Täufer.* Zürich, 1887.

Gerbert, Camille. *Geschichte der Straßburger Sectenbewegung 1524-35*. Strasbourg, 1889.

Goerters, J. F. G. G. *Ludwig Hätzer (ca. 1500-1529)*. Gütersloh: C. Bertelmann, 1957.

Goertz, Hans–Jürgen. *Die Täufer: Geschichte und Deutung*. München: C. H. Beck, 1980.

— *Innere und Äussere Ordnung in der Theologie Thomas Müntzers*. Leiden: E. J. Brill, 1967.

— *Umstrittenes Täufertum 1525-1975. Neue Forschungen*. Göttingen: Vandenhoeck, 1975.

Goetze, A. *Frühneuhochdeutsches Glossar*. Berlin: Walter de Gruyter, 1967.

Gothein, Eberhard. *Wirtschaftsgeschichte des Schwarzwaldes und der angrenzendes Landschaften*. Vol. 1: Städte– und Gewerbegeschichte. Strasbourg, 1892.

Grimm, Jakob and Wilhelm, eds. *Deutsches Wörterbuch*. Leipzig: S. Hirzel, 1854-1960.

Guderian, Hans. *Die Täufer in Augsburg*. Pfaffenhoff: Ludwig Verlag Pfaffenhausen. 1984.

Hege, Christian, ed. *Gedenkschrift zum 400–jährigen Jubiläum der Mennoniten oder Taufgesinnten 1525-1925*. Ludwigshafen a. Rh., 1925.

Hulshof, Abraham. *Geschiedenis van de Doopagezinden te Straasburg van 1525-1527*. Amsterdam, 1905.

Jehle, Marianne u. Frank. *Kleine St. Gallen Reformationsgeschichte*. St. Gallen: Zollikofer Fachverlag, 1977.

Kießling, Rolf. *Bürgerliche Gesellschaft und Kirche in Augsburg im Spätmittelalter*. Augsburg: Hieronymus Mühlberger, 1971.

Kittelson, James M. *Wolfgang Capito from Humanist to Reformer*. Leiden: E. J. Brill, 1975.

Kiwiet, Jan J. *Pilgram Marbeck. Ein Führer in der Täuferbewegung der Reformationszeit*. Kassel: Oncken, 1957.

Klaassen, Walter. *Michael Gaismair. Revolutionary and Reformer*. Leiden: E. J. Brill, 1978.

Klassen, William. *Covenant and Community*. Grand Rapids, Mich.: Eerdmans, 1968.

Kraus, Jürgen. *Das Militärswesen der Reichstadt Augsburg 1548-1806*. Augsburg: Hieronymus Mühlberger, 1980.

Lienhard, Marc, ed. *The Origins and Characteristics of Anabaptism*. The Hague: Nijhoff, 1977.

Löscher, Hermann. *Das erzgebirgische Bergrecht des 15. und 16. Jahrhunderts*. Berlin, 1957.

Loserth, Johann, ed. *Pilgram Marbecks Antwort auf Kaspar Schwenckfelds Beurteilung des Buches der Bundesbezeugung von 1542*. Wien, Leipzig, 1929.

McLaughlin, R. Emmett. *Caspar Schwenckfeld: Reluctant Radical*. New Haven, Conn.: Yale University Press, 1986.

Maier, P. *Caspar Schwenckfeld on the Person and Work of Christ*. Assen: Royal Van Gorcum, 1959.

Maurer, Justus. *Prediger in Bauernkrieg*. Stuttgart: Calver, 1979.

Mecenseffy, Grete. *Geschichte des Protestantismus in Österreich*. Graz: H. Boehlaus Nachf., 1956.

Metz, Johannes Baptist. *Theology of the World*. Trans. William Glen–Doepel. London: Burns and Oates, 1969.

Ottenthal, Emil von, and O. Redlich. *Archiv Berichte aus Tirol*. Vols. 3-4. Wien u. Leipzig, 1903.

Ozment, Steven. *Mysticism and Dissent*. New Haven, Conn.: Yale University Press, 1973.

Paas, Martha White. *Population Change, Labor Supply, and Agriculture in Augsburg 1480-1618*. New York: Arno, 1981.

Packull, Werner. *Mysticism and the Early South German–Austrian Anabaptist Movement, 1525-1531*. Scottdale, Penn.: Herald, 1977.

Russell, Paul. *Lay Theology in the Reformation: Popular Pamphleteers Southwest Germany 1521-1525*. Cambridge: Cambridge University Press, 1986.

Roth, Friedrich. *Augsburg Reformationsgeschichte*. Vols. 1-4. München: Theodor Ackermann, 1901-11.

Schmid, Josef. *Des Cardinals und Erzbischofs von Salzburg (1519-1540) Matthäus Lang: Verhalten zur Reformation*. Fürth i.B., 1901.

Schmidt, Heinrich. *Reichsstädte, Reich und Reformation. Korporative Religionspolitik 1521-1529/30*. Stuttgart: Franz Steiner, 1986.

Schmoller, Gustav. *Straßburg zur Zeit der Zunftkämpfe und die Reform seiner Verfassung und Verwaltung*. Strasbourg, 1875.

Schoeps, Hans. *Vom himmlischen Fleisch Christi*. Tübingen: Mohr, 1951.

Schornbaum, Karl, ed. *Bayern II Abteilung. Quellen zur Geschichte der Täufer*. Vol. 5. Gütersloh: Gerd Mohn, 1951.

Schultz, Selena G. *Caspar Schwenckfeld von Ossig (1489-1561)*. Norristown, Penn.: Board of Publishing of the Schwenckfelder Church, 1947.

Soelle, Dorothee. *Political Theology*. Trans. and ed. John Shelley. Philadelphia: Fortress, 1971.

Stafford, William S. *Domesticating the Clergy: The Inception of the Reformation in Strasbourg, 1522-1524*. Missoula, Mont.: Scholars, 1976.

Stark, Franz. *Das Ungeteilte Land. Appenzeller Geschichte*. Vol. 1. Appenzell, 1964.

Stayer, James. *Anabaptists and the Sword.* 2d ed. Lawrence, Kans.: Coronado, 1976.

Steiger, Hugo. *Geschichte der Stadt Augsburg.* München u. Berlin: R. Oldenbourg, 1941.

Stetten, Paul von. *Geschichte des Heiligen Römischen Reichs Freyen Stadt Augsburg.* Frankfurt and Leipzig, 1743.

Stolz, Otto. *Geschichte des Landes Tirols.* Vol. 1. Innsbruck: Tyrolia, 1955.

Stops, Friedrich. *Die Chronik der alten Stadt Rattenberg.* Rattenberg: n.p. 1980.

Williams, George H. *The Radical Reformation.* Philadelphia: Westminster, 1962.

Winckelmann, Otto. *Das Fürsorgewesen der Stadt Strasbourg.* Leipzig, 1922.

Wittmer, C. and C. Meyer. *Le livre de bourgeoisie de la ville de Strasbourg 1440-1530.* Vol. 2. Strasbourg, 1954.

Wolfftriegl–Wolfskron, Max Reichsritter von. *Der Tiroler Erzbergbau von 1300-1665.* Innsbruck, 1903.

Zeman, Jarold Knox. *The Anabaptists and the Czech Brethren in Moravia 1526-1628.* The Hague and Paris: Mouton, 1969.

Zorn, Wolfgang. *Augsburg: Geschichte einer deutschen Stadt.* Augsburg: Hermann Rinn, n.d.

Articles

Baring, Georg. »Hans Denck und Thomas Müntzer in Nürnberg 1524.« *ARG 50* (1959): 145-81.

– »Ludwig Hätzers Bearbeitung der Theologia Deutsch: Worms 1528.« *Zeitschrift für Kirchengeschichte* 70 (1959): 218-30.

Bender, Harold. »Pilgram Marpeck, Anabaptist Theologian and Civil Engineer.« *MQR* 38 (1964): 231-65.

Bergsten, Torsten. »Pilgram Marbeck und seine Auseinandersetzung mit Caspar Schwenckfeld.« *Kyrkohistorisk Arsskrift,* 1957, 39-100, and 1958, 53-87.

Bossert, Gustav. »Beiträge zur Geschichte Tirols in der Reformationszeit.« *Jahrbuch der Gesellschaft für Geschichte des Protestantismus in Österreich.* Innsbruck, 1885, 145ff.

Boyd, Stephen. »Anabaptism and Social Radicalism in Strasbourg, 1528-1532: Pilgram Marpeck on Christian Social Responsibility.« *MQR* 63 (1989): 58-76.

– »Hans Schlaffer.« *Bibliotheca Dissidentium, Répertoire des non–conformistes religieux des seizième et dix–septième siècles.* Vol. 15. Ed. André Séguenny. Baden–Baden: Valentin Körner, forthcoming.

– »Leonhart Schiemer.« *Bibliotheca Dissidentium, Répertoire des non–conformistes religieux des seizième et dix–septième siècles.* Vol. 15. Ed. André Séguenny. Baden–Baden: Valentin Körner, forthcoming.

– »Marpeck, Pilgram.« *ME.* Vol. 5. Ed. C. J. Dyck. Scottdale, Penn.: Herald, 1990.

- »Pilgram Marpeck.« *Bibliotheca Dissidentium, Répertoire des non–conformistes religieux des seizième et dix–septième siècles.* Vol. 15. Ed. André Séguenny. Baden–Baden: Valentin Körner, forthcoming.

Brady, Thomas. »Social History.« *Reformation Europe: A Guide to Research.* Ed. Steven Ozment. St. Louis, Mo.: Center for Reformation Research, 1982.

Brunner, Otto. »Souveränitätsproblem und Sozialstruktur in den deutschen Reichsstädten der früheren Neuzeit.« *Vierteljahrschrift für Sozial– und Wirtschaftsgeschichte.* Vol. 50. Ed. Hermann Aubin. Wiesbaden: Steiner, 1963, 329-60.

Bücking, Jürgen. »The Peasant War in the Habsburg Lands as a Social Systems Conflict.« *The German Peasant War: New Viewpoints.* Ed. Bob Scribner and Gerhard Benecke. London, 1979, 160-73.

Chrisman, Miriam U. »Urban Poor in the Sixteenth Century: the Case of Strasbourg.« *Social Groups and Religious Ideas in the Sixteenth Century.* Ed. Miriam U. Chrisman and Otto Gründler. Kalamazoo: Medieval Institute, Western Michigan University, 1978, 63-67.

Clasen, Claus–Peter. »The Anabaptist Leaders: Their Numbers and Backgrounds in Switzerland, Austria, South and Central Germany 1525-1618.« *MQR* 49 (1975): 122-64.

Correll, Ernst. »Anabaptism in the Tyrol.« *MQR* 4 (1927): 49-60.

Dedic, Paul. »The Social Background of the Austrian Anabaptists.« *MQR* 13 (1939): 5-20.

Deppermann, Klaus. »Die Straßburger Reformatoren und die Krise des oberdeutschen Täufertums im Jahre 1527. Eine Antwort auf J. H. Yoder 'Der Kristallisationspunkt des Täufertums.'« *MGB* 30 (1973): 24-41.

Dollinger, Philippe. »La tolerance à Strasbourg au XVIe siècle.« *Hommage à Lucien Febvre.* Vol. 2. Paris, 1953, 141-49.

Doorkaat–Koolman, J., ten. »Graubünden.« *Mennonitisches Lexicon.* Vol. 2. Ed. C. Hege and C. Neff. Frankfurt–Weierhof.

- »Leopold Scharnschlager und die Verborgene Täufergemeinde in Graubünden.« *Zwingliana* 4 (1926): 329-37.

Dörrer, Fridolin. »Tiroler und andere Geldsorten (2. Teil).« *Haller Münz–Blätter* 1, no. 14 (April 1975): 19-27.

Fast, Heinold. »Bemerkungen zur Taufanschauung der Täufer.« *ARG* 57 (1966): 131-51.

- »'Nicht was, sondern das'. Marpeckhs Motto wider den Spiritualismus.« *Evangelischer Glaube und Geschichte: Grete Mecenseffy zum 85. Geburtstag.* Ed. Alfred Raddatz and Karl Lüthi. Wien: Evangelischer Oberkirchenrat, 1984, 66-74.

- »Pilgram Marbeck und das oberdeutsche Täufertum. Ein neuer Handschriftenfund.« *ARG* 47 (1956): 212-42.

- »Variationen des Kirchenbegriffs bei den Täufern.« *MGB* 22 (1970): 5-18.

Fischnaler, Konrad. »Aus dem Bürgermiliz– und Schützenwesen in Rattenberg.« *Geschichts–, Kultur– und Naturbilder aus Alttirol.* Innsbruck: Mar. Vereins-buchhandlung, n.d.

Friedmann, Robert. »Leonhard Schiemer and Hans Schlaffer: Two Tyrolean Anabaptist Martyr–Apostles of 1528.« *MQR* 33 (1959): 31-41. Also in *Hutterite Studies.* Ed. Harold Bender. Goshen, Ind.: Mennonite Historical Society, 1961.

– »The Oldest Church Discipline of the Anabaptists.« *MQR* 29 (1955): 162-66. Also *ME* 4:252-54.

– »Schiemer, Leonhard.« *ME* 4:452-54.

– »Schiemer, Leonhard.« *ML* 4:56-58.

– »Schlaffer, Hans.« *ME* 4:457-59.

– »Schlaffer, Hans.« *ML* 4:63-65.

Fuchs, François–Josef. »Le Droit Bourgeoisie à Strasbourg.« *Revue d'Alsace* 101 (1962): 19-50.

Gothein, Eberhard. »Beiträge zur Geschichte des Bergbaues im Schwarzwald.« *Zeitschrift für die Geschichte des Oberrheins, N. F.* 2 (1887): 385-448.

Hauthalter. »Cardinal Matthäus Lang und die religiös–soziale Bewegung seiner Zeit.« *Mittheilungen der Gesellschaft für Salzburger Landeskunde* 36 (n.d.): 319-49.

Hege, Christian. »Pilgram Marbeck und die oberdeutschen Taufgesinnten. Neue Forschungsergebnisse.« *ARG* 37 (1940): 249-57.

Hein, Gerhard. »Leopold Scharnschlager. Ein Mitarbeiter Pilgram Marpecks.« *MGB* (1939): 6-12.

– »Leupold Scharnschlager, d. 1563: Swiss Anabaptist Elder and Hymn Writer.« *MQR* 17 (1943): 47-52.

Hillerbrand, Hans. »An Early Anabaptist Treatise on the Christian and the State.« *MQR* 32 (1958): 29-47.

Hirsch, Emanuel. »Zum Verständnis Schwenckfelds.« *Festgabe von Fachgenossen und Freunden Karl Müller.* Tübingen: J. C. B. Mohr, 1922, 145-70.

Hollaender, Albert. »Ein Bergknappenaufstand zu Schwaz 1525.« *Tiroler Heimat-blätter* 13 (1935): 29-33.

Keller, Ludwig. »Marbeck.« *Allgemeine Deutsche Biographie* 20 (Leipzig, 1884): 290-91.

Kittelson, James. »Wolfgang Capito, the Council and Reform of Strasbourg.« *ARG* 63 (1972): 126-41.

Klaassen, Walter. »Church Discipline and the Spirit in Pilgram Marpeck.« *De Geest in het Geding.* Ed. I. Horst, A. De Jong, and D. Visser. Willink: Tjeenk, 1978, 169-80.

– »Eine Untersuchung der Verfasserschaft und des historischen Hintergrundes der Täuferschrift. *Aufdeckung der Babylonischen Hurn... .« Evangelische Glaube und Geschichte.* Ed. Alfred Raddatz and Karl Lüthi. Wien: Peter Karner, 1984.

– »Investigation into the Authorship and Historical Background of the Anabaptist Tract Aufdeckung der Babylonischen Hurn.« *MQR* 61 (1987): 251-61.

Klassen, William. »Leupold Scharnschlager's Farewell to the Strasbourg Council.« *MQR* 42 (1968): 211-18.

– »The Limits of Political Authority as seen by Pilgram Marpeck.« *MQR* 58 (1982): 342-64.

– »Pilgram Marpeck: Freiheit ohne Gewalt.« *Radikale Reformatoren. 21 biographische Skizzen von Thomas Müntzer bis Paracelsus.* Ed. Hans–Jürgen Goertz. München: C. H. Beck, 1978.

– »Pilgram Marpeck's Two Books of 1531.« *MQR* 33 (1959): 18-30.

– »The Relation of the Old and New Covenants in Pilgram Marpeck's Theology.« *MQR* 40 (1966): 97-111.

Köhler, Walther. »Marbeck.« *Die Religion in Geschichte und Gegenwart III.* 2d ed. Tübingen, 1927-32.

Kolde, Thomas. »Stephan Agricola.« *Realencyclopedie für protestantische Theologie und Kirche.* Vol. 1. Ed. Albert Kank. Leipzig, 1896, 254-55.

Krahn, Henry G. »Martin Bucer's Strategy Against Sectarian Dissent.« *MQR* 50 (1976): 163-80.

Kreider, R. »The Anabaptists and the Civil Authorities of Strasbourg 1525-55.« *CH* 24 (1955): 99-118.

Lienhard, Marc. »Les autorités civiles et les anabaptistes: Attitudes du magistrat de Strasbourg (1526-1532).« *The Origins and Characteristics of Anabaptism.* Ed. Marc Lienhard. The Hague: Nijhoff, 1977, 196-215.

Looß, Sigrid. »Butzer und Capito in ihrem Verhältnis zu Bauernkrieg und Täufertum.« *Weltwirkung der Reformation.* Ed. Max Steinmetz and Gerhard Brendler. Vol. 1. Berlin, 1969, 226-32.

Loserth, Johann. »Der Anabaptismus in Tirol von seinen Anfängen bis zum Tode Jakob Huters (1526-1536).« *Archiv für Österreichische Geschichte* 78 (1892): 427-604.

– »Marbeck, Pilgram.« *Mennonitisches Lexikon,* 3:28f. And *Mennonite Encyclopedia.* Vol. 3. Scottdale, Penn.: Herald, 1957, 491-500.

– »Recent Research in the History of the Tyrol–Moravian Anabaptists.« *MQR* 1 (1928): 5-15.

– »Studien zu Pilgram Marbeck.« *Gedenkschrift zum 400–jährigen Jubiläum der Mennoniten oder Taufgesinnten, 1525-1925.* Ludwigshafen a. Rh., 1925, 134-77.

– »Zwei Tiroler. Ein Beitrag zur Geschichte des tirolisch–mährischen Täufertums im 16. Jahrhundert.« *Zeitschrift des deutschen Vereins für die Geschichte Mährens und Schlesiens* 30 (1928): 1-9.

Mecenseffy, Grete. »Die Herkunft des oberösterreichischen Täufertums.« *ARG* 57 (1956): 252-59.

– »Täufer in Rattenberg.« *Das Buch von Kramsach, Schlernschriften.* Vol. 262. Innsbruck – München, 1972, 197-214.

– »Ursprünge und Strömungen des Täufertums in Österreich.« *The Origins and Characteristics of Anabaptism.* Ed. Marc Lienhard. The Hague: Nijhoff, 1977, 42-61.

Meyer, C. »Die Anfänge des Wiedertäufertums in Augsburg.« *Zeitschrift des Historischen Vereins für Schwaben und Neuberg* 1 (1874): 207-53.

Müsing, Hans – Werner. »The Anabaptist Movement in Strasbourg from Early 1526 to July 1527.« *MQR* 51 (1977): 91-126.

– »Karlstadt und die Entstehung der Straßburger Täufergemeinde.« *The Origins and Characteristics of Anabaptism.* Ed. Marc Lienhard. The Hague: Nijhoff, 1977, 169-95.

Oberman, Heiko A. »The Gospel of Social Unrest: 450 Years after the So – Called 'German Peasants' War' of 1525.« *Harvard Theological Review* 69 (1976): 103-29.

Oyer, John. »The Influence of Jacob Strauss on the Anabaptists.« *The Origins and Characteristics of Anabaptism,* Ed. Marc Lienhard. The Hague: Nijhoff, 1977, 62-82.

Paulus, N. »Ein Gutachten von Staupitz aus dem Jahre 1523.« *Historisches Jahrbuch der Görresgesellschaft* 12 (1891): 773-77.

Preus, James S. »The Political Function of Luther's Doctrina.« *Concordia Theological Monthly* 43 (1972).

Quiring, Horst. »Die Anthropologie Pilgram Marbecks.« *MGB* 2 (1937): 10-17, and *MQR* 9 (1955): 155-64.

Röhrich, T. W. »Zur Geschichte der Straßburgischen Wiedertäufer in den Jahren 1527-1543.« *Zeitschrift für die historische Theologie* 30 (1860).

Rott, Jean. »La Guerre des paysans et la ville de Strasbourg.« *Etudes alsatiques: La Guerre des paysans, 1525.* Ed. Alphonse Wallbut (1975), 23-32.

Ruckdeschel, Wilhelm. »Die Brunnenwerke am Roten Tor zu Augsburg zur Zeit des Stadtsbrunnenmeisters Casper Walter (um 1750).« *Zeitschrift des Historischen Vereins für Schwaben* 69 (1975): 61ff.

– »Das Untere Brunnenwerk zu Augsburg durch vier Jahrhunderte.« *Zeitschrift des Historischen Vereins für Schwaben* 75 (1981): 87-113.

Ruf, S. »Dr. Jakob Strauß und Dr. Urban Rhegius.« *Archiv für Geschichte und Altertum Tirols* 2:67-81.

Russell, Paul. »Common People and the Future of the Reformation in the Pamphlet Literature of Southwestern Germany to 1525.« *ARG* 74 (1983): 122-24.

Schiess, T. »Aus dem Leben eines Ilanzer Schulmeisters.« *Bündnerisches Monatsblatt* (1916), 73-89.

Séguenny, André. »Christian Entfelder.« *Bibliotheca Dissidentium, Répertoire des non – conformistes religieux des seizième et dix – septième siècles.* Vol. 1. Ed. André Séguenny. Baden – Baden: Valentin Körner, 1980, 37-48.

– »Sebastian Franck et la Philosophie Spirituelle.« *Archiv für Geschichte der Philosophie* 60, no. 3 (1978): 293-313.

Sölch, Georg. »Die Holzbringung im oberen Kinzigtal.« *Der Forstmann in Baden – Württemberg* 7 (1957): 158-63.

Stayer, James. »The Anabaptists.« *Reformation Europe: A Guide to Research.* Ed. Steven Ozment. St. Louis, Mo.: Center for Reformation Research, 1982, 135-60.

– »Die Anfänge des schweizerischen Täufertums im reformierten Kongregationalismus.« *Umstrittenes Täufertum 1525-1975: Neue Forschungen.* Ed. Hans – Jürgen Goertz. Göttingen: Vandenhoeck and Ruprecht, 1977.

Stolz, Otto. »Zur Geschichte des Bergbaues im Elsaß im 15. und 16. Jahrhundert.« *Elsaß – Lothringisches Jahrbuch* 18 (1939): 117-71.

Stupperich, Robert. »Straßburgs Stellung zu Beginn des Sakramentsstreites, 1524-1525.« *ARG* 38 (1941).

Waldner, F. »Dr. Jakob Strauß in Hall und Seine Predigt vom grünen Donnerstag... 17 April, 1522.« *Zeitschrift des Ferdinandeums für Tirol und Vorarlberg.* Series 3, vol. 26. Innsbruck, 5-39.

Waring, George. »The Silver Miners of the Erzgebirge and the Peasant's War of 1525 in the Light of Recent Research.« *Sixteenth – Century Journal* 18 (1987): 231-48.

Weingartner, Josef. »Aus der alten Schwazer Bergwerkgeschichte.« *Schlernschriften* 251 (1962): 161.

Wenger, John C. »Additional Notes on the Life and Work of Pilgram Marpeck.« *MQR* 12 (1938): 269-70.

– »The Life and Work of Pilgram Marpeck.« *MQR* 12 (1938): 137-66.

– »A Letter from Wilhelm Reublin to Pilgram Marpeck, 1531.« *MQR* 23 (1949): 67-75.

– »Pilgram Marpeck, Tyrolese Engineer and Anabaptist Elder.« *CH* 9 (1940): 24-36.

– »The Theology of Pilgram Marpeck.« *MQR* 12 (1938): 205-56.

Widmoser, Eduard. »Das Tiroler Täufertum.« *Tiroler Heimat* 15 (1951): 45-89, and *Tiroler Heimat* 16 (1952): 103-28.

Williams, George H. »Francis Stancaro's Schismatic Reformed Church, Centered in Dubets'ko in Ruthenia, 1559/61-1570.« *Harvard Ukranian Studies* 3-4 (1979-80): 931-57.

– »German Mysticism in the Polarization of Ethical Behavior in Luther and the Anabaptists.« *MQR* 48 (1974): 275-304.

- »Popularized German Mysticism as a Factor in the Rise of Anabaptist Communism.« *Glaube, Geist, Geschichte: Festschrift für Ernst Benz.* Ed. Gerhard Müller and Winifried Zeller. Leiden: E. J. Brill, 1967, 290-312.
- »Sanctification in the Testimony of Several So–Called Schwärmer.« *MQR* 42 (1968): 5-25.
- »Sectarian Ecumenicity: Reflections on a Little Noticed Aspect of the Radical Reformation.« *Review and Expositor* 44 (1967): 141-60.

Wiswedel, W. »Hans Schlaffer, ein ernster Beter und eifriger Verteidiger der göttlichen Wahrheit.« *Bilder und Führergestalten aus dem Täufertum.* Vol. 2. Kassel: J. G. Oncken, 1952, 191-201.
- »Leonhard Schiemer, der erste Täuferbischof Oberösterreichs.« *Bilder und Führergestalten aus dem Täufertum.* Vol. 2. Kassel: J. G. Oncken, 1952, 174-86.
- »Pilgram Marbeck und seine Bedeutung für das Schriftum der Täufer.« *Bilder und Führergestalten aus dem Täufertum.* Vol. 2. Kassel: J. G. Oncken, 1952, 69-80.
- »Die Testamentserleüterung.« *Blätter für Württembergische Kirchengeschichte* 41 (1937): 64-76.

Wray, Frank. »The 'Vermanung' of 1542 and Rothmann's 'Bekentnisse'.« *ARG* 47 (1956): 243-51.

Yoder, John H. »'Anabaptists and the Sword' Revisited: Systematic Historiography and Undogmatic Nonresistance.« *Zeitschrift für Kirchengeschichte* 85 (1974): 270-83.

Zani, Karl Granz. »Michael Gaismair. Mit einem Beitrag über Armut und Unterdrückung in Tirol.« *Der Schlern* 49 (1975): 584-97.

Zeman, Jarold Knox. »Historical Topography of Moravian Anabaptism.« *MQR* 40 (1966): 266-78, and *MQR* 41 (1967): 40-78, 116-60.

Ziegler, D. J. »Marpeck versus Butzer: A Sixteenth Century Debate over the Uses and Limits of Political Authority.« *Sixteenth Century Journal* 2 (1971): 95-107.

Zimmer, Jürgen. »Die Veränderungen im Augsburger Stadtbild zwischen 1530 und 1630.« *Welt in Umbruch.* Vol. 3. Ed. Städtischen Kunstsammlungen Augsburg und dem Zentralinstitut für Kunstgeschichte in München, 1981.

Dissertations and Papers

Angerer, Anton. »Die Augustiner Eremiten in Nordtirol. Unter besondere Berüchsichtigung des Klosters Rattenberg.« Doctoral dissertation, Innsbruck, 1980.

Gerhard, Werthan. »Zur Geschichte der Augsburger Täufer im 16. Jahrhundert.« Wissentschaftliche Prüfung für Lehramt am Gymnasien im Frühjahr 1972, München.

Grams, Warnfrid Werner. »Die Straßburger Almosenordnung von 1523 im Spannungsfeld der Geschichte. Eine Untersuchung zur Frage des Sozialwesens.« Doctoral dissertation, Heidelberg, 1975.

Källstigen, Olof. »Der Mensch Christus als Eckstein. En analys av Kristologi och församlingssyn i Marbecks–drifterna.« Licentiate dissertation, Stockholm, 1964.

Schmelzer, M. »Geschichte der Löhne und Preise in Rattenberg vom Ende des 15. Jahrhunderts bis in die. 2. Hälfte des 19. Jahrhunderts.« Doctoral dissertation, Innsbruck, 1972.

Seebass, Gottfried. »Müntzer's Erbe. Werk, Leben und Theologie des Hans Hut (gestorben 1527).« Habilitationsschrift, Erlangen, 1972.

Stayer, James. »Theses on the Resistance Movement of the German Commoners in 1525.« Unpublished paper, Anabaptist Studies Colloquium, Goshen College, Ind., November 22-23, 1985.

Uhland, Friedwart. »Täufertum und Obrigkeit in Augsburg im 16. Jahrhundert.« Freudenstadt, Germany: Private printing, 1972.

Widmoser, Eduard. »Das Täufertum im Tiroler Unterland.« Doctoral dissertation, Innsbruck, 1948.

INDEX

Adolf, Thomas, 52

Agricola, Stephan (son of Stephan
  Castenbaur), 132

Albrecht Alcibiades, 131

Alsace, 102, 108, 144

Amon, Hans, 103

Anabaptism:
  in Appenzell, 112
  in Augsburg, 132-134, 141,
    143-144
  Bucer and, 63-67
  Capito and, 63-65
  Franck and, 60
  Marpeck and, 110-115, 138-144
  in Moravia, 98-102
  »Pilgramite« groups, 99, 101,
    145-146
  in Rattenberg, 24
  early opinion of Schlaffer, 37
  in Schwaz, 24
  South Germany, 3, 132
  in Strassburg, 47-52, 59-63
  Streicher and, 105
  Swiss, 103, 107, 161
  in the Tirol, 21
  See also Hutterites; Swiss Brethren

Anngst, Bartlme, 22

Ansbach-Beyreuth, 60

Apostles' Creed, 139, 158

Appenzell, 98, 107-108, 111-112, 134,
  142, 144-145, 161, 164

Ascherham, Gabriel, 101

Augsburg, 2, 21, 37, 50, 55, 60, 64,
  97-112 passim, 127-147,
    153, 156, 159-166 passim, 170

Augsburg Confession, 132

Augsburg Interim, 130, 160

Auspitz, 103

Austerlitz, 52, 99-100, 102, 108, 144

Babenhausen, 61

Bächlin, Leonhard, 132

Bader, Augustin, 65

Bader, Sabina, 65

Ban: Marpeck and, 111

Baptism:
  Bucer and, 46, 63
  Capito and, 65
  Franck and, 60
  Gross and, 49
  Marpeck and, 56, 67, 92, 118, 120,
    124, 153, 158
  Schiemer and, 34, 35
  Schlaffer and, 39, 40
  Strauß and, 15
  Hans Wolff and, 48, 63
  Clement Ziegler and, 47

Bartholome, Sixte, 133

Basel, 48-50

Baumgartner, Hans, 134, 160

Bavaria, 17, 22, 30

Beckenknecht, Hans, 132

Benfeld, 48, 50

Berchtesgaden, 13

Berndarffer, Leonard, 12

Betschold, Martin, 47

Blaurer, Ambrosius, 64

Blaurer, Margaret, 64

Böcklin, Wolfgang, 47

Bonifatius, Wolfart, 140, 142

Bosch, Sigmund, 61

Brendlin, Abraham, 145, 164

Brenner, Gilg, 61, 67

Brixen, 13, 20

Brixlegg, 37

Bruchen, Claus, 59

Bucer, Martin, 13, 45-46, 49-50, 53,
    59, 63-67, 80, 88-96
    passim, 108, 159

Bünderlin, Johannes (Hans), 59-60,
    84, 87, 89, 101, 103, 105,
    132, 158

Butenbach, Schertlin von, 129, 141

Campanus, John, 60

Capito, Wolfgang, 45-46, 48, 50, 56,
    63-65, 159

Carlstadt, Andreas Bodenstein von,
    48

Carthusians: Schlaffer and, 36

Castenbaur, Stephan
    (father of Stephan
    Agricola), 9, 15-18
    21, 24, 159, 169
    and Luther, 16, 18

Catholics, 159, 161, 165

Cellarius, 49, 63

Charles V, 127-132, 141, 159-160

Christ:
    Denck on, 49
    descent into hell, 28, 140, 151
    in *Theologia Deutsch*, 27-28
    Marpeck on the body of, 74-75, 82,
    124
    Marpeck on the person of, 62, 69,
    71, 88, 100, 112-121, 123,
    144-145, 157-158, 170
    Marpeck on the realm of, 80-83,
    111, 157, 161-162, 170
    Marpeck on the reich of, and the
    church, 158
    Marpeck on the work of, 69,
    72-75, 110, 113, 148
    Marpeck's critique of the

Magisterial Reformers and, 90
    Marpeck's critique of Spiritualist
    Christology and, 104
    Schlaffer on the body of, 38
    Schlaffer on the work of, 36-37
    Schwenckfeld on the person of,
    115
    Second Strassburg Conference on
    the person of, 145-146
    Streicher on the person of, 104
    See also Theology of the Cross

Christoph of Reith, 18, 19, 24

Chur, 108, 144

Church:
    Marpeck and, 95-96, 120, 144,
    154-155, 157-158
    Marpeck and the community of
    saints, 158
    Marpeck on the relationship of the
    person of Christ and, 123
    Marpeck on the relation to the
    state, 95
    Schlaffer and, 40
    Schwenckfeld and, 105-106

Civil government:
    Anabaptists and, 132
    and faith, in Marpeck, 159-161
    and the realm of Christ, in
    Marpeck, 161-168
    Bucer and, 63
    Capito and, 63
    Michael Ecker and, 50
    Jakob Gross and, 49
    Marpeck and, 62, 93, 101,
    109-110, 157
    Sattler and, 50
    Hans Wolff and, 48

Civil sword. *See* Sword

Communion. *See* Lord's Supper

Community of goods, 112, 139, 143
    and Anabaptism in Strassburg, 48-49
    and Marpeck's group in
    Strassburg, 62

Constance, 64

Constantine, 60

Covenant(s), 72, 92, 139
 Marpeck and the Old and New, 88-89, 92, 151
 Schwenckfeld and the Old and New, 115

Czech Brethren, 101, 145

Dachser, Jakob, 133

Danube River, 143

Denck, Hans, 22, 37, 49, 51, 59, 63, 89, 132

Diet of Augsburg, 132

Diet of Worms, 22

Dillingen, 129-130

Duntzenheim, Konrad von, 47

Eberlin, Hans, 141

Ecclesiology. *See* Church

Eckel, Fabian, 116

Ecker, Michel, 50

Ecksel, Wilhelm, 49

Eibenschitz, 60, 99, 101, 108, 145

Eichwald, 57

Einbach, 57, 61, 67

Entfelder, Christian, 59-60, 84, 87, 89, 99, 101, 103, 105, 158

Erasmus, 54

Eschatology:
 Hut and, 133
 Marpeck and, 83
 Schiemer and, 35
 Schlaffer and, 40, 83, 133

Esslingen, 108

Eucharist. *See* Lord's Supper

Evangelicals, 108, 166

Faber, Johann, 143

Faith: Schiemer and, 34
 Streicher and, 105

Felix, Hans, 99

Ferdinand I, 6-12 passim, 16-24 passim, 37, 41, 52, 99, 128, 130-132, 159, 162

Feuchtner, Sebolt, 133

Flinner, Johann, 143

Franck, Sebastian, 59-60, 87-88, 99, 169

Frankfurter, the anonymous, 26-29, 31, 69, 71-76 passim, 89, 149

Freyberg, Helena von (Helena von Münchinau), 24, 102, 105-106, 133-134, 139

Freyberg, Jörg Ludwig von, 104

Frick, Leonhard, 23

Frisch, Hans, 61

Fuggers of Augsburg, 10-11, 37, 127-129, 159-160, 170
 Hans Jakob Fugger, 144

Fürstenberg, Elizabeth von, and family, 56-57, 67

Füssen, 135

Gaismair, Michael, 20

Geister. *See* Spiritualism

Germany, South, 102, 104, 107-108, 130, 144

Glait, Oswald, 30, 37

Glatz, 101, 116

God:
 Marpeck and the doctrine of, 117, 121-122
 in *Theologia Deutsch*, 26

»Gospel of All Creatures«:
 Hut and, 32
 Marpeck and, 77-79, 89
 in *Theologia Deutsch*, 26-29
 Schiemer and, 32, 33
 Schlaffer and, 37

Gottesheim, Conrad, 47

Gottesheim, Friedrich von, 47

Grace:
 Marpeck and, 77-80
 Schiemer and, 32-33

Grafenwerdt, 143

Graubünden, 102, 144

Gross, Jakob, 49-51, 63, 132

Guilds:
  in Augsburg, 127
  Marpeck and »gardener=
    wagoners,« 53, 58-59
  in Rattenberg, 7, 9-12
  in Strassburg, 43

Hackfurt, Lukas, 45, 50-51, 54-55
Hafner, Ludwig, 102
Hall, 10, 13-15, 21, 37
Hallau, 48
Haslach, 56
Hätzer, Ludwig, 37, 49, 51, 59, 64,
    89, 132
Hausach, 56-57
Hedio, Caspar, 45, 63
Held, Johann, 130, 141, 143
Helding, Michael, 130
Hell:
    descent into,
      in *Theologia Deutsch*, 28
    See also Christ
Henry II (king of France), 131
Henry VIII, 128
Herbrot, Jakob, 128, 131, 141, 159
Herlin, Martin, 47
Hieber, Leonhard, 143
Hieber, Sabina, 133, 143
Hildebrand, Anthony, 137-138
Hiller, Matthis, 49
Hofmann, Melchior, 59-62, 88, 91,
    146
    See also Melchiorites
Holy Spirit:
    Capito and, 65
    Denck and, 49
    Franck and, 60
    Marpeck and, 67, 73-83
    passim,
    86, 91-92, 101-125
    passim,
    151-170 passim
    Streicher and, 105
    Hans Wolff and, 48

Hopfgarten, 61
Horb, 61, 64
Hoser, Simprecht, 144
Huber, Caspar, 131
Hubmaier, Balthasar, 30, 48, 132
Hut, Hans, 21-22, 30, 32, 37, 40, 60,
    132-133
Hutterites, 97, 103, 110-115 passim,
    139, 143, 145-146, 161, 170

Ickelsamer, Valentin, 102, 105
Ilanz, 102, 108, 140, 144
Ilsing, Melchior, 135
Incarnation:
    Capito and, 65
    Marpeck and, 71, 87
    See also Christ
Innsbruck, 6-23 passim

Jamnitz, 145
Jerusalem, 34-35, 60, 104, 112
Jesus Christ. *See* Christ
John Frederick, 130
Jost, Lienhard, 60
Jost, Ursula, 60
Justice:
    and Christ, in Marpeck, 72, 78, 87,
    147, 152, 156, 169-170
    Schiemer and, 31
    Schlaffer and, 39
    in Theologia Deutsch, 26
Justification:
    Marpeck and, 78-79
    Strauss and, 15
Justingen, 102, 104

Kautz, Jacob, 37, 49, 51, 54-55, 59,61,
    64, 89, 132
Kehl, 57-58, 96
Keller, Michael, 129, 159-160
Kern, Wilhelm, 9, 19, 21, 24, 169
Kessler, Johannes, 98
Kinzig Valley, 56-58, 102
Kitzbühel, 5, 8, 24, 61

Klöpfer, Hans, 143
Kniebis, Nikolaus, 47
Knoll, Ulrich, 141
Kraft, Georg, 141
Krumau, 52
Kufstein, 11, 16, 19

Lang, Matteüs, 22, 159
Langenau, 107-108, 145, 164
Langenmantel, Joachim, 135
Leber Valley, 58, 102, 108
Lebertal, 145-146
Lech River, 134-138, 143
Liechtenstein, Christoph Philipp
        von, 6, 9, 17-18
Linz, Wolfgang Bandhuber zu, 37
Lord's Supper, 64, 130
        Bucer and Capito and, 46
        Marpeck and, 118, 120-121,
        124, 144, 158
        Schlaffer and, 39
        Strauß and, 15
        Streicher and, 105-106
Loscher, Georg, 137-138
Luther, Martin, 13, 15, 18, 21-22, 30,
        34, 36, 39-40, 45, 54, 64, 92, 94,
        115, 169
        and opinion of Schiemer, 33
        and *Theologia Deutsch*, 29
        and theology of glory, 29
        and theology of the cross, 29
Lutheranism, 13, 21, 41, 65, 128,
        130, 132, 141, 159
        Franck and, 60
        Marpeck and, 20-21
        Schiemer and, 33, 34

Magisterial Reformers, 84, 97, 103
        Marpeck's criticism of, 90
        Marpeck's debate with Bucer
        over, 63-67
        relation to Anabaptists in
        Augsburg, 143

Maler, Gregor, 132
Maler, Jörg, 98, 112, 133, 138-145
        passim, 164-165
Marburg, 60, 64
Marpeck, Pilgram: and oath of
        citizenship, 8
        Anna, 7, 52, 139, 146
        daughter, Margareth, 7
        father, Heinrich, 5, 6
        first wife, Sophia Harrer, 6
        parents, 13
Marquart, Balthasar, 143
Marschalk, Walpurga, 106
»Martyr's Synod« (August 1527), 30,
        132
Maurice of Saxony, 131
Maximilian I, 10-11, 17
Meckart, Georg, 132
Meckart, Johann, 143
Melancthon, Philip, 132
Melchiorites (Hofmannites), 144, 146, 150
Melhorn, Georg, 132
Mennonites, 145
Meyger, Fridolin, 50-55 passim, 59,
        82
Mining: in Rattenberg, 8-19
        in Schwaz, 10, 20
        in the Tirol, 9-11
        See also Guilds
Moravia, 52, 61, 98-103, 108-109,
        133, 143-145
Moser, Ulrich, 37
Mueg, Daniel, 47
Mühldorf, 17
Müller, Constantius, 136
Münster, 97, 108, 133, 142
Münsterites, 97, 103, 108-109, 142,
        159
Müntzer, Thomas, 22
Musculus, Wolfgang, 131

Nagensenfftig, Barbara, 139
New Being. *See* New Birth

New Birth:
    Marpeck and, 76-80, 91, 110,
    124, 147, 152-153
    Schiemer and, 32-35
    Schlaffer and, 38
    in *Theologia Deutsch*, 28-29
Newenbach, 57
Nicolsburg, 30, 37, 59, 101
Nuremberg, 30, 37

Oaths, civil, 142, 164
    Bucer and, 63
    Capito and, 64
    Michael Ecker and, 50
    Hut and, 133
    Marpeck and, 53, 58, 94, 164
    165
    Sattler and, 50
    Jörg Tucher and, 49
Oecolampadius, 64, 132
Österreicher, Georg, 131
Ott, Matheus, 133
Ottomans. *See* Turks

Papacy, 84, 103, 108
    Castenbaur and, 18, 21
    Marpeck and, 21, 84
    Strauß and, 21
Pappenheim, Magdalena Marschalk
    von, 104-106
Passau Treaty, 131
Peace of Augsburg, 127, 132
Peasant War, 108
    in Schwaz, 20
    in Strassburg, 55, 90
    in the Tirol, 19-21
Pelagianism:
    Marpeck and, 147
Penance, 29
    Marpeck and penitential
    discipline, 114, 139, 153-154
    Strauss and, 14
Penntz, Hans, 143

Pernstain, Jan von, 98-99, 101, 110 165
    sister, Bohunka, 99
Pfarrer, Mathis, 47
Philip of Hesse, 130
Poppitz, 145
Prussia, ducal, 99, 101

Rattenberg (on the Inn), 1, 5-22
    passim, 37, 41, 59, 61, 83,
    89, 139, 163-164, 167
    See also Guilds Mining
Rayserin, Magdalena, 143
Rebirth. *See* New Birth
Rechlinger, Heinrich, 135
Regel, Anna, 144
Regel, Regina, 134
Regensburg, 22, 37, 99
Rehlinger, Ulrich, 134, 143
Reith, 9, 18-19, 24
Reublin, Wilhelm, 48, 54-55, 59,
    61-63, 99
Rhegius, Urbanus, 14-15, 21
Rode, Hinne, 46
Rosenheim, 5-6
Rothenfelder, Jörg Probst, 133
Rothmann, Bernhard, 97, 103, 108,
    119, 169
Rülich, Jakob, 132

Sacraments:
    Marpeck and sacramental
    theology, 122, 125, 170
    Schwenckfeld and sacramental
    theology, 121-122
    Strassburg Reformers and, 46
Sailer, Leonhard, 143
Sailer, Wolfgang, 102
St. Gallen, 98, 134, 136, 144-145,
    164, 170
Salvation:
    Schiemer and, 35
    in Theologia Deutsch, 28
Salzburg, 16-18, 30, 55

Sanctification:
    Marpeck and, 72, 79,
        101, 156
Sattler, Michael, 49-51, 64
Schakwitz, 100-103, 108, 112, 143
Scharnschlager, Anna, 98
Scharnschlager, Leupold, 52, 61,
        98-99, 139-140, 144
Schehe, Cornelius, 61
Schiemer, Leonhart, 3, 22-25, 30-38
        passim, 41, 52, 55, 61, 69, 72,
        76-78, 83, 89, 169
Schlaffer, Hans, 3, 23, 25, 30, 36-41,
        69, 72-77 passim, 83-84, 89, 169
Schleiffer, Hans, 141
Schlettstatt, 50
Schloßer, Philip, 133
Schmalkalden, 102
Schmalkaldic League, 90, 127,
        129, 159
Schmalkaldic War, 135, 141, 144 156,
        165-166, 170
Schmidt, Anna, 139
Schmidt, Bernhart, 133
Schmidt, Hans, 139
Schmotzer, Ulrich, 9
Schneider, Hans Jakob, 134, 139,
        141-142, 164-165
Schultheiss, Wolfgang, 63
Schwaz, 13, 15-16, 23, 37
        See also Mining
Schwebel, Johannes, 45
Schweblin, Johannes, 50-51
Schwenckfeld, Caspar, 64, 88, 97-106 passim,
        115-122 passim, 133-134, 140, 144,
        147, 158, 163, 169
        Marpeck's controversy with
        104-107, 115-126
Schwenckfeldians/ers, 143
        in Glatz, 101
Scriptures:
        Marpeck on the
        interpretation of, 93

Seid, Katherine, 60
Seifrid, Jörg, 140-143
Silesia, 101, 116
Sin:
        Denck and, 49
        Marpeck and, 69-70, 110, 144,
        147-150
        Schiemer and, 31
        Streicher and, 105-106
        in Theologia Deutsch, 27
Speyer, 52
Spiritualism (Geister), 69-70, 72,
        77-79, 103, 132
        Franck and, 60
        Marpeck and, 84-89, 100-101,
        115, 158-159
        in Moravia, 101-102
        and the person of Christ
        150-151
Staupitz, Johann, 18
Steiger, Christman, 61, 67
Steyr, 30
Strassburg, 2, 13, 21, 43-67, 69, 81,
        85, 89-90, 93, 96-104, 108, 112,
        115, 122, 127, 131, 133, 135, 144,
        146, 156, 159-160, 163-164, 167,
        170
        First Strassburg Conference, 146
        Second Strassburg Conference,
        146
        Third Conference, 146
Strauß, Jakob, 13-15, 21
Streicher, Helena, 104-105, 121
Sturm, Hans, 55
Sturm, Jakob, 47, 67, 93
Suffering, 25, 78
        Marpeck and, 69, 76
        See Theology of the Cross
        Swiss Brethren, 97, 103, 110, 132,
        146, 170
Switzerland, 98, 107-108, 110,
        133-134, 144, 156

Sword:
        Bucer and, 63
        Hut and, 133
        Maler and, 142
        Marpeck and, 108-112, 165
        Schneider and, 142

Theologia Deutsch, 3, 25-31, 34, 41,
        49, 69, 78, 89, 114, 149, 169
        on Christ, 27
        Luther and, 29
        on salvation, 28
        Schlaffer and, 37
        on suffering, 29
Theology of the Cross:
        Luther and, 29
        Marpeck and, 62, 69, 71-75, 83,
        91, 100, 108-125, 147,
        153, 156-158, 160-161, 170
        Schiemer and, 30
        Schlaffer and, 37
Tirol, 5, 10, 19-22, 30, 98
        See also Mining
Tregor, Conrad, 45
Treübel, Eckhart zum, 45, 51
Truchseß, Otto, 129-130, 135,
        159-160
Tucher, Jörg, 49, 51
Turks, 103, 109, 161, 169

Ulm, 104-108, 145
Unsinn, Bernhard, 143
Usury:
        and social radicals in
        Strassburg, 54

Vallenperger, Lienhart, 17
Veh, Cornelius, 100, 102-103, 145
Vienna, 30, 143, 145
Vogelsberger, Sebastian, 131

Walch, Johannes, 56, 58
Waldshut, 48
Wanner, Albrecht, 50-51
Weckerlin, Jörg, 133, 141, 144
Weckerlin, Pauls, 133
Weißhauptin, Regina, 143
Welser, Anthony, 135
Welser, Ulrich, 144
Wertach River, 133
Westphalia, 108
Wiedemann, Jacob, 37
Wiedenmann, Conrad, 137-138
Wilhelm of Bavaria, 135
William of Hesse, 131
Witikon, 48
Wittenberg Concord, 132
Wolfach, 56
Wolff, Hans, 48, 63
Worms, 49
Wurmser, Bernhard, 47, 57

Zell, Mattheus, 45-48
Ziegler, Clement, 47-51
Ziegler, Jörg, 48-49, 51
Znaim, 99, 101, 103, 108, 145
Zurich, 15, 48, 50, 61, 108
Zwingli, Ulrich, 20, 48, 64-65, 132,
        169
Zwinglianism, 108, 128, 132
        Franck and, 60